5.00

André Malraux
and the
Tragic Imagination
*

André Malraux

and the
Tragic Imagination

by

W. M. Frohock

STANFORD UNIVERSITY PRESS
STANFORD, CALIFORNIA
LONDON: GEOFFREY CUMBERLEGE
OXFORD UNIVERSITY PRESS

STANFORD UNIVERSITY PRESS, STANFORD, CALIFORNIA
LONDON: GEOFFREY CUMBERLEGE, OXFORD UNIVERSITY PRESS

THE BAKER AND TAYLOR COMPANY, HILLSIDE, NEW JERSEY
HENRY M. SNYDER & COMPANY, 440 FOURTH AVENUE, NEW YORK 16
W. S. HALL & COMPANY, 457 MADISON AVENUE, NEW YORK 22

Library of Congress Catalog Card Number: 52-10712

For
Natalie Barrington Frohock
Natalie Helen Frohock
Sarah Frohock

*

Introduction

THE THREE BOOKS on Malraux already in print are all helpful, and one, Gaëtan Picon's, is truly excellent. But all three were written shortly after the war, when Malraux had just quit his twenty-year love affair with the Communists and emerged at the right hand of General Charles de Gaulle. It was widely rumored not only that he wrote the General's speeches but also that he was rewriting his own novels to make them "conform to his new political beliefs." Moreover, he had suddenly become a literary ancestor as well as a political leader, for the Existentialists were exploiting the old vein of Absurdity that Malraux had pioneered as early as 1925: Sartre's *Nausée* clearly owed much to Malraux's early novels, and the debt of the then much-admired Albert Camus extended to the borrowing of specific phrases. Further, he still had to be considered an active novelist, for though he had written but one brief fiction since 1937, the lapse seemed due to his having been involved in two wars in a row. His Swiss publisher had announced the continuation of *Les Noyers de l'Altenburg*,* in a series called *La Lutte avec l'ange*. He was also supposed to be working on a novel about the adventurer, Mayrena, and to have finished his study of T. E. Lawrence, *Le Démon de l'absolu*. *The Psychology of Art* was in the offing. Any of these supposedly forthcoming books might reveal latent and unsuspected meanings in the old ones. *Circa* 1945, only tentative judgments were possible.

Today it is a decade since Malraux has written a novel. He has announced that he will not try to continue *La Lutte avec l'ange*.[1] The book on Lawrence is still unpublished. *The Psychology of Art* and its revised version, *Les Voix du silence*, are very revealing in many ways but do not force one to change one's opinion of the novels. The Communists claim, of course, that when Malraux jettisoned the faith he also threw overboard all he had to say. They may be right. What is certain is that any novel Malraux writes after this long silence may properly be thought to be part of a second cycle of activity. Meanwhile the furor about Existentialism has subsided, and the likelihood of Malraux's being sud-

* Titles of Malraux's untranslated works are given in French. The titles of the translated works are those of the American, not the English, editions. Translations quoted are my own. Page references are always to the French editions.

[1] The prefatory note in the Gallimard (1948) edition offers the book to those "interested in what might have been," and remarks on the impossibility of continuing a novel after so long a lapse.

denly precipitated into political prominence again seems far enough in the future for it not to incite one to commit great errors of judgment.

Thus 1952 is a much more favorable year than 1945 was for rereading Malraux attentively and without distraction. And if one is a foreigner, for once there is no loss in being born outside the French literary tradition. Malraux's techniques depart radically from those common in France. His themes are universal: human suffering, human solitude, humiliation and human dignity, the constant imminence and irrevocability of death, the inanity of life. His heroes are rarely French: Perken, Kyo, Kassner, Garine, Manuel, and Vincent Berger are either people of indefinite origins, or of mixed blood, or foreigners. And the values Malraux deals in are perhaps less remote from us than from the French. Action and violence are not radical departures for us, at least in literature.

For Americans, Malraux has the special interest of being what America rarely produces, an artist who is also an intellectual. Of the serious novelists writing in America in the 1930's who moved leftward under the impact of the Sacco-Vanzetti case and the depression, John Dos Passos alone demonstrated the possession of even an elementary grasp of the political intricacies and intellectual obligations of his new attitude. As Philip Rahv remarks in his recent *Image and Idea*, "They succeed in representing incidents of repression and revolt, as well as sentimental conversions, but conversions of the heart and mind they sketch in on the surface, or imply in a gratuitous fashion . . . The sympathy of these ostensibly political writers with the revolutionary cause is often genuine, yet their understanding of its inner movement, intricate problems, and doctrinal and strategic motives is so deficient as to call into question their competence to deal with political material" (p. 17). Mr. Rahv is severe, and one is not obliged to agree with him that the deficiency he describes makes such writers deficient as novelists, but one can hardly deny that their intellectual inability to encompass the political problem defines the kind of novelists they are.

In contrast, Malraux is a writer whose ideas are as important as his emotions. His novels are a product of both intellect *and* sensibility and, even more, of a need to establish an equilibrium between intellect and sensibility with respect to what Mr. Rahv calls "the political problem." For the central, crucial experience of Americans and Europeans alike has been the familiar political choice between passivity and revolution, and Malraux's name is high on the list of writers who moved away from democratic capitalism in the 'twenties and 'thirties, only to move back again when events culminating in the Non-Aggression Pact of 1939 revealed that the brave new world was not so perfect either. His novels had their first and greatest success as the work of the most distinguished of French fellow travelers. They are nourished by the imperious need he felt to clarify his experience by transposing it into art; their special excellence lies in his ability to feel the relations between politics and the characteristic ideas, preoccupations, apprehensions, and anxieties that torture our time. This excellence is one that our American novelists, however fine otherwise, do not have.

Critics like those of the British *Scrutiny* group deny that Malraux's six fictions may properly be called novels at all. In one sense they are right. Certainly these hurried stories, often overpopulated, always embarrassed by the size of what they try to contain—hard, brilliant, nervous, and closely related to drama as they are—are the antithesis of the kind of narrative which is defined by the unhurried thoroughness of its method. They are not patient, massive, rich; they seem to be deficient in Ortega's "thick texture of life." Malraux's fictions do not "create a world" of their own so much as they illuminate the hidden nature of a world which already exists. They mean to "reveal reality," as Lionel Trilling thinks a novel should, but to reveal it in flashes, with great demands upon the visual imagination of the reader as well as upon his comprehension, and probably not at all in the way that Mr. Trilling has in mind. Yet such strictures merely make it clearer than ever that what Malraux tries to do with fiction requires a special form—one, precisely, which will permit establishing a balance between sensibility and intellect.

Malraux rather luxuriates in the epithet "intellectual" and clearly delights in ideas. But "intellectual" does not have to mean "philosopher." A philosopher is more or less obliged to have a rationally discursive mind. The intellectual, on the other hand, may quite permissibly feel himself less committed to logic. He is at the service of ideas, but ideas are not necessarily his servants. We grant the title of intellectual to a man if "ideas mean a lot" to him, if what he does betrays his preoccupation with them. His ability to align them in the form of rational discourse is not what makes him an intellectual.

Only by such a definition can Malraux be counted among the intellectuals. His ideas are deeply felt but not, properly speaking, *thought*. Rarely has he chosen—or perhaps been able—to develop them discursively. When he tries to do so, as in the books on art, his prose does indeed have unity, but not because it develops a rectilinear argument. It owes such unity as it has to the fact that every paragraph is related, if not

always to the paragraphs adjacent, to the eternal, unchanging preoccupations of his mind. The style is oracular; ideas are juxtaposed to other
ideas with scant attention to those little matters of conjunction and subordination which make such a difference to the reader. The parts of *The
Psychology of Art*, for example, were so far out of rational order that the
new version, *Les Voix du silence*, is an improvement less because of its
added materials than because of its superior clarity and coherence. So
long as *The Psychology of Art* succeeds as well as it seems to be succeeding
now in making readers aware of the significance of styles in art and of the
relations of various arts to each other, the weakness in its structure is not
fatal. It is merely a detriment, and hardly important to us here. What is
important is that when we look back to this "intellectual's" novels after
reading the art books, we see that the novels are incoherent in just the
same way.

The logic of the stories—of situation and circumstance and inevitable
outcome—invariably leads in one direction, to one conclusion, and the
conclusion is invariably unpalatable. *La Tentation de l'occident* (which
happens not to be a novel but which contains an implicit story) demonstrates the inanity of Occidental life; *The Conquerors* demonstrates
the absurdity of *all* life, East or West; *The Royal Way* presents the
final ignominy of death; *Man's Fate* illustrates our inability to rise
above the human predicament and our inability this side of death to
achieve a fitting dignity. And so on, with the exception of *Days of Wrath*,
through the whole Malraux canon. Malraux does not reject these conclusions—how could he?—but he turns their logic, juxtaposing to them
some picture, figure, image, or poetic symbol which affirms, oracularly,
the opposite of what the rational discourse affirms. Thus in *Man's Fate*
the manner of Katow's death makes the reader forget how thoroughly
both he and Katow are subject to human bondage. The technique here
is the technique of the art books: it consists of omitting links—of not
setting down, for example, a reason why Katow's behavior as he goes out
to be burned in the locomotive is at all relevant to what we have seen, for
several hundred pages, to be man's fate. But in the art books we call this
incoherence a defect and in the novels we call it an artistic technique. His
craft is a craft of ellipsis.

The cost of disregarding the character of Malraux's craft runs high.
For example, almost the entire October 1948 number of *Esprit*, a publication noted for serious and acute criticism, was devoted to what it labeled
"The Malraux Case." The contributors, among whom were some extremely gifted critics, were mainly interested in Malraux's recent political

shift. But to illumine his politics they had to account for his novels, and most especially for *Les Noyers de l'Altenburg*, since this one had been written after the Hitler-Stalin Non-Aggression Pact. What they succeeded in proving was not so much something about politics as about literary criticism: viz., one should not talk about the meaning of any book until one has examined the meanings inherent in the way it is put together. In their industry they quoted and glossed every idea expressed by the characters in this novel. But not a single critic remembered that the essential import of the story resides in a central and very conspicuous symbol, the same walnut trees from which the book gets its title. Vincent Berger, the hero, has been listening to the gathered intellectuals of the Altenburg colloquy prove (by discursive logic) that the notion of the continuity of man, based upon the notion of the continuity of successive cultures, is completely untenable. Berger dislikes the conclusion, though he cannot refute it. Finally he breaks away and goes out for a breath of air. There on the hill outside the Altenburg Priory loom the clumped walnuts, and suddenly he sees in them an unmistakable symbol which affirms the continuity and uninterrupted identity of man. In other words, for Vincent Berger, those walnuts *deny* the argument which has prevailed within the Altenburg, and since the most persuasive speaker to advance the latter had been the proto-Nazi Möllberg, the fact is not without its political significance. The critics missed the point.

Malraux's books invite such critical behavior. When an intellectual writes novels, the presence of ideas in the fiction constantly incites the critic to extract the idea from its context, and to ascribe it directly to the author. Malraux's way of constructing characters also lends itself to the same treatment; they are motivated by inner, obsessive drives, and what most frequently obsesses them is an idea. A given character acts as he is forced to by his attitude toward death, sex, human dignity, power, liberty, or something similar. He appears at once as an individual and as the incarnation of his special drive. Thus he becomes easy to label: Garine is The-Man-Haunted-by-the-Absurd, Hong is the Terrorist, Gisors is the Paralyzed Intellectual. Such labels reek of allegory, and it is a tradition of Western literature that allegory should teach a lesson.

But looking in Malraux's novels for *clear* lessons is as fruitless as asking them to be conventional novels, and extracting theses from them is like extracting theses from Shakespeare. The mere fact that he returns to worry the same old ideas, twisting and turning them over and over, should be a warning. As a matter of record, he is a man of a very few seminal ideas, though these few are important. To them he comes back like the

dog in the Bible: *Les Noyers de l'Altenburg* and *The Psychology of Art*
take up again themes already present in 1925 in *La Tentation de l'occident*.
In view of the technique of ellipsis which is natural to him, we have to accept the fact that the novels are extremely slippery documents on what, at
the time of writing, Malraux *thought*.

They are excellent documents on how he *felt*—which is to say that
his work should be treated primarily as the work of a poet. It is dramatic
poetry by an intellectual, for whom ideas become themes. To make this
assumption is, of course, to assume a heavy responsibility not to destroy
the context in which the themes are embedded and to tolerate such para-
doxes as turn out to be present in the work rather than to insist on resolv-
ing them by an act of the reader's will. In rational discourse paradox is
an inconvenience. In poetry, as we have recently been brought to realize,
it may lie very close to the heart of the matter.

I have tried to avoid removing Malraux's ideas from their context, and
have preferred to let his techniques of ellipsis and juxtaposition lead me
to an interpretation which has at least the merit of taking a man who has
spent his life writing books to be above all a literary artist. In turn, this
means treating the political aspects of his books as if politics were merely
a very engrossing literary theme, or as if it were a sort of context which
permits the outlines of human destiny to appear in all sharpness. This
is not to deny the importance of politics in the novels, but to define it.
We all subscribe, and Malraux more firmly than most, to the belief that
the political problem is the crucial problem of our lives. The importance
of politics in the novels is precisely that the crucial nature of the political
problem makes their poetry possible.

The poetry of the novels, as we were saying, rises out of the tension
created by Malraux's craft of ellipsis. The logic of events in his novels is
opposed by the magnificent picture of the human individual, placed *in
extremis* by the events, which he juxtaposes to the logic. For this juxtaposition to be plausible, obviously, the character involved has to be of a
certain size. My only quarrel with Harry Levin's remark, that Malraux's
people go about the world looking for situations which will enhance their
size to the stature of tragic heroes,[2] is that he sounds as if he thought they
had not found the situations. They find them (I think) less in geography
than in politics. For precisely because politics is the central problem of
our lives, they become our surrogates. Their "wandering" serves to put

---

[2] *James Joyce*, New Directions, 1941, p. 211. His ideas on the disappearance of the hero
from fiction are elaborated in "From Priam to Birotteau," *Yale French Studies*, VI (December
1950), 75–82.

them where we can see them, to lift them out of the familiar and always indecisive humdrum of our Western bourgeois cities. For an example of how completely a Malraux character can be taken as a surrogate, see Emmanuel Berl's *La Mort de la pensée bourgeoise*. If Garine, whose character inspired M. Berl's commentary, moves us more deeply than does Perken, the reason is that the situation in *The Conquerors* is political and of general import, whereas the hero of *The Royal Way*, who is in no sense a political figure, seems involved in a more private and personal situation.

But politics is neither an end in itself for Malraux nor the end of the critic's effort. "As a writer," he makes one of his autobiographical characters exclaim, "what have I ever dealt with . . . except the nature of man?" (*Les Noyers*, p. 24). Politics is only one of the contexts in which man's nature stands out with great clarity. Malraux makes anthropology another. His interest in art—all the arts including literature—had taken an anthropological turn as early as 1921. I have tried to take advantage of this fact to make the novels give up a bit more meaning than perhaps they have yielded up to date, and to underline the unity which runs through the novels, the art books, and the legend surrounding Malraux's life.

Now no subject has inspired more nonsense from literary critics in the last few years than anthropology and especially the part of it that deals with myth. We have discovered so many mythic patterns in all sorts of human behavior that we would do well to stop before we become grotesque. Yet no serious treatment of Malraux's work can avoid anthropology, because *Les Noyers de l'Altenburg* not only identifies its hero with a mythic type dear to cultural anthropologists, but also contains a specific invitation to the reader to look back and find the fundamental mythic experience recurring in Malraux's previous books. With this much to guide a rereading, at least three of the earlier novels turn out to have characters in them who have undergone the same experience. And when, after the novels, we re-examine the legend of Malraux's life of action, it becomes clear that the hero of the legend has had the experience also. With all due respect for the dangers involved, the opportunity is one that an interpreter can do nothing but welcome.

One personal word. One hardly devotes several years of one's life to studying a writer unless he feels the writer's work to have a special, personal appeal. I have read and reread Malraux, and applied to him all the explicative techniques I know, because to me his books seemed especially significant, and especially baffling. This does not mean that I accept and share his philosophy of life. I do not—any more than I share either his past or his present political views. I might point out that I am particularly fond of Balzac also, and find it possible to admire him without sharing his royalism, just as I am reasonably fond of Shakespeare without sharing his religious beliefs, and without, as a matter of fact, knowing what his beliefs were. I am extremely grateful to my subject for his help, particularly in bibliographical matters, and to his publishers, Gallimard and Grasset, for permission to quote his copyrighted works. I also thank Richard Chase and his publisher, the Louisiana State University Press, for permission to quote a page of *The Quest for Myth*.

My debts to my friends are many. I should especially like to thank Norman Torrey, Henri Peyre, and Jean Hytier for their encouragement, Margaret Gilman, Parker Peckham, and Herbert Dieckmann for reading and criticizing parts of the manuscript, and James Agee, whose scenario of *Man's Fate* originally interested me in Malraux. Specific debts, for aid with specific problems, I have acknowledged in the notes.

Contents

Contents

André Malraux

and the
Tragic Imagination

*

CHAPTER ONE

The Legend of a Life of Action

*"Perhaps he could have destroyed the mythic per-
sonage he was coming to be, if he had tried. But he
didn't want to. His legend flattered him. Even more
—he loved it."*
—LES NOYERS DE L'ALTENBURG, p. 51

P ROBABLY nothing about Malraux is so important as the legend that has
grown up, more or less spontaneously, about him. No authorized biographical account exists. He has taken the position that while his books
belong to the public, his private life is entirely his own business; the public,
free to do exactly what it pleases with what it knows—or thinks it knows—
of his personal affairs, has made the most of its opportunity.

Malraux is given to disappearing on long and secret trips to the more
agitated ends of the earth. His books are full of desperate characters and
bloody deeds. They often sound like autobiography. Such a man quite
naturally creates his own legend anyhow, and Malraux's personality makes
the process even easier. "He has an irresistible air of adventure, decision,
and melancholy about him," wrote the ubiquitous Maurice Sachs some
twenty-five years ago. "He has the very fine profile of an Italian Renaissance character and something of the young officer, the dilettante, and the
romantic poet; he talks fast and well, infallibly dazzles one, and leaves one
with the impression of having just met 'the most intelligent man of the century'" (*Au temps du boeuf sur le toit*, p. 204). Later, when both men
were working for the publisher Gallimard, and Sachs knew Malraux better,
he also had the feeling that Malraux was something of a "charlatan" and
"prestidigitator" (*Le Sabbat*, p. 420). Sachs's judgments are rarely to be
trusted, but his impressions are suggestive, especially when his tone implies
that he has heard certain gossip. Gossip there has always been. If Malraux's personal reticence was ever intended to keep him out of the
public eye—if he is not one who, like his character Vincent Berger, enjoys
having and being a legend—then it is the most signal failure of his career.
Instead of one authorized account there are dozens of unauthorized ones
among which one may pick and choose.

This is certainly not the moment to try to set the record straight. Many
of Malraux's early exploits took place in Asia, where even in the best
circumstances the records would be out of reach. He had a knack of as-

sociating himself with the kind of lost causes which, by definition, leave fragmentary histories at best, and the nature of what he did was clandestine. Furthermore, he was long associated with the Communist party, which is not a noteworthy source of verifiable information. A serious biography simply could not be written at this time.

Fortunately we do not need one, so much as we need a full statement of the legend as it exists at this writing, accompanied by certain comments and corrections at points where one's attitude toward the legend is likely to affect one's interpretations of the written works. What follows immediately, then, is presented as legend, *not as truth but as what people have publicly assumed to be the truth*, a composite of what is in circulation in the year 1952.

Georges-André Malraux was born in Paris on November 3, 1901. His father's family were from Dunkerque and had followed seafaring trades. Louis Malraux, his great-grandfather, had died at sea. Alphonse-Emile, the grandfather, was a master cooper and outfitter, and, according to recent versions of the legend, was once mayor of Dunkerque; he died a suicide. The writer's father, Fernand-Georges, had a business at Suresnes, near Paris, and in 1930 likewise committed suicide. The father, a brilliant and somewhat nervous man for whom his son had great admiration, had separated from the mother many years before and young Malraux had been brought up by women. He was educated at the Lycée Condorcet and after the baccalaureate studied at the Ecole des Langues Orientales.

His studies finished, he went to work in the art department of the publisher Kra. There he met a brilliant and attractive young German-Jewess named Clara Goldschmidt (she has since written several novels and has been the editor of a review called *Contemporains*) and shortly married her. They were to separate in the 1930's.

Malraux's early interest in art was already coupled with an equally strong one in archaeology. He had read about the ruined Buddhist temples along the abandoned Royal Road of Cambodia and had an idea that he knew precisely where to look for the remains of some valuable Khmerian sculpture. In no time he and his wife were on their way to Indochina.

They were in the bush for some ten months, traveling by oxcart and suffering from fever, and they did in fact find the sculpture for which they were looking. Finding it was only the beginning of their adventures. Malraux had a government mission to look for the sculpture, but the colonial authorities felt that whatever he found was public property and not to be appropriated by an individual. Malraux felt that but for the effort and risk of an individual named Malraux the sculptures would still be vine-covered rubble—and that individual initiative should be rewarded. This divergence of views resulted in his being "detained," haled into court at Pnompenh, found guilty and sentenced to three years in jail. In midsummer of 1924 his wife had to return to Europe alone in search of help.

A variant of the episode says that the charge against Malraux was a trumped-up one: colonial officials suspected him of subversive politics and wanted a quick way of getting him out of Indochina. This version is supported by the fact that, on a second trip to Indochina, Malraux became involved in political activity with so little delay that he must already have known the ground and been in touch with some of the heads of the nationalistic, Communist-tutored, Jeune-Annam movement.

In any case, back in Paris, a petition, signed by a series of notables including André Gide, had its effect.[1] Malraux was released and allowed to return to France in the autumn. He stayed two months, and then was off again for Indochina. This time he was in Saigon, where, in collaboration with the Jeune-Annam, he helped operate a newspaper, L'Indochine, which was frowned upon, but not forthrightly suppressed, by the colonial administration. This is one of the rare points on which Malraux himself furnishes any light: his Preface to Andrée Viollis' Indochine S.O.S. tells of some of the difficulties the paper experienced, particularly in the matter of obtaining French type-characters, and of how a native printer solved the problem by helping himself to a handful in the shop of another local newspaper. How long Malraux stayed in Saigon (the legend never being clear on dates) is a matter of conjecture.

Here the legend thickens. Up the coast at Canton the Russians had accepted Sun Yat-sen's invitation to help his Nationalist movement. The extremely competent Mikhail Borodin was installed as political counselor to the Kuomintang. He was accompanied by the gifted soldier Galen who, under the name of Blücher, was later to command the Soviet troops in Siberia. Ostensibly their mission was to aid in the establishment of the

[1] "Pour André Malraux," Nouvelles Littéraires 3e année, No. 99 (September 6, 1924), p. 1. "The undersigned, moved by the condemnation that has fallen upon André Malraux, express their confidence in the respect which justice habitually shows toward all those who contribute to the enlargement of the intellectual patrimony of our country. They are eager to stand guarantors for the intelligence and real literary value of this personage whose youth and work already done permit the highest hopes. They would greatly deplore the loss resulting from the application of a penalty which would hinder André Malraux from accomplishing what all have the right to expect from him. Signed: Edm. Jaloux, Jacques Rivière, R. Gallimard, Pascal Pia, André Gide, Max Jacob, Philippe Soupault, André Houlaire, François Mauriac, François Le Grix, Florent Fels, André Desson, Pierre Mac Orlan, M. Martin du Gard, Louis Aragon, André Breton, Jean Paulhan, Charles Du Bos, Pierre de Lanux, Marcel Arland, André Maurois, Gaston Gallimard, Guy de Portalès."

Nationalist government as the government of the whole of China, which for the moment meant loosening the hold of the Occidentals, particularly the English, on the coast cities. China had been in a bubbling ferment since the middle of 1924, and it was hardly a secret that the real purpose of Borodin and his lieutenants was to take advantage of the tumult to turn the Chinese revolution into a Communist enterprise. It was Borodin—still according to the legend—who sent for Malraux to come from Saigon to help in the task.

In China, Malraux's revolutionary activity is supposed to have reached its height. As the revolution moved north from Canton to Shanghai his role increased in importance. His specialty was propaganda, but actually he took part in all the kinds of back-alley, after-dark conspiracy which are part of revolution in Asia. He was a competent agent and not an obscure one. There was a moment when he sat on the Kuomintang Committee of Twelve with Chiang Kai-shek and served as its secretary. Later he was director of propaganda in Kwangsi and Kwangtung. Then Chiang Kai-shek broke with the Communist wing of the Kuomintang, Malraux broke violently with Chiang, and shortly he was back in Europe with his Asiatic career behind him.

He had been writing since 1920. With Marcel Arland and other friends he had contributed to small and largely unknown publications like *Université de Paris, Dés, Action, Aventure, 900, Signaux*, had projected one book, *Journal d'un pompier de jeu de massacre*, had worked on another called *Écrit pour une idole à trompe*, on a third, *Lunes en papier*, and started on still a fourth, *Royaume farfelu*. Much in this first writing suggested that the writer was playful and brilliant, but not particularly interested in a literary career. Certainly nothing in it hints at the seriousness of the interest we know that he had in art, to which the voyage to Indochina itself eloquently testifies. Another book, begun in 1921, *La Tentation de l'occident*, gives evidence of much more serious intentions and does refer to art, but it was not finished until 1925 and most probably was not put into final form until after the first Indochinese venture.

But now, after his second return from Asia, he turned seriously to writing. "D'une jeunesse européenne," an essay published in the last number of the *Cahiers Verts*, with others by André Chamson, Jean Grenier, and Henri Petit, in 1927,[2] proclaimed a personal alienation from European culture to match the one expressed by the focal character in *La Tentation*; he finished *Royaume farfelu* and wrote his first full-dress

---

[2] See Bibliography. Because the book is an anthology, Malraux's essay has frequently escaped the attention of his critics.

novel, *The Conquerors*, which Grasset published in 1928. The novel was a success and Malraux was launched. In 1930 he brought out his second novel, *The Royal Way*, and in 1933 won the Goncourt prize with his third, *Man's Fate*. Meanwhile he had gone to work for Gallimard; he was helping edit other men's books, writing reviews for the *Nouvelle Revue Française*, arranging art exhibitions at the gallery of the N.R.F., criticizing other exhibitions—and frequently interrupting these occupations for archaeological expeditions, of which he made at least three, in 1929, 1930, and 1931. The 1931 trip took him as far as China. In 1934 his report that he had discovered from the air the lost city of the Queen of Sheba, near Rub' al Khali in southern Arabia, failed to stir an apathetic world.

From 1927 on, Malraux had been an increasingly conspicuous public figure, one of the luminaries, with Gide, Ramon Fernandez, Drieu La Rochelle, Léon Bopp, Jean Paulhan, and the rest, gathered together by Gallimard. He had taken part in the famous colloquies at Pontigny, where Paul Desjardins assembled the elite of Europe in the famous "decades." Stories of his immense intelligence and impressive verbal fluency had got about. Winning the Goncourt prize added to his public stature, and the publicity department of the house of Gallimard doubtless earned a share of the credit, at this point, for the further growth and spread of the legend. The moment was not a bad one for Gallimard to have in his stable an important writer of marked Communist sympathies. Fascism in Italy and the rise of Hitler were doing in Europe what the great depression had done in America. The intellectuals were moving leftward almost in a body. Visits to the Soviet Union were in order and conversions were no less common for being somewhat impermanent. And when such disparate figures as Gide, Romain Rolland, and Louis-Ferdinand Céline took the road to Russia, Gallimard had the bellwether.

Malraux naturally became one of the spokesmen of the Left. The Russians made much of him. It was by no means clear that he was an orthodox, line-toeing Communist: *Man's Fate* was suspect of Trotskyite "deviationism." Ilya Ehrenburg reported to his countrymen that Malraux was something of a dilettante (*Duhamel, Gide etc. vus par un écrivain de l'U.R.S.S.*, pp. 189–202). But the Soviets of the Five-Year Plan were eager to welcome foreign fellow travelers, and, as Ehrenburg added, Malraux's heart was obviously in the right place. Did Malraux have a party card? The legend holds that he did not. And on his trip to the 1934 Writers' Congress in Moscow, where he was greeted with considerable enthusiasm, he behaved with a certain independence. He was billed on the program as a "Marxist humanist" and, according to reports, placed his emphasis much more on the human than on Marx. His hearers were displeased, especially by his insisting that what the artist *qua* artist needed most was freedom. His speech brought a heated reply from Karl Radek and the atmosphere became so thick with acrimony that in the end the Soviet hosts had to dust off old Maxim Gorky to find something good to say about everyone's thesis, including Malraux's. In the same year Malraux and Gide made their much-publicized trip to Germany in behalf of the imprisoned Dimitrov.

Malraux was in demand to speak at mass meetings, gradually developed a platform manner, and became, in spite of his nerves and low voice, an effective orator, a Voice of the Left. At the June 1935 Congress of Writers in Defense of Culture, held at the Palais de la Mutualité in Paris, he was on a list of speakers which included Gide, E. M. Forster, Aldous Huxley, Heinrich Mann, and Ehrenburg. He signed the anti-Fascist counterblast to Henri Massis' manifesto in favor of Mussolini's Ethiopian enterprise. In 1935, also, he published *Days of Wrath*—somewhat hurriedly, if we judge by the number of changes made between magazine and book publication. He was seriously preoccupied with reconciling the claims of art and the claims of propaganda. He seemed as unready as he had been in Russia, the year before, to sacrifice the needs of the artist to the needs of the revolution. From the contents of this novel one gathers that he had certain doubts about Communism; yet he entertained none at all about the evils of Fascism, and where practical action was concerned, at least, he was heart and soul against the Rightist dictatorships.

This was still his mood when the fighting started in Spain. He was separated from his wife now and felt much freer than before to lead a life of action. Two days after the Civil War broke out he was across the Pyrenees. He helped organize the Republican air force, flew as member of a plane crew, was wounded, sat in the highest councils of the Republicans, made a trip to America in search of aid for the cause, and still had time to write *Man's Hope*.

Then came the defeat of the Republicans, Munich, the Non-Agression Pact, and the new war. Malraux enlisted in the French army, as a private in the tanks—which doubtless meant, given the shortage of material in France in 1940–41, that he was indistinguishable from the other infantrymen. He was again wounded and ended up, after the breakthrough, in the P.W. camp at Sens. In the lull that followed he began a new novel, *La Lutte avec l'ange*; the Swiss publisher Skira got the one volume of it we now know, and the Gestapo got the rest.

But before Skira published the part that had been saved, in 1943, Malraux was off again, helping organize what became the Resistance in south-western France. He was in and out of German hands. On one occasion they stood him against a wall before a firing squad, like one of his own characters, in an effort to get him to talk. Gradually he acquired new stature and once more rose to leadership. What the Alsace-Lorraine Brigade did to hinder the arrival of the Deutsches Reich Panzerdivision in Normandy has been highly publicized, as have also its campaign in Alsace and its role in the eventual liberation of Strasbourg. The Colonel "Berger" who was one of its commanders was Malraux.

Then, in a highly spectacular political development, he appeared as the lieutenant of De Gaulle. How long since he had turned his back on the Communists? Had he felt, as others did, that the Russians had sold out the Spanish Republicans? Had he had new light on the Communists during the Resistance? Was this dramatic turnabout merely the continuation of a gradually growing dislike for those whom one of his characters calls "the Curés of the Revolution?" Or was he, as his adversaries contended, playing a sharp game of political opportunism? In any case, there he was. In the short-lived De Gaulle government of November 1945 he was Minister of Information. The very spectacle of the author of *The Conquerors* and *Man's Hope* playing a ministerial role in a government so unrevolutionary did nothing to quiet the legend. His political development became the subject of published controversy. And when the De Gaulle government fell, in 1946, the controversy went on. Malraux retired to private life, but hardly to privacy.

Even before the war he had published, in fragmentary magazine articles, about half of what is now the first volume of *The Psychology of Art*. With his retirement he got to work on it again. Skira brought out *Museum Without Walls* in 1947, *The Creative Act* (which is Volume II) in 1949, and *The Twilight of the Absolute* in 1950. The same year also saw the publication of *Saturne*, his book on Goya.

Such is the mixture of verifiable fact and unverifiable gossip which surrounds Malraux and which, precisely because it is an inextricable mixture, is best thought of as a legend.

For the attentive reader of fiction, interested in novels and not in gossip, only the early part of the legend needs examination here. Critics have always been tempted to read *The Conquerors* and *Man's Fate* as though these novels were eyewitness accounts of the events they describe. They know that there is much autobiography in *The Royal Way, Man's*

Hope, and *Les Noyers.* They assume that there must be autobiography in the other novels (except *Days of Wrath*) as well. They speak of Malraux as *"le témoin capital"* and allow the words to imply that the witness was always physically present. The transition from such assumptions to the belief that *all* of Malraux's books involve an element of journalism is easy.

Now "eyewitness" (or "journalist") is not necessarily a term of disparagement. But to treat as a kind of reporting these novels which are actually built not of historical but of imagined action is to fail to recognize the *nature,* if not the quality, of Malraux's achievement. If we know that the ferocious violence of *The Conquerors* and *Man's Fate* is in these books *because Malraux's fictional world needs to be violent to be complete,* and not just because he saw torture, suffering, and death while he was in the Orient, we know something decisively important about his peculiar originality as an artist.

For this reason it is pertinent to scrutinize, point by point, the legend of his early years.

That the novelist was born on November 3, 1901, is completely verifiable, and the year should be underlined. Had he been born much earlier, he would have been old enough to serve in the first World War and would doubtless not have escaped its traumata. Malraux's writing shows no trace of the feeling that somehow the world has done him a personal injury; it has no equivalent for the feeling of slightly older writers, like Henry de Montherlant, that the war was more or less devised by an older and stay-at-home generation to assure the unhappiness of the young. When one thinks of the tone of the war literature of Dos Passos, Hemingway, Bernanos, Céline, and even T. E. Lawrence, Malraux seems by contrast to have been beneficiary of a major historical accident. He appears in this respect to belong to another generation—whence, possibly, his appeal to younger French critics—and to have avoided the classical stereotype which his elders accepted. For the Lawrence of *The Mint* as for the Dos Passos of *Three Soldiers,* the depths of human humiliation and the plight of the common soldier in the modern army are identical; for Malraux, humiliation is the specialty of prisons and prison camps, of physical and spiritual torture and of gas chambers, and of giving one's epidermis to be made into a lamp shade.

His birth date also makes it impracticable to explain his "morbid fascination with death" by the two suicides which are supposed to have occurred in his family. In the first place, it is highly unlikely that Alphonse-Emile Malraux, the grandfather, committed suicide at all. His death certificate places his death in the civilian hospital of Dunkerque (of which town, incidentally, he had *not* been mayor). If he died from other than natural causes, Dunkerque, including its newspapermen, did not know about it. In any case, the old man's death took place on November 20, 1909, when the novelist was a child of eight years and some days. The fact that a grandfather very like Alphonse-Emile figures in both *The Royal Way* and *Les Noyers* might strengthen the argument that Malraux draws very heavily on his personal experience, had the novelist not been so young when the old man died. No doubt Malraux's grandfather did furnish a model, but the model must have been one of the dimmest of childhood memories and, given the time elapsed, the figure in the novels must, after all, be largely a creature of the imagination. Moreover, the death of his father took place in 1930, *after* the books in which the fascination of death is most powerful had been written. The shock of the suicide may be behind Malraux's increasing attention to the relations between father and son in *Man's Fate*, *Man's Hope*, and *Les Noyers*; it certainly had nothing to do with the choice of themes in the earlier books.

Coming from a family connected with the sea appears to have affected Malraux's imagination not at all. Sea voyages in his books are nothing but bores. Travel is important, but only as a means either of getting away from somewhere or of reaching a scene of action; nothing significant happens in the course of the voyage, and traveling characters fret to have the journey over with. And in the book that draws most heavily upon reminiscence, *Les Noyers*, he transposes the salt-water men of his family into a race of Alsatian foresters. Truly, if Malraux is the exoticist that he is sometimes alleged to be, he is one of the rare ones whose exoticism is not amphibious.

The significant fact about Malraux's education is that before he was twenty-two he had picked up a very adequate working knowledge of art, archaeology, and anthropology, three domains which have always blended into each other in his work. Ancient art has always interested him as much as modern art, and on the same grounds: as far back as the subject can be traced in his work, art appears as one of the keys to the culture that produces it. How adequate his early knowledge was should not be overlooked. The Indochina venture did indeed end in an absurd fiasco, but it is no less true that Malraux found the Khmerian sculpture exactly where he had expected it to be. His failure was not the failure of the archaeologist but of the young man who did not know how to deal with colonial officials, and this whether or not his troubles in Indochina were, or were not, of political origin.

There is room to doubt that the ultimate value of the trip for Malraux lay in the first heady experience of dangerous adventure. That *The Royal Way* is based on his own expedition into the jungle is true, but the jungle which in the novel gives young Claude Vannec the creeps is not quite so hostile to whites as the novel suggests. (It appears even hospitable in the novel, *Portrait de Grisélidis*, that Mme Clara Malraux set in the same general locale.) Actually, it had long been inhabited by white men, and in 1924 French airplanes had even landed in the hinterland. The country around Banteaï-Srey, where the sculpture was found, was not particularly dangerous. The expedition ran the risks of bugbite and fever which are standard in any tropical swamp country. Although it is true that the tropic fever Malraux caught did him considerable physical damage, such fevers can be contracted as easily in the capitals of southern Asia as they can back in the bush. All this does not suggest that the crucial experience involved the kind of derring-do that his novels make us associate with his name.

Much more probably, the central experience was his break from the life he had led up to that time. The mere fact of a voyage is important: he was away from home. Home was Europe, the slightly insane Europe of the giddy early 'twenties. Europe was a set of values which—as is clear from *La Tentation de l'occident*, finished just after this trip—he could not accept, and the home of an unsatisfactory kind of life he was already trying to analyze. European values, moreover, were represented in Indochina by the colonial administration with which he found himself on bad terms. In the colonial court he had had the occasion to learn something of the experience that Garine, the hero of *The Conquerors*, undergoes in the court in Switzerland. Throughout his trial, Garine is conscious only of the absurd discrepancy between the (to him) minor nature of his crime and the vast importance attached to it by the State. For him the experience is crucial: he sets off afterward on his career of revolution. In view of the number of instances in Malraux's novels where the experience of humiliation is linked either with a prison, with a court, or with a legal interrogation of which the hero is victim, one cannot help surmising very strongly that to Malraux the Indochina episode was crucial also. It gave him a first experience of humiliation, for which he could hold Europe—and European values—responsible. Hence the feeling of estrangement which, together with an awareness of the Absurd, characterizes the early novels.

On the basis of such evidence as exists, the first visit to Indochina appears more important in determining Malraux's subsequent attitudes than does anything that happened to him in the five years that followed it. He went back on his second visit already an "enemy of the law," and apparently quite ripe for his twenty-year experience of Communism. Nor is it clear that his adhesion to Communism was merely a matter of intellectual conviction. His detention in Indochina had caused a small scandal in Paris. There had been stories in the newspapers.[3] In such circumstances, the thought of vengeance would normally be pleasant.

In any case, the tone of high seriousness that marks all of Malraux's mature work appears in his writing immediately after the years of absence in Asia. Superficially, he appears here to have shared a common experience. For every writer in modern literature who, like Proust, left home as little as possible, there seem to have been two who have needed their years before the mast, or their exile in Siberia, to unfetter their talents.

Some, like Saint-John Perse and Paul Claudel, appear to have needed the mere feeling of being away from home. Others, like Saint-Exupéry, had to have both this feeling and the kind of activity that was available to them only abroad. And still others, like Dostoevski, required that the experience of absence should be an experience of humiliation also. Malraux seems to belong in this last category. Absence, coupled with humiliation, turns up as a constant element in the pattern of experience which we shall find recurring from book to book.

Meanwhile, the real center of action in Asia was not Saigon but Canton. Since January 1924 Communists had been admitted to the Kuomintang. Freighters from Vladivostok were docking weekly in Canton to unload arms and ammunition. Subsidies of as much as two million dollars Mex. a month were coming from Moscow. (It is true that Moscow was also contributing prudently to the war chest of Fêng Yü-hsiang, the archenemy of the Kuomintang who controlled the road from Siberia to China.) Obviously the International expected a large return on its investment. Borodin's sphere included not only China proper but also the general area of Southeast Asia. His project was to make the party indispensable to Dr. Sun Yat-sen and eventually to usurp the leadership of a political alliance which included such unlikely bedfellows as Wang Ching-wei, then known as a "radical democrat," the capitalists T. V. Soong and H. H. Kung, "old socialists" like Sun himself, and pro-Communists like Sun's independent wife.

[3] André Breton, "Pour André Malraux," *Nouvelles Littéraires*, 3e année, No. 96 (August 16, 1924), p. 1. ". . . Thus we read in the papers that the young author of *Lunes en papier* . . . has been 'guilty' . . . [of a] theft of no importance. . . ." Breton's version is that Malraux had been caught in a poet's prank.

To the great detriment of Communist plans, however, the Kuomintang had also admitted the young commander of the Soviet-backed military school at Whampoa, Colonel Chiang Kai-shek. Chiang's star was rising. After the civil war of the summer of 1925 in Canton had made the Kuomintang secure in that quarter, the next step of Sun Yat-sen's program was to invade the North and thus bring the parts of the country together under one regime. The moment called for a good soldier who was also an adroit politician. Chiang was both—and he was no friend of the Soviets. So long as he had to take any backing he could get, Chiang had no choice but to accept the Communists, but as early as March 1926, when his army took the local governments of Canton and Swatow out of Communist hands, the International must have suspected that open rupture was not remote. How soon it would come depended upon how rapidly Chiang gained strength. In March 1927 he arrived in force at Shanghai.

Shanghai had been a Communist stronghold since 1920, when Professor Ch'ên Tu-hsiu, having been dismissed from the University of Peking for his part in founding the New Chinese Youth Society, had come there. The youth club he formed in Shanghai became the nucleus of the Chinese Communist party a month later. In 1927, when Chiang arrived, the city was in turmoil and the local Kuomintang was in the process of taking over the government from the existing proforeign regime. Chiang marched in and, in Chinese fashion, "restored order." Certain authors refer to Chiang's "conversion" at Shanghai. Probably what converted him was that he found there the financial support he needed; that some of it was not Chinese but European is of course entirely possible. In any case, Chiang no longer needed the Communists. In May he cleared them out of Hankow, where they had fled from Shanghai, and by July Borodin and his colleagues had departed either for the remote Western provinces or for Russia.

How much of this segment of history did Malraux witness in person? He had returned from France to Indochina in January 1925. On the next June 17 his name appeared on the masthead of Volume I, Number 1, of *L'Indochine*, a daily devoted to closer Franco-Annamite relations. The co-editor was Paul Monin, a Saigon lawyer and member of the Colonial Council. "*L'Indochine* is a free paper," they announced in the first number, "open to all, unattached to banks or business groups. It will make a principle of respecting the temperaments of contributors, regular or otherwise. Polemicists will write with asperity, moderates with moderation." The paper was in eight pages, most of which were filled with boiler plate from *Candide* in Paris. The front page carried two political articles and the usual double column of cable news—which, other Saigon papers shortly declared, was cribbed from their own day-old dispatches. The political pieces were confected with the heavy irony, diatribe, and character assassination common in a press unrestrained by an adequate libel law.

Some eighteen are signed by Malraux. That the editors were not among those whom their declaration of policy referred to as moderates is clear from the start. Within the first week of the paper's existence Malraux was inviting a duel with the editor of the *Courrier-Saigonnais,* and on July 9 he complains at length that he has seen nothing of his adversary's seconds! The title of one of his articles suggests the general tone of the rest: "First letter to Mr. Henry Forward-March-to-the-Rear, Severe Moralist and Healthy Journalist," the individual so designated being the editor of the Saigon *Impartial.* The article (July 8) was signed: "André Malraux, Audacious Adventurer and Unhealthy Journalist."

L'Indochine enraged the other Saigon papers. On June 21 a note appeared prominently in the *Courrier-Saigonnais* welcoming the new daily. On the twenty-second the editors of the *Courrier* denied in print that they felt any of the warmth expressed in the previous note or any knowledge of how the note had got into their paper! (How had Malraux and Monin contrived the insertion? One suspects that the typographers of the two papers were less on the outs than their editors, a suspicion strengthened by the ability of the editors of *L'Indochine* to announce forthcoming items to be printed by the other papers.) The latter were shortly busy branding as false an interview with the temporary Governor General which Malraux had published (*L'Impartial,* June 24); denying that *L'Indochine* had the support of Prime Minister Paul Painlevé (*ibid.,* July 6); publishing Malraux's court record (June 7, and thereafter); printing a photograph of one of the now notorious Khmerian sculptures (July 10); accusing Monin of having "sold out to the Kuomintang," with the added inference that he had made Bolshevism a present danger in the colony (July 13); asking ominously just where the new paper was getting its money; and accusing the editors of stealing cable news from their competitors (July 30). Then, during the first week of August, a strike was called at the Saigon arsenal and eight hundred men left their jobs. The Saigon papers, led by *L'Impartial,* were quick to hint very broadly at a connection between *L'Indochine* and the success of the strike (August 6).

Suddenly references to *L'Indochine* dropped out of the other papers. They do not even reply when Malraux calls the editor of *L'Impartial* "the former stool pigeon" (August 11), and a week later the clear trail ends and we lose track of Malraux. Where he disappeared to nothing even suggests.[4]

Whatever explains Malraux's silent withdrawal from Saigon journalism, and whether or not he withdrew in the direction of China, one thing is abundantly clear. He cannot possibly have left in time to have witnessed any of the action at Canton which he describes so graphically in *The Conquerors*. The novel opens on June 25 and the last scene takes place on August 18. The events at Canton are events that were reported in the Saigon papers while Malraux was still in Saigon. He was not running his paper from a distance, because his articles in *L'Indochine* almost invariably answer articles published in the other papers a day or so previously. Even if he had left Saigon on August 11, when his last article was printed, he could not have reached Canton in time to witness the events in his story. So it is entirely out of order to treat *The Conquerors*, as so many critics have done, as the direct transcription of a personal adventure.

No doubt Malraux's keen and detailed understanding of the military and political situation at Canton is responsible for much of the feeling of historical accuracy the reviewers found in the novel and which no literate person could help perceiving. Yet it is hardly anything which an interested observer in Saigon, in contact with the Kuomintang of Canton as the people in Saigon were, could not have reconstructed for himself. Part of Borodin's propaganda work must have been to keep the subsidiary groups in Southeast Asia well informed of the progress of the Kuomintang in actual combat (especially since the Kuomintang was winning) and quite probably to make such lessons as were learned at Canton available to others who might need them later. There is, in other words, nothing in *The Conquerors* that required the author to be on the spot, provided the author were otherwise well informed, intelligent, and imaginative. These things André Malraux certainly was.

Even so, *The Conquerors* contains far more specific detail, of a kind that suggests that the author may have been on the ground, than does *Man's Fate*. The anonymous narrator, seeing Singapore, Hong Kong, and Canton for the first time, does see the names of hotels and business firms, the shapes of a few buildings, a vague outline of the topography of the towns—although he sees absolutely nothing that could not be picked up from an atlas and a few hours' study of the *National Geographic Magazine*. And he does feel an atmosphere, of course, which seems quite authentic to the Occidental reader—although Malraux was entirely familiar

---

[4] Copies of the newspapers mentioned are on file in the Versailles branch of the Bibliothèque Nationale.

with the atmosphere of the cities of Indochina, and for purposes of convincing an Occidental reader there is little difference between the atmosphere of Saigon and that of a city even a thousand miles away. In *Man's Fate* there is even less recognizable geography and the atmosphere is even less specific.

One learns more about the physical detail of Shanghai from one chapter of a book like O. P. Gilbert's *Mortelle Asie* than from the whole of Malraux's novel. Almost any city, provided it were unfamiliar to the reader, would suit his book as well. No doubt a foreign scene was necessary in the alchemy of creation: Malraux appears always to need the exotic backdrop. The strangeness of the scenery is useful in that it permits him to exhibit his characters in relief. Stripping them of humdrum Western surroundings makes their human predicament more plainly visible. But the strange scene is kept vague; the focus is always on the specific characters rather than on the specific backgrounds. And the subordination of the background is what permits the characters to have such a high degree of tragic generality.

And not only is the background not specifically and recognizably Shanghai; what happens in the book is not always faithful to the history of the Shanghai insurrection. In the novel, the end of the first day of fighting brings the central characters to the discovery that what since early afternoon has seemed a great victory is turning into something else: Chiang Kai-shek is in the offing and, with his order for the Communists to disarm, is readying to liquidate the revolutionary enterprise. The whole economy of the book depends on their being trapped by this turn of events. It has to catch them off balance, so that Kyo and Tchen will have to make their trip to Hankow to find out from the representatives of the International just what the situation is and then make the momentous decisions which determine the outcome of their lives. In actual fact, the Communists had no reason to be surprised at all. Borodin had received orders from Moscow in 1926 telling him under no conditions to allow the Kuomintang to split. The policy of compromise with Chiang was well established. The one question was when Chiang would repudiate the compromise. The leaders of so important a Communist movement as the one in Shanghai would certainly have known the danger. But if Kyo and Katow had been allowed to know what was in the wind, their plight would have been fraught with far fewer tragic possibilities—and *Man's Fate* is a tragic novel.

There seems to be a similar departure from the facts of the biography of the historical figure who, almost certainly, furnished the model for the hero of the novel. Chou En-lai had been born in southern China in 1898, was the son of a professor, and had been educated, in part, in Japan—all of which is also true of the hero of the book, Kyo Gisors. Chou had a varied revolutionary career. At one point he organized a branch of the Chinese Communist party at Paris. At another, he was political commissar of the Chinese First Army. Finally he got the assignment to organize the workers of Shanghai. When Chiang Kai-shek arrived with his army and broke the insurrection, Chou, like Kyo in the novel, was in fact captured. But here the parallel ends abruptly: instead of taking poison he gave his captors the slip, fled to Hankow, moved from there to Canton when Chiang emptied Hankow of Communists, and before the year was out was back in Shanghai again reorganizing the shattered Communist remnant! Chou has since risen high in Communist circles and is at this writing Mao Tse-tung's Premier and Foreign Minister. Such resilient stuff doubtless makes excellent revolutionaries. The same resiliency makes impossible tragic heroes. And the tragic novel needed a tragic hero.

But the thing which really clinches the argument and makes it quite evident that Malraux was not attempting a journalistic job is one further departure from the history of the insurrection. According to the history, Chou En-lai had been in Shanghai organizing the city's working population for the Kuomintang. When the zero hour came, Chou's 600,000 workers simply swamped the police, whose distaste for resistance against such odds was comprehensible, and took over the government with not much more fighting than it took to save face. *The Left Wing Kuomintang coup at Shanghai was very nearly bloodless;* Chou had done his work so well that violence was not needed. But an atmosphere of violence is absolutely necessary to a Malraux novel, and so the day of insurrection in *Man's Fate* is marked by some of the bloodiest and most savage fighting to be found anywhere in Malraux's work. As his novel needed a tragic hero, it also needed violence, and when history did not provide what he wanted he took matters into his own hands.[5]

In his controversy over *The Conquerors* with Leon Trotsky, which took place in 1931 and thus occurred, chronologically, between the two novels which are most frequently suspected of being mere personal histories

[5] No account of Malraux's years in the East can be completely verified at the present time. My report is essentially negative: I have read numerous books, and consulted numerous persons who were on the ground, without finding any proof that Malraux participated in events either at Canton or Shanghai. That he was at Canton at one time or another, and saw action somewhat similar to what he describes in *The Conquerors*, is easily possible. I have found nothing to indicate that he was present during the time of the actual events of the novel,

lightly disguised as fictions,[6] Malraux's burden is that he was more interested in writing a novel than in reporting a revolution. He could now say the same thing of all of his novels up to, though not including, *Man's Hope*. His intimates appear to have assumed that he never meant to do anything else. For Malraux's close friend Emmanuel Berl, whose entire *Mort de la pensée bourgeoise* develops the implications of Malraux's presentation of the character of Garine, the importance of *The Conquerors* was that this novel portrays a new kind of revolutionary. He is interested in the disaffected and disabused bourgeois intellectual, and not at all in a possible vicarious experience of revolution. Malraux's staunch friend Bernard Groethuysen, a convinced Communist whose apartment in Paris was a crossroads for visiting Communists, and who would certainly have known what was going on in the world, says absolutely nothing in his review[7] of *The Conquerors* about Malraux's having played the role in the East that we have heard so much about, and nothing about his having seen either the Canton or the Shanghai civil wars.

When the purveyors of the legend appear, toward the end of 1933, during the mild furor attendant upon winning the Goncourt prize, they were not Malraux's intimates, and one suspects that it was at that moment

---

and much to indicate that he was not. Nothing suggests that he was ever in Shanghai before 1931.

As for the political aspect of Malraux's Oriental experience, I have seen no list of Canton Kuomintang Committee members which included his name and, in fact, have found no list showing the name of any European; even Borodin appears to have played, officially, only the role of adviser. That Malraux was of *some* service to the Communists in the East, however, is attested by the ease with which his archaeological expeditions were permitted, later, to cross Soviet territory. The details may be left for his biographers to straighten out. What is important to us here is that his novels cannot be direct transcriptions of experience.

I am especially indebted to Professor C. Martin Wilbur and Professor Nathaniel Peffer, my colleagues, and to M. René Hussenet, former Vice-Consul of France at Kunming, for their suggestions regarding Malraux's political role in China; they are, of course, in no way responsible for my conclusions. For an account of political events in China during the years in question, see Harold Isaacs, *The Tragedy of the Chinese Revolution* (rev. ed., Stanford University Press, 1951). On the Shanghai insurrection J. J. Brieux, "La Chine de Mao Tse-tung," *Esprit*, 17e année, No. 11 (November 1949), pp. 766–86, is extremely useful, and I am grateful to John L. Brown for mentioning the study to me. On the subject of Oriental atmosphere, compare Malraux's novels with such journalistic accounts as Hallett Abend, *My Life in China, 1926–1941*, and O. P. Gilbert's *Mortelle Asie*.

[6] See Bibliography. What is frequently referred to as if it had been a lengthy controversy consists, so far as I can discover, of a single article by Trotsky and a single reply by Malraux.

[7] "Les Conquérants; Royaume farfelu," *Nouvelle Revue Française*, 16e année, No. 187 (April 1, 1929), pp. 558–63. Groethuysen insists at length on the importance of Garine's character, which he finds to be compounded of the Will to Power and of repugnance for the existing social order.

that the novels began to nourish the legend. Since *The Royal Way* was so palpably a novelization of Malraux's own experience in Indochina, why not assume that the brute material of the others had a similar source? And since the contours of Garine's personality seemed so like those of Malraux's, why not believe that much of Garine's story was a transposition of personal experience? After such assumptions it can have been no great effort to go one step more and take for granted that the novels were disguised *reportage* and not quite the major works of imaginative art that they really are. The issue has persistently beclouded interpretations of Malraux's work ever since.

To what extent the legend is factually true at other points than those which touch his two "China novels," and to what extent it is a tissue of exaggerations and possibly of falsehoods, are questions that need not delay us, since they do not affect the interpretation of his other books. But we shall have to return to the legend later from another angle. For, although there is no evidence to show that Malraux actively discouraged the formation of his legend, it is quite clear that if he had wanted to he could at one time have stopped it dead with one word of denial. He never did so, and hence must bear some of the responsibility. The legend has become a part of the public personality of a man active in public life, and, as such, something he has had a share in creating. We thus have to study it, as much as his other creations. The time to do so, however, is not now, but after examining the other aspects of his creative achievement.

CHAPTER TWO

The Implacable Urge

> *"The artist has an 'eye,' but not at fifteen, and how much time does it take a writer to come to write with the sound of his own voice?"*
> —*Museum Without Walls*, p. 114

> *"The implacable urge which constrains the artist to destroy the forms to which he has been born . . ."*
> —*The Creative Act*, p. 98

ARD as this is to believe, the author of some of the grimmest novels of this century began his career writing stuff that is playful to the point of frivolity. *Circa* 1920 Malraux was almost a textbook case of surrealism. His early pieces show the delight in imaginative irresponsibility and the mastery of the techniques of projecting metaphors into action, and of implausible metamorphosis, which one would expect any bright young man of that moment to have acquired. The two he has republished are tucked away in the back of the *Tentation de l'occident* volume of the Skira edition, and not even these get into the anthology of his work published by Gallimard in 1946. The rest (I have found a half-dozen) have been left to crumble with the evanescent little magazines where they appeared, and where their author would doubtless be content to leave them undisturbed.

But in an article in the *Partisan Review* (July-September 1948) Nicola Chiaromonte does his best to make them important by reviving the opinion of earlier critics to the effect that the style of these first writings indicates a "revolt of the imagination." Chiaromonte's theory is that Malraux's mind has always shown a tendency to turn away from the real toward the fantastic. According to him, Malraux has always been conscious of the tendency, considered it common to many of his generation, and feared that it may sap their capacity for action.

The load is heavy for such slight evidence to bear. It seems more likely that Malraux began writing as he says that all artists begin their work, using a style not so much his own as common to many writers of the time. In other words, the first writings use not a "style of revolt" but a style *against which he would revolt* when the time was ripe for him to establish his own characteristic way of expression—and from which, to use a favorite expression of the *Psychology of Art*, he would "wrest his originality."

In spite of a convention which makes bibliographers list *Lunes en papier* as poetry, this piece is really a fantastic tale. The epigraph comes from the *Tales of Hoffman*: "Keep close watch," said the Silversmith, "for here you are involved with some rather strange people." Strange is not the word. The characters first appear as funny little balloons, born of moonbeams striking on water on a quiet night. They are quickly transformed into fruits, and these in turn become weird little men who have "the advantage of existing only in the imagination." They take the names of the Seven Deadly Sins and set off on an expedition with the object of killing Death. Their journey takes them first through a fantastic forest where they are menaced by the Cable, which becomes a serpent and slithers about picking living hearts off trees. They progress to a miraculous inn where they are further beset by numerous unlikely creatures. Eventually they come to the Realm of Death, or "royaume farfelu." Death happens to be ill and calls her new physician, who persuades her to try his healing bath. The bath turns out to be a corrosive acid which eats away the aluminum vertebrae of Death's up-to-the-minute skeleton, and when the physician unmasks himself he is one of our strange little people. While Death lies dying, the pillows of the royal chamber burst open and out step the other members of the weird band. They congratulate each other, but then, when one remarks that he has forgotten the purpose of the execution, all look at each other in surprise: no one in the group can remember why they undertook to kill Death in the first place. Incidentally, we learn, Death has been contemplating suicide anyhow.

The structure, of course, is familiar. We have the supernatural—or perhaps extra-natural—origin of the voyagers, their miraculous voyage through country populated by monsters that have to be vanquished by quasi-miraculous means, the enchanted wood and the castle where the travelers are further tested, and finally the evil monarch who is to be bested by whatever prowess or guile the heroes possess. But the dangers are burlesqued and met with burlesque weapons; for example, the serpents at the inn turn out to be dangerous only because the songs they sing are so enormously stupid that after ten minutes the listener either takes flight or goes mad; they are overcome when one of the little men (who, conveniently, has been a musician in a previous incarnation) takes up the horn of an old phonograph and toots such lugubrious notes that the serpents are paralyzed by envy. Out of the clash between classical material and burlesque treatment comes the playful, somewhat insane, irony of the piece. Today we recognize both the playfulness and the irony as elements of the "black humor" of the surrealists. Every page of *Lunes en papier* dates it and attests its kinship with the mood of the Age of Mystification which produced that maddest of all mad images, André Breton's Soluble Fish. It is *enfant terrible* literature.

The Prologue opens with a cascade of metaphors of a kind that make the identification unmistakable. Certain of them, like one that compares the changing moon to the light of a varicolored sign and another that equates the forked wake on the water with the hands of a clock, achieve a juxtaposition of the order of nature with an order of things completely artificial and man-made, that catches the reader by complete surprise. Several of the others obtain the same effect, with more and more difficulty as the passage progresses, by rapidly repeated transpositions of the senses. The moon gives off musical notes, one of which falls like a tiny frog; others become the moon's teeth and then come tumbling down together into the water; their light—presumably the light of the notes, but possibly of the teeth—forms pale streaks in the sky like the trails of stars grown too heavy, and the notes, afloat on the water, open out like wetted paper flowers. The reader's comprehension is forced to switch violently back and forth between auditory and visual imagery, and he is not always entirely sure, as for instance in the case of whether the moonbeams equate with musical notes or with teeth, just what his imagination is leaving behind and what it is moving toward.

This is certainly a specimen of the confusion of the senses which Rimbaud recommended to poets some years before Malraux was born. But with a slight difference: it is the kind of stuff not that dreams are made on, but that they would be made on if we had enough control over them to keep our dreams consistently fantastic. In other words, it is a waking fantasy on a dream pattern. The surprising relationships created by the metaphors, the "events" such as the emergence of an Auvergnat from a floating box and his subsequent flight on awkward wing (never to reappear in the story), the incessant metamorphoses of the characters and the fact that the shapes they assume are always deformations of familiar forms, are all the work of an imagination functioning *as if* in sleep. The Prologue creates, and the rest of the story inhabits, a sort of child's world full of wounds that leave no scars and of death that "doesn't hurt."

This self-conscious dream-imagination runs wildest in the enchanted-wood sequence. The leaves on the lower parts of the trees are arranged in geometric patterns—spheres, cubes, and prisms, from each of which hangs a human heart. The Cable now rises up and becomes a snake with a cupping glass for a head. The snake goes about picking the hearts, like fruit, between the lightning flashes. He goes through any substance like a needle through parchment, leaving a perfectly clean hole where he has passed, and carries the hearts like beads about his neck. Each time one is picked the stem bleeds slightly, but quickly heals and puts down a tendril from the wound to the ground. Meanwhile fat kangaroos flit awkwardly about on trapezoidal wings. The largest, bumping a cloud, falls calamitously upon a whole sheaf of the tendrils. They stick in him like *banderillas* in the neck of a bull. When he gets up he looks like a porcupine. And now the broken stems join together into a parallelepiped and the Cable climbs up it with the hearts he has gathered. Pleased with himself, he rises playfully on the end of his tail. The string of his necklace breaks; he lunges after the escaping hearts, but they run off in every direction, looking like cupids that have been spanked too hard.

Today Malraux's manner seems only too familiar. The forest with its mad geometry, the crazy metamorphosis of the Cable into a snake, followed by the diversion of attention to the kangaroo's mishap, and then the apotheosis of the dream with the breaking of the necklace of hearts, create a sequence that has lost its power to surprise. Almost any Cocteau movie or Dali painting luxuriates in such effects. Elsewhere Malraux even uses the device, so dear to the surrealists, of the little human figure with its eyes stuck out on antennae away from its head, which has since been employed by a writer as unsurrealistic as Céline. But he was working before the great surrealist year of 1924, and doubtless his manner seemed fresher then than it does now.

The other pieces that Malraux published between 1920 and 1924 are extremely like this one, peopled by fantastic creatures, decorated with metaphor which dissociates the common data of experience, and enlivened by monsters to be slain with unlikely weapons. One, *Écrit pour un ours en peluche*, is the story of the capture and killing of a monster, the "Key of C," that sounds remarkably like the "Cable" but behaves somewhat more lethally. Taken as a whole these pieces are the work of a talented beginner whose vocation has preceded his finding a subject. He has not yet had the experience which will give him something to say, nor found a style of his own in which he can say it.

One piece, however, shows his imagination reaching out toward the crucial experience, as though Malraux had already had an intuition of what he needed. *Royaume farfelu* is again dream stuff, but this time a dream populated by human beings and involving human adventure.

The narrator is an old soldier who has come by ship to Trebizond. The demon that has pursued the ship now abandons it, but after the passengers have gone ashore and watched a bird merchant burn a phoenix, and have refused to buy a dragon, the narrator is suddenly seized by "the Functionary" who has been following them. He is clapped into prison. The next day he is taken before the Petit Mogol. After listening to reports that the hanging gardens are now dust, that the "sad songs of Hell" are myth since there is no singing there, and that his daughter has been married to the Fish-Eating Tsar over whose kingdom she now reigns, the Prince dictates a heartsick letter to the Princess of China (whom he has never seen) and orders the narrator off to the army. As historiographer royal the latter goes off to the siege of Ispahan. The army is a strange one, poorly equipped and disciplined, but Ispahan is completely undefended. They encamp under the walls of the city, but the inhabitants have sealed the gates so thoroughly that the invaders are unable to find their way in. The besiegers are shortly surrounded by animals. Scorpions invade the camp and gradually kill off the troops. Food is exhausted. Such officers as are left take to fishing in the fountains. Demons come to haunt the soldiers, one to each man, whispering disaster in their ears. Then comes a whole crawling horde of scorpions and the invading army disperses, every man for himself. The narrator does not remember how he got back to Trebizond. He only knows that he hopes to persuade the Prince to let him leave his life of selling pretty shells and depart on a new adventure.

Obviously this piece is not so imitative, technically, as *Lunes*, and, at the same time, the dream has moved from the never-never land of the little men to what is geographically identifiable as the Orient. The style avoids the fabulously far-fetched metaphor in favor of a lushness appropriate to a fantastic East; the content of the dream itself is full of spices, silks, strange animals, and exotic people—the kind of thing that one writer or another has been imagining ever since Marco Polo.

The writing is still very far from the hard, jerky, fast, nervous prose of *The Conquerors*. If *Royaume farfelu* sounds, even so, somewhat maturer, somewhat less of a set piece than does *Lunes*, the reason is probably that Malraux touched it up before publishing it in 1928. Malraux's friend Groethuysen, who reviewed the story in the *Nouvelle Revue Française* at the same time that he did *The Conquerors*, refused to take *Royaume farfelu* at all seriously.[1] Doubtless he was right. The tale is a slight thing indeed and *The Conquerors* could not fail to dwarf it. Yet when read in its proper place in the chronological series of Malraux's works, the piece takes on a certain interest. The story starts by being a tiresome sea voyage and the hero arrives at a place new and strange to him. The pattern will be exactly

---

[1] See April 1, 1929, issue (pp. 558–63). A brief mention of *Royaume farfelu* is appended to a long review of *The Conquerors*. Groethuysen tends even to parody Malraux's style.

the same for the beginnings of *The Conquerors, The Royal Way*, and also for the story implicit in the essayistic *Tentation de l'occident*—we shall have to wait until *Man's Fate* for a story which does not open with a trip, an arrival, and a subsequent adventure. As so often in Malraux's work, the adventure involves a siege and the siege ends in frustration. Death hovers over the whole enterprise. A malevolent fate defeats the army from Trebizond. Malraux's imagination is already preoccupied with insects and other crawling things, as it will be in *The Royal Way*. And in general, one recognizes numerous elements of which Malraux will make more impressive use later: *Royaume farfelu* is a fantastic tale of strangely violent men; they die in an adventure of which death is the only possible reward; their death is perilously close to having no meaning. Take out the word "fantastic" and the formula fits, with fair accuracy, Malraux's subsequent full-dress novels.

The real importance of these first writings is less literary than psychological. They represent the kind of art against which he will shortly rebel. The result of the rebellion will be the tone of high seriousness which will mark everything he writes after his return to Europe from Indochina. Already in 1925, the structure of *La Tentation de l'occident* constitutes an implicit rejection of the form of imagination that takes the world apart and then reassembles the parts according to its pleasure: a Prologue written in the manner, tone, and color of *Royaume farfelu* precedes a text written in a style which aims at the opposite extreme. The Prologue is loaded with apostrophe, ejaculation, metaphor and color adjective. "Why have I not met you [it starts], you surprising savages who used to bring the navigators horn-shaped fruits on barbarian trays. . . ." The putative author of the Prologue is on a ship going east, away from Europe, and his mind is playing over images of Asia he has found in books.

Chaque printemps couvre les steppes de Mongolie de roses tartares, blanches au coeur de pourpre. Des caravanes les traversent; des marchands sales conduisent de grands chameaux velus porteurs de paquets ronds, qui, à l'étape, s'ouvrent comme des grenades. Et toute la féerie du royaume des neiges, pierres couleur de ciel clair ou de rivière gelée, pierres aux reflets de glace, et plumes pâles d'oiseaux gris, fourrures de givre et turquoises aux empreintes d'argent s'écroulent sur leurs doigts agiles. (P. 20.)

Each springtime covers the Mongolian steppes with roses of Tartary, white, purple-centered. Caravans cross; dirty merchants drive great shaggy camels loaded with round bundles which, at the halts, open out like pomegranates. And all the fairy stuff of the kingdom of the snows, stones the color of open sky or of frozen river, stones that flash like ice, and pale feathers of gray birds, frost-silvery furs and turquoises veined with silver, pour over the nimble fingers.

Vocabulary, syntax, and imagery are so similar to those of *Royaume farfelu* that the Prologue could easily be a suppressed passage from the earlier book. The Prologue is still dream stuff. The text that follows is waking reality. Style and mood in the body of the book are so much closer to Malraux's later manner that there is no doubting he intends the contrast. The rest of the text rejects the style of the introductory pages as thoroughly as "A.D." rejects the dreamworld he has been living in before his trip to the Orient. The following illustration comes from the last page of *La Tentation*:

Europe, grand cimetière où ne dorment que des conquérants morts et dont la tristesse devient plus profonde en se parant de leurs noms illustres, tu ne laisses autour de moi qu'un horizon nu et le miroir qu'apporte le désespoir, vieux maître de la solitude. Peut-être mourra-t-il, lui aussi, de sa propre vie. Au loin, dans le port, une sirène hurle comme un chien sans guide. Voix des lâchetés vaincues ... je contemple mon image. Je ne l'oublierai plus.

Image mouvante de moi-même, je suis pour toi sans amour. Comme une large blessure mal fermée, tu es ma gloire morte et ma souffrance vivante. Je t'ai tout donné, et, pourtant, je ne t'aimerai jamais. Sans m'incliner, je t'apporterai chaque jour la paix en offrande. Lucidité avide, je brûle encore devant toi, flamme solitaire et droite, dans cette lourde nuit où le vent jaune crie, comme dans toutes ces nuits étrangères où le vent du large répétait autour de moi l'orgueuilleuse clameur de la mer stérile. (P. 124.)

Europe, great cemetery where only conquerors sleep and whose melancholy deepens as it wraps itself in their illustrious names, you leave only an empty horizon about me and the mirror of that old master of loneliness, despair. Perhaps even he will die, too, from the weight of his own life. Far off, in the port, a whistle howls like an abandoned dog. Voice of the cowardice I have conquered . . . I contemplate my own picture. I will never forget it.

Shifting image of myself, I have no love for you. Like a wide and unhealed wound, you are my dead glory and my living suffering. I have given you everything, and yet I shall never love you. Each day I shall bring you my tribute of peace, but without bowing down. Hungry lucidity, I burn still before you, a solitary and upright flame, in this heavy night where the yellow wind cries, as in all those foreign nights where the sea wind repeated about me the prideful clamor of the sterile sea.

Two years after this, in the essay called "D'une jeunesse européenne," Malraux will make the reasons for the change in styles explicit and clear, for when he rejects the idealist, subjective aesthetics of artists like Kandinsky, he also rejects the aesthetics of his own explorations of the private world of the imagination. Meanwhile, the rupture we have just seen expressed in the juxtaposed styles is not expressed by style alone. It inheres also in the tone. The second of the passages quoted is solemn and grim. The auditory image of the howling siren is the same used in later books to mark grave moments. The similes—*grand cimetière, large blessure mal fermée, flamme solitaire et droite*—are grandiose, to say the least. The *"vent du large"* sets off the speaker's figure in dramatic loneliness. The rhythm is heavy and solemn: *lucidité avide/je brûle/encore/devant toi/ flamme solitaire/et droite/dans cette lourde nuit/où le vent/jaune/crie* ... We are out of the dream now and into the reality of Asia. Reality is grim business.

La Tentation de l'occident consists of sixty-five hermetic pages, made up of sixteen letters supposed to be exchanged between two young men, alert, educated to the brink of erudition, particularly well versed in art, and dedicated to the search for quintessences. The author of five of the letters is the young European traveling in the Orient, "A.D." The rest are written by "Ling W.-Y.," a young Chinese traveling in Europe.

The more Ling moves about Europe, the more he is convinced that European culture rests upon a base of confusions. Europeans seem unable to distinguish being from acting, or order from civilization. Gradually he comes to the point of saying that the European's notion of reality is itself confused and self-contradictory. And at last what he has seen brings him to use a phrase which re-echoes through the remainder of the book: *in the depths of European man, where it dominates the great moments of his life, there resides an essential absurdity.* The italics are in Malraux's text.

"A.D." replies that he agrees that Western man is the creature of the Absurd and takes over the rest of the book to enumerate additional reasons for thinking so and to explore the possible consequences. European man, he says, lives an unconscious life entirely at odds with his conscious one; he depends on dreams to carry him into realms of action he could not reach otherwise—reading is the opiate of the West and the motion picture is its source of vicarious heroism. Through these the European achieves greatness by proxy. The European conviction of the transiency of all things, the corroding awareness that nothing is permanent, is really, he continues, an admission of life's essential meaninglessness. Value after value, "A.D." reports, disappears as the effort to understand advances, and we are eventually left face to face with the incomprehensible, the Absurd. He has learned that the anxiety of the Europeans has even invaded the Orient and that there is a new generation of Chinese who have cast aside their native culture, received no equivalent in return, and have nothing left them but a furious desire for destruction. (Ling agrees: he sees signs that already the will to destruction is organizing and taking up arms. Soon millions of Chinese will be animated only by their awareness of injustice and suffering, having no idea of the opposites, happiness and justice.) "A.D." concludes, sadly, that there is a certain bitter pleasure in contemplating an anarchic reality, one that cannot be expected to make sense, and his last letter ends in the promise to himself, to live in lucid awareness of the predicament he shares with the rest of Europe, without blinking the transcendent presence and power of the Absurd.

Obviously, to a man like "A.D." not only God is dead, but, going beyond Nietzschean formula, Man is dead also. At least, one of his manifestations, the European, has succumbed. He has managed to destroy his accustomed mode of consciousness of himself. His ideals and his idols have deserted him. In an empty world, under an empty heaven, he stands alone and for his loneliness there is no palliative. Recent readers of *The Psychology of Art* cannot fail to recognize in this a first statement of the central thesis of the *Psychology* (and of *Les Voix du silence*), to wit, that Europeans must forge a new and adequate idea of man.

But in 1925 Malraux is framing only the negative premise, that the old idea of man has fallen apart, and this is as far as his thought goes at the moment. His first two novels are based upon the same negative conviction. *The Conquerors* and *The Royal Way* will exploit at length this awareness of the meaninglessness of life and thus do much to turn the abstraction of the Absurd into one of the most essential bases of the common metaphysic of our time. They will, however, go further than does *La Tentation*. For the man confronted by the Absurd in *La Tentation* is Western man; the dilemma is the dilemma of the Occidental. The East is in danger only to the extent that it may be contaminated by the West. Malraux has not yet reached the tragic assumption that life is absurd for all men everywhere. Even in the first two novels, the heroes who are most completely aware that they are powerless against the Absurd are Europeans, scions of the middle class who, like "A.D.," have forsaken class and country. But the degree of completeness will be greater, because, when they meet their destiny through their discovery of the Absurd, they do so less because they are Europeans than because they are men.

To the attentive reader, this midway position in the development of Malraux's attitude seems entirely appropriate to the moment when the book was written. The dedication to Clara Malraux, and the fact of the book's having been finished in 1925, authorize the suspicion that *La Ten-*

tation de l'occident represents the state of his feelings as they were at the end of the first Indochina enterprise. The tone of the letters is primarily one of repudiation, and what he is repudiating is Europe. His adventure had contained everything necessary to make him aware of the differences between Europe and Asia and—ending so perilously close to a colonial jail—had been such as to make him acutely aware of certain kinds of absurdity. The book as a whole thus stands as a further announcement of the rupture.

So far as I know, Malraux has never revealed, in public, the intimate motivations that led to the break. But a famous essay by Marcel Arland, exactly contemporary with Malraux's first trip to the Orient, pictures the youngest literary generation of the first half of the 'twenties as completely fed up. They were, Arland said, victims of a new *Weltschmerz*. After the premature collapse of the Dada movement they had nowhere to go. Literature had become merely something to while away the time, on a plane with occupations like marriage, running for office, and certain "interesting crimes." They had Nietzsche at their fingertips, and (Arland notes) they were full of Dostoevski. "Never," Arland writes, "have Frenchmen felt closer to certain heroes in *The Possessed* and *The Brothers Karamazov*."[2]

Arland was one of Malraux's most intimate friends, and may well be speaking for Malraux in his article. In Nietzsche, Malraux could have found whatever incitement he needed to abandon values that no longer appealed. In Dostoevski he could have found the same values closely associated with the notion of the Absurd. In both—as also in Gide, whose "seriousness" he had praised in an early article[3]—was the invitation to break with everything, to escape the spiritual weariness of home that Arland talks about.

His book announces a rupture, but not a program. Malraux is so frequently represented both by friends and adversaries to be the great apostle of action that his skepticism about the value of action in *La Tentation* is a real surprise. To Ling the European cult of action is one of the more trying incomprehensibles with which he has to cope. To "A.D." the value set upon action is the source of Western man's conflict between dream and reality; it contains that promise of a final outburst of destruction which

---

[2] *Nouvelle Revue Française*, 11e année, No. 125 (February 1, 1924), pp. 149–58. See especially p. 156: "No doctrine can satisfy us, but the absence of a doctrine torments us. It is possible that someday such torments may appear to have been naïve, and people may be astonished by this taste for somber pleasure, this masochism, this anxiety."

[3] See Bibliography. The article is too brief to permit even a guess as to how well Malraux knew Gide and Gide's work, or as to what specific aspects of the work appealed to him.

threatens to be his bloody destiny. Most of the European's metaphysical discomfort rises from his yearning to act. The author of *La Tentation* knows already how certain his future man-of-action heroes are of being defeated. The certainty will not prevent Malraux himself from seeking an adventurous life or from writing stories which attach value to action. But he already realizes that his hero's plight is one from which he can be rescued only by an act of poetry—the creating of a poetic situation which somehow turns defeat into victory.

This poetic strategy is already at work even in *La Tentation*, in those last paragraphs of the book which exhibit the young European in his determination to face down the fact of life's absurdity. The lyric tension of the passage has already been underlined. René Lalou, an attentive reader of Malraux and a generally trustworthy critic, has called these final paragraphs noble. And certainly this picture of a man defeated has something that makes the reader forget the defeat: a human being's ability to face the Absurd with open eyes, and in so doing to transcend it, becomes more important than his being beaten. One need hold no high opinion of the quality of this particular poetry as poetry: it has something about it of the self-satisfaction of "Invictus" and some of Kipling's weaker stuff, and is not far from the dividing line between poetry and mere oratory. But for the moment quality is not at issue. The nature of the passage is what is important.

Two years later, in the essay, "D'une jeunesse européenne," Malraux foregoes the poetry. The central figure is again the abstract Western man who, Malraux says, wants to rid himself of the burden of his civilization as he once wanted to be rid of the burden of God. The notion of reality which his civilization has given him no longer suits the European's taste, and he no longer has the Christian assurance of the unity, permanence, and responsibility of humanity. Thus, Malraux says, he has to attain a new notion of man. Meanwhile he is full of anxiety, loneliness, and a Nietzschean *inquiétude* regarding himself. Nietzsche's work, for Malraux, merely expresses a despair and violence which already existed.[4]

The great obstacle in the way of "creating a new reality"—the expression is synonymous with attaining a new notion of man—is the modern ego. The notion of God has been replaced by the great new passion of indi-

---

[4] How well Malraux knew Nietzsche at this time is an open question. The "Nietzschean accents" of the early novels are evident—but not such as to indicate that Malraux had read much of Nietzsche. The Adventurer characters are Nietzschean only in the popular sense. Malraux appears to have renewed his philosophical studies after his return from Asia, at which time he began frequenting the "Decades" at Pontigny and became the intimate of Groethuysen.

vidualism. And individualism places men in unhappy straits. There is nothing on which to found a new conception of man except the consciousness each man has of himself. And here we totter, he says, on the brink of the Absurd, for there is no way for a man to know himself. The instruments we use in judging others cannot be brought to bear. Even our memory is conditioned, and what we remember of our own acts is private, and dependent on all the forces which condition our memory. There is no way of examining our past lives which does not employ subjective and thus completely undependable means. Walled up in his own ego, the European finds himself unable to establish satisfactory relationships with other individuals. His situation is ironical: he experiences two orders of sensations, those he feels in himself and those he attributes to his vis-à-vis. Love, for example, would be entirely different if it did not suppose a constant and involuntary effort to penetrate the sensations of the beloved . . .

By this reasoning, Malraux concludes that to carry the search for one's ego to the ultimate extreme, accepting (as one must) one's own vision of the world as the valid vision, is to give in to the Absurd. Our civilization has no spiritual goal upon which individuals may establish common ground. Our thought and our sensibility are at odds. We are uncomfortable in our individualism; the burden is heavy and our hearts are no longer in carrying it. The best reflection of ourselves is the resultant anxiety.

A man who knows his thought to be only a system of allegories knows, Malraux says, that he cannot comprehend himself. In addition, the young men of Europe, those who have come to maturity in the years since the war, realize that certain ideas alone have the power of defending men against the gradual, constant wear of time. They are thus uneasily searching for the Idea which will preserve them from their own individualism and at the same time hold them permanent amid the flux of the years. Malraux does not allege that they have found the idea. He does not mention communism.

The reader, following Malraux's already somewhat oracular utterances—written in declarative sentences which state, without qualification and with scant regard for the relations between them, ideas which are presented as aspects of universal truth—is ready at any moment to find Malraux proposing that European youth take the road to Moscow. Roger Stéphane, one of the critics who has taken Malraux most seriously, declares that the proposal is latent in every page of the "D'une jeunesse ..." essay.[5] But actually the essay leads up to the proposal and stops short of it. And unless one is prepared to read into the text more than the words say, the

---

[5] "Malraux et la révolution," *Esprit*, 16ᵉ année, No. 10 (October 1948), p. 461.

essay must be taken as a negative document. It simply refuses to accept the conditions of European civilization. Like *La Tentation de l'occident*, the essay is at once a diagnosis of what is wrong with Europe and a rejection. And like "A.D.," Malraux has closed a door behind him.

There had already been a literature of globe-trotting in the 'twenties, typified by the work of Paul Morand—full, at its best, of urbane curiosity and, otherwise, of rather cheap sensationalism. There was shortly to be another, the work of young men who would take up the tone and manner of such stern predecessors as T. E. Lawrence and Ernest Psichari. Malraux was in the vanguard of the new group. His departure from Europe coincides closely with the first epic flights of Antoine de Saint-Exupéry. Their search for a new kind of life pretty much marks the beginning of the New Seriousness. In 1925 it was new indeed.

Current historians believe that the years 1925–30 saw French literature pass a kind of climacteric. The first World War had been, in the novelist Radiguet's much-quoted phrase, "a four-year vacation," and had been followed by the general letdown which Maurice Sachs has called "the witches' sabbath." The immediate postwar period had brought the various forms of Modernism, from Futurism through Cubism and Dadaism to Surrealism. The movement, according to one very alert observer, Mme Claude-Edmonde Magny, had produced nothing but fuss; the surrealists, instead of making a real revolution in literature, had turned out to have nothing in common but their dislikes, had never managed to set up a constructive program, and had fizzled out in what she calls "a series of school-girl quarrels." Otherwise, the literature of the 'twenties had specialized, Mme Magny says, in eluding essential issues and in confirming the bourgeoisie in its characteristically sterile habits of mind. There was, she continues, a Maginot Line in literature; its defenders were François Mauriac, André Maurois, Jules Romains, Georges Duhamel, and their kind. And then, finally, in the middle of the decade there emerged a new group who may have had little else in common but did at least have their seriousness and their willingness to face the essential problems. Men as different as Malraux, Bernanos, Céline, Montherlant, and Giono brought the basic questions into fashion.[6]

One does not have to accept such a simplistic analysis as the final word on the subject. Where freshness of mind is concerned, some of the older generation whom Mme Magny refuses to consider—Gide and Valéry for instance—were rather more youthful and malleable than young men like Louis Aragon. But when all the objections have been raised, it is still true

[6] *Histoire du roman français depuis 1918*, I, 24 ff.

that one finds a marked difference between the anodyne writing which was the common pabulum of the early 'twenties and the harsh, bitter rejections of middle-class Europe that fill the books of the newly emerged group of 1925–30, and that is implicit in *La Tentation de l'occident*.

The immediate effect of Malraux's experience in Asia seems to have been both to make Malraux ask these "basic questions" and to answer them in a tone of discouragement. His first novels are dark with the apprehension of death and sad with the vanity of life, and haunted by the inevitable, tragic defeat of man's attempts to impart real meaning to what he does. They contain hardly a hint that in some way life may acquire meaning through the fraternity of revolutionary action and sacrifice. This suggestion will come in 1933, in *Man's Fate*.

In 1927 he appears to have been in the predicament of a young and able composer whose head teems with more materials than he can use in a single piece of music. Not only do *La Tentation* and the "Jeunesse" essay contain in germ what will go into the first novels; they also adumbrate the themes of all the later works. What remained to be done was to establish the relationships between the themes and to find the people to incarnate them.

The man who lives in calm distress, aware of the conflicts between his acts and his inner life, will be Garine, the hero of *The Conquerors*. The one who is willing, as "A.D." puts it in his last letter, to risk death in the name of hatred alone, will be Hong, the terrorist in the same novel. Out of "A.D.'s" somewhat Dostoevskian remark, "the taker of a life . . . may discover that he is penetrated either by his crime *or* by the new universe which his crime forces upon him," will come the figure of Tchen at the beginning of *Man's Fate*, murdering a man in a hotel bedroom and then discovering that his act has admitted him to a new, private, and very lonely world. And it will turn up again, most significantly, in connection with the hero of *Les Noyers de l'Altenburg*. Perken, in *The Royal Way*, will be a victim of the eroticism which puts the protagonist of the sexual drama in the intolerable position of having to experience both his own sensations and those of his partners. (This is the same situation which makes Ling first suspect the absurdity of European life; it is later seen in "D'une jeunesse" as an inevitable product of European individualism.) Ferral, in *Man's Fate*, will suffer the same torment. The great conflict between acting and being, which so impresses Ling, will underlie Garine's decision to join the Communists in *The Conquerors*, will be dramatized by the gradual rise to power of the Communists and the death of Hernandez in *Man's Hope*, and will have a decisive influence on Vincent Berger's career in *Les Noyers*.

The great question, whether it is possible for man to be considered a permanent, continuously identical entity, is a central theme of both *Les Noyers* and the books on art. The fear of growing old, and of discovering that time itself has decided one's destiny, will be another source of Perken's anguish.

Such are the themes, already stated and soon to be made flesh. Certain additional ones are present by implication. We have heard nothing so far of human dignity, for which Kyo is willing to die in *Man's Fate,* or of virile fraternity, the experience of which is vouchsafed to heroes like Kyo's friend Katow, and to Kassner in *Days of Wrath.* But these themes are really responses to earlier questions. Human dignity is an opposite of the Absurd, since it supposes the discovery of meaning in life, and virile fraternity is the counterpart to man's feeling of estrangement.

At this point in Malraux's career, the theme of the Absurd predominates. Most criticism of Malraux focuses its interest on the nature of his heroes and the way they are animated by concern about these central themes. The tendency, however understandable, has the disadvantage of falsifying the picture of Malraux's work. For it seems impossible to carry such discussions far without selecting some one of the themes and declaring, by fiat, that this one is the essential preoccupation of heroes and author alike. Thus Mme Magny, for example, is persuaded that Malraux's central subject is man's inability to communicate with man, and that he "has never written about anything else."[7] Roger Stéphane takes essentially the same position.[8] On the whole, such judgments assume more stability than is actually present in Malraux's work. Of course there are places in the novels where man's fate seems to be an eternal condemnation to solitude. But there are others where solitude seems to be a relatively minor consideration. In *La Tentation,* for example, its importance, though real, is quite secondary. For Malraux, at that moment, the pivotal fact is that Western civilization places men in an absurd position. In comparison, solitude is a mere by-product: we are isolated from our fellows *because of* our untenable notion of reality. In "D'une jeunesse" we are cut off *because of* the individualism inherent in our civilization. Both pieces make solitude a function of something far more fundamental—the Absurd.

As epigraph for "D'une jeunesse" Malraux uses a line from *La Tentation,* to the effect that the highest achievement of a refined civilization is "a scrupulous refusal to cultivate the ego." The words are in one of the letters ascribed to Ling, but their import belongs in an Occidental, not an Oriental, context. Malraux's generation had read Barrès and been nour-

[7] "Malraux le fascinateur," *Esprit,* 16ᵉ année, No. 10 (October 1948), p. 513.
[8] *Portrait de l'aventurier,* p. 96.

ished on the idea that one's sacred duty toward oneself is to develop the individual personality as far as possible. "Feel as deeply as possible," Barrès had declared his slogan, "while analysing as completely as possible."[9] (As late as 1936, Malraux will make one of the characters of *Man's Hope* declare that the best thing one can do with one's life is "to transform into consciousness the broadest possible experience"—p. 391.) To older men, like Gide, Barrès' counsel had been of immense value. Certain of Malraux's contemporaries, like Henry de Montherlant, were still busy, in 1927, pursuing it to its ultimate absurdity of arbitrariness. For Malraux, in the same year, it seems to have arrived at a dead end. However completely he develops his individuality, the individual must still find the Absurd waiting for him when he has finished.

Other writers of the late 1920's had also convicted the world of its desolate vanity. Hemingway, for example, had done it in *The Sun Also Rises*, and had taken a title straight from Ecclesiastes for a book that has been said to speak for a whole generation, and doubtless does. But Malraux's first novels will begin with the affirmation with which Hemingway's stops: he grants the world's inanity, just as he grants the political and cultural bankruptcy of bourgeois civilization. In the natural logic of his emotional response to the world about him, Hemingway will come directly to his position expressed in *Death in the Afternoon*, "let those who want to save the world." The logic of Malraux's emotions will not be quite so simple. The Absurd will haunt and frustrate the heroes of his first two novels, but at the same time—by a reasoning which refuses to submit to the constraints of a syllogism—awareness of the Absurd never appears to him a valid justification for withdrawing from the world. It still leaves the door open to political action. Man's position is absurd, but his position is clearly the work of his civilization. Change his civilization and it is possible that the menace of the Absurd will become less real.

Thus by 1927, with his Asiatic *Wanderjahre* behind him, Malraux had obeyed the "implacable urge" to destroy the forms which he had found ready and available at the very beginning of his career. In 1924 André Breton had written of him as if he had in mind one of the promising *enfant terrible* poets of the decade. In 1928, after the publication of *The Conquerors*, such a judgment of Malraux would have seemed ridiculously inappropriate. He had found his own "voice."

[9] *Un homme libre*, Emile-Paul, 1912, p. 11. Original edition, 1889.

CHAPTER THREE

The Metallic Realm

". . . A hopeless conflict . . . prepares us for the metallic realm of the Absurd."
—LA TENTATION DE L'OCCIDENT, p. 122

M ALRAUX's own esteem for his first two novels is strictly limited. He has called *The Conquerors* "the book of an adolescent"[1]—which, since he was twenty-five when he wrote it, can only mean that he finds the book itself immature—and he omits *The Royal Way* entirely from the Pléiade edition of his novels. He is right.

At least he is right to the extent that these two novels constitute a dry run. He had a basic theme: the Absurd—and some subsidiary ones as well. He had a basic magma of material: what he learned about life and about himself from his first experiences in the Orient. And he had a basic fable: a man goes out to the East, meets another man, somewhat older, with whom he has a special bond, and watches his friend go through the calvary of discovering his limitations as human being. He had discovered his basic, tragic mood. What he did not have was a corresponding experience of techniques which would allow him, on the first try, to put everything else he had into one book; he still had to practice his hand and clarify his vision. After he had done so, but only then, he could start *Man's Fate*.

He conceived *The Conquerors* as political by its setting and action, tragic by its tone, and metaphysical by its implications. Since revolutionary events move fast, he had to find a form and a style that would keep up with their fundamental rhythm and preserve the feeling essential in all his novels up to *Man's Hope*, that history will not wait for an individual to settle his destiny at leisure.

Actually the shape he gave *The Conquerors* is the exact opposite of the one he finally settled upon for *Man's Fate*. The latter novel opens with its focus entirely upon one character and broadens until it encompasses the whole revolutionary picture. But in 1928 he starts from the widest possible focus and narrows it through the three parts of the narrative until at the end one individual occupies the whole scene. The first part, labeled "The Approaches," takes in the whole play of revolution in Southeast Asia; the second, called "The Powers," studies the fighting at Canton which his

---

[1] "Postface," in the Grasset (1949) edition of *Les Conquérants*, p. 247.

hero, Garine, is directing; and the third, "The Man," studies Garine him-self. As the narrator's ship moves up out of the Indian Ocean toward Hong Kong and Canton, characters are introduced, issues at stake made clear, and the apprehension of the passengers, coupled with the narrator's im-patience to reach the scene of action, builds up the nervous tension and unifies the feeling of the novel as a whole. Next the story moves in upon the battle for Canton and follows the detail of revolution. Finally it turns to Garine, who is the nerve center of the fight, and fixes upon him. Thus the perspective moves, evenly, from wide pan to close-up.

The narrative itself is entrusted throughout to the same first-person narrator. He is unnamed and his personality is kept intentionally unob-trusive; though he is a participant, his acts are always the carrying out of orders and are not significant. He has known Garine a long time, and the latter has put him to doing some vague sort of liaison work for the Commu-nists, but his one real function is to be the Jamesian "central intelligence."

His record is virtually a diary. Action is noted in the present tense and as though at the narrator's first moment of leisure, as soon as possible after it has taken place, *and without his knowing what will happen next*. The device adds greatly to the effect of immediacy and to the reader's feeling of being present at the action. The account starts *in medias res* and with a rush. (This is not a novel where events grow out of contacts between char-acters; the events would happen anyway even if these characters did not exist.) Radio bulletins alternate with fragmentary explanations and bits of conversation. Each notation bears a date (from June 15 to August 18, 1925) and often an hour. As the story hurries along the reader is always kept aware of time, not the time which wears men away and in this sense works upon and changes characters, but the time which sets a limit in which a man must do what he has to do. The characters rarely relax, sleep fitfully, hardly eat, and are always under dramatic tension.

The style of the diary is impressionistic, in places telegraphic, and rarely in need of the grammatically complete sentence.

Silence. Dès que nous attendons quelque chose, nous retrouvons la chaleur, comme une plaie. En bas, une faible rumeur; murmures, socques, inquiétude, la cliquette d'un marchand ambulant, les cris d'un soldat qui le chasse. Devant la fenêtre, la lumière. Calme plein d'anxiété. Le son rythmé, de plus en plus net, de la marche des hommes qui arrivent, au pas; le claquement brutal de la halte. Silence. Rumeur ... Un seul pas, dans l'escalier. Le secrétaire. (P. 128.)

Silence. As soon as we expect something to happen we feel the heat again, like a sore. Below, a quiet stirring; murmurings, shoes, nervousness, the clatter of a street vendor, the cries of a soldier driving him off. Opposite the window, the light. Stillness full of uneasiness. The rhythmic sound, clearer and clearer, of men marching up, in step; the heavy stamp of the halt. Silence. Stirring . . . A lone step, on the stairs. The secretary.

Such writing can do with a minimum of syntax because impressions noted in series require little to link them. There is no need to subordinate some to the others, because all have the same value, i.e., the value of events. The rhythm of this particular series goes: silence, noise, silence again, new noise, significance of the noise (the last handled by the event of the secretary's entrance which explains the new noise). The development of the series is dramatic: silence comes over the room; during the wait they become aware of the heat; then a noise brings a tension; tension falls when the source is recognized; they are calm again but still tense when the soldier has driven off the pushcart man. A new noise comes, but is too quickly recognized for tension to mount; there is silence again, then another noise which registers after a moment (note the comma between *pas* and *dans*) as a step, and then in walks the secretary. The punctuation serves, most frequently, to separate stimulus from interpretation: one step (comma for a pause while they ask themselves *where*) in the stairway (period while they ask themselves *who*) and then the answer. Naturally the whole book does not maintain this pace or this impressionistic brevity, but there are many other passages as loaded and as rapid as this one, and the net effect is to add to the feeling of haste and to the nervous tension.

Whenever possible, running narration is avoided in favor of dramatic scenes, even when doing so calls for real ingenuity. To introduce Garine, for example, the narrator is made to dig a captured British Secret Service dossier out of a trunk, and read it aloud, supplying the hero's motives as he reads and arguing with the document when the information is faulty. This in spite of the fact that he has known Garine for years and might well simply tell us the essential facts on his own authority—except for the nagging question: what happens to the dramatic excitement of the book while he does so? The concern for dramatization is carried so far that when, because of its confidential nature, the narrator cannot plausibly hear a conversation, Garine reports it to him later in dialogue and even imitates the voices.

Malraux sees his scenes much better than he hears them; in places the dialogue may be too smooth to be true, and too elliptical for the characters to have understood each other, but his eye is as true as Hemingway's, and his study of gesture so complete that at times he can get on without dialogue. The scene where finally the captured terrorist Hong is brought before him is handled without a spoken word. Hong enters between two soldiers, with marks on his face from the fight; he stops, arms behind his back, feet spread; Garine looks at him, waiting, fatigued by his fever, his head moving slowly sideways; he pulls in a deep breath, shrugs. Hong catches the shrug, lunges toward Garine, is brought down by a rifle butt on the head. And that is all: each movement is significant and motivated, and —remembering Garine's instinctive sympathy for Hong and his saying that he has few enemies he understands so well—the gestures translate without loss the emotions of the scene.

Malraux sees the scene with the precision of a good movie lens, and to what extent his eye is cinematographic becomes clear in the pages directly following the confrontation with Hong, when Garine and the narrator go to see the mutilated bodies of their murdered friends. They are in a shed where a Chinese sits at the door, kicking away a dog that persistently tries to get in. The dog leaps and dodges, and keeps coming back. Garine and the narrator approach. The Chinese leans his head against the wall, eye half-closed, pushes the door open for them. The large, dirt-floored room has dust piled in the corners. In spite of the blue shades the light is too strong and blinds them. The narrator drops his eyes, raises them again, and sees the corpses *standing up*, not laid out but leaned against the wall. Garine tells the guard to get covers. The guard has to be told three times before he can understand; Garine lifts a fist, then tells him that he will get ten *taels* for bringing covers within half an hour. The narrator's muscles relax when he hears spoken words, but tighten again as he sees that the mouth of a dead friend has been mutilated, widened with a razor. He squeezes his arms against his sides and leans against the wall. A fly lights on his forehead and he does not drive it away. . . .

Recent criticism says much about this kind of immediacy of sensation. The visual detail and the narrator's visible reaction to the detail are passed on to the reader for interpretation: no need to tell the reader what the fly's remaining on the narrator's forehead means. And because the reader interprets he participates. He is as close to the action as he can be, and seems to live it rather than contemplate it. In other words, aesthetic distance has been cut to a minimum.

The effect is one of compelling authenticity. Malraux seems quite aware of what he is doing, and even introduces a gratuitous but particularly striking and immediate image on occasion to re-enforce the reader's feeling of being present. Thus when Borodin reveals to Klein and the narrator how he has worked on Hong's emotions, so as to be sure that Hong will murder the Gandhi-like Tcheng-dai without delay, and adds that from that moment Hong's terrorists will have the Communist group on their list of prospects: "Borodin, chewing his moustache and buckling the uniform belt that bothers him, rises and leaves. We follow. Stuck against the light bulb a large butterfly projects upon the wall a great black stain" (p. 151). The shadow of the butterfly is completely irrelevant to the action and has no symbolic significance, but after Borodin's speech about Hong, full of implications about impending murder which naturally project the mind into a near and ominous future, the image pulls one back into the reality of the present with great force.

The sharpness of Malraux's visual imagination is of course a vast advantage. When he is ready to write *Man's Hope* ten years later, he will return to the device of telling his story in brief, sharply cut episodes like these and make the most use possible of the visual effects. But the Spanish War novel is a complicated one, and much of its meaning is conveyed through juxtaposition of scenes that vary greatly in tone, color, and emotional mood, whereas the story of *The Conquerors* is simple and rectilinear, a matter of aligning the scenes one after the other in the order of the chronology of narration—from the passage of the ship up the South Asia coast to the moment when Garine realizes that his strength is exhausted and he must leave Canton while he still can, in public victory but in private defeat.

Technically, so far as telling a story is concerned, *The Conquerors* was a success. The sharp-focused point of view, the skillfully maintained pace, the extremely immediate imagery, are achievements which Malraux has never bettered.

But Malraux's technique is one that makes the presentation of character inordinately difficult. Personal relations such as the traditional novel exploits can hardly exist here. The only event that could be alleged to develop out of a personal relationship—Garine's refusal to let Hong be tortured—can be attributed more accurately to his understanding a human case very like his own. Otherwise the important relationship for each character is his political role, and his connection with the other characters is professional.

The characters are primarily types, defined by their attitudes toward life and politics. Borodin is the man who has submerged his individuality in the Revolution. Hong is the Terrorist. Nicolaïeff is the Torturer. Tcheng-dai is the Moral Force. Rebecci is the Anarchist who has talked away his energy. The fact that they are also men emerges very slowly, even in the case of Garine.

Like Tartufe in the play, he is familiar long before we see him, but familiar as a type. At Saigon, Rensky, the art collector, drops the tempt-

ing remark to the narrator that he doubts that Garine is really a Marxist
Bolshevik. At the next port of call another minor character adds that
Garine has joined the Revolution for the same reason men join the Foreign
Legion: he cannot abide life in ordinary society. He also remarks that
where Borodin is a man of action, Garine is a man *capable* of action, and
pays tribute to Garine's ability as organizer. Still a third minor character
later adds that Garine seems to him a sick genius and not entirely depend-
able. Thus in the first seventy pages of a 215-page book we learn about
the central figure only what kind of man he is.

Here the narrator breaks out the Intelligence report on Garine and gives
us a biography, with footnotes on motives, yet even now the emphasis on
Garine as an individual human being is not complete. We learn why
Garine's type is not Borodin's—why he is a Conqueror rather than what
Malraux will later label a "Curé" of revolution, a maker rather than a
custodian. Only when we reach Canton, enter Garine's office, see him,
feel the presence and power of the man's personality, does the type recede
behind the image of the driving, intense, desperately earnest, desperately
sick individual. The fact of his being a type remains in the background
through the tense days of the fighting, maneuver, murder, and torture, but
it is still there and emerges again in the final pages, when Garine has decided to leave Canton rather than die on the scene of his triumph. We are
reminded by a series of dialogue passages that it is just as well he leave,
since the Revolution has no permanent berth for the Conqueror: such
types are too undisciplined.

The key to Garine's character is his *Angst*, which has its source in his
violent awareness of the vanity of life. His "dedication to a great action"
has been an escape, to let him live in awareness of the Absurd without
giving in to it. As a student in Switzerland he had financed a number of
abortions. Tried as an accessory, he had felt his trial to be a grotesque,
unreal farce. The (to him disproportionate) penalty for his offense had
finished the job of convincing him of the absurdity of his plight. "I don't
think of society as evil—and thus capable of improvement—but as absurd. Not the absence of justice itself bothers me but something deeper,
the impossibility of accepting any social form whatsoever" (p. 78). He
had not served his jail sentence, but the first World War had brought him
again face to face with the Absurd and he had deserted: the knives issued
for a trench wipe-up had reminded him too powerfully of kitchen knives.
Later he had joined the Bolsheviks while they were still in exile, prefer-
ring them to the Anarchists because they were technicians rather than
preachers, and feeling that the Bolsheviks were likelier to offer the ex-

perience of a great action and the experience of power. This hope had
overweighed his knowledge that he could not tolerate party discipline,
had no interest in social amelioration, and, in general, disliked people.
He had arrived in the Orient in time to plunge into the young revolution
"with absolute absence of scruple," to build a propaganda service, combine it with the police, and have it ready to deliver to the International
after the death of Sun Yat-sen. He and Borodin *are* the Canton revolution. But dysentery and swamp fever have wasted him to the point where
he has had to choose between returning to Europe and seeing the victory
at Canton. He has chosen to stay. The success of the Canton enterprise
attests his sustained vitality. But with his decline in strength, the awareness of the Absurd has returned, and he is now persuaded that not merely
society but life also is absurd. His driving energy collapses when Hong's
terrorists murder Klein and his companions; the sight of the tortured,
mutilated faces plunges him back into the emptiness of his accomplishment. At most he is able to affirm that one thing still counts—not to be
conquered. Occasionally he rouses from his despair, but the final collapse
is inevitable. As his health weakens, he grows increasingly obsessed by
the Absurd. He becomes increasingly a private individual struggling with
a private problem rather than the leader of great action. Then when he
refuses to make a political speech at Klein's funeral—disobeying Borodin's
order—the individual asserts himself completely: "I didn't throw Europe
into a corner like a pile of rags and take the risk of ending up like some
Rebecci just to teach people obedience. Or to learn to obey, myself,
either . . ." (p. 199).

This is his ultimate *non serviam.*

We are a long way from Communist orthodoxy here. Technically
Garine is no anarchist, but his sensibility is anarchistic: his ultimate authority is the satisfaction of his intimate, private needs. This is why he
has been able to understand young Hong's rejection of the party discipline in favor of direct personal action. Either of these men could have
said what Garine does say: that action had made him indifferent to everything else, including its outcome, and that if it was easy for him to join
the Revolution, that was because the result was distant and always un-
certain.

Consequently, Garine's plight is sad; the Revolution offers him the
best available possibility of meeting his private needs through participation in a "great action," but at the cost of his own destruction: there is
no permanent place for the transcendent ego of the Conqueror type in
the revolution he makes. There is no exit from the dilemma.

What Garine needs, said Leon Trotsky in his resounding article, is a good dose of Marxism. To Trotsky's mind, the character with real stuff in him is not this "revolutionary who scorns Revolutionary doctrine," but young Hong, whose refusal to compromise is the beginning of virtue. He makes no bones of calling Malraux amateurish and doctrinally timid, and alleges that his sympathies have been corroded by excessive individualism and aesthetic caprice.

(What Trotsky really means is that in letting the bourgeoisie of Canton share the Canton revolution, people like the historical Borodin and the fictional Garine were playing Stalin's hand and not Trotsky's. Malraux has gone wrong by not having read his Trotsky.)

Malraux's reply amounts to an ex post facto statement of intention: he meant *The Conquerors* to be a novel and not a declaration of faith. The judgments represented in the book are not his, but those of distinct, autonomous individuals, in particular circumstances, at a particular time. The purpose of the book, he declares, is less to picture a revolution than to make clear the nature of man's eternal fate. Trotsky has mistaken the human and fallible characters of a novel for immutable archetypes of political allegory.

This interchange between Malraux and Trotsky does much to reveal the essential nature of Malraux's book. To Trotsky, Garine is merely a defective revolutionary; his trouble is quickly reduced to excessive individualism; and man's fate, as Malraux calls it, is nothing but Garine's inability to adjust himself to the brave new world—whereas Malraux's "aesthetic caprice," as Trotsky calls what we would call the intention of the artist, is to show a man in a situation he has created, the only situation in life which he finds tolerable, and one which is absolutely certain to work the ruin of its creator. Trotsky is looking for a revolutionary, and Malraux is giving him a tragic hero who happens to be involved in a revolution.

Now the reason for the incessant haste of the style becomes clear—the story must hasten toward its outcome with something of the rush appropriate to tragedy. *And the point of view must be focused relentlessly upon Garine because he is meant to have the general significance of a tragic hero.*

But does he? Trotsky, for all his special predispositions, was an intelligent reader, and he took what Malraux meant for tragedy to be the report of a revolution. (Trotsky even puts quotes around the word *roman.*) And the other critics who read the book as Trotsky did were numerous. Were they so terribly wrong in neglecting the tragic aspect of the book?

Not entirely. For putting men in the situation of revolution reveals many other aspects of the fundamental human situation besides Garine's, and the book is evidence that these other aspects were extremely interesting to Malraux. These subsidiary interests are what spoil in some degree his technical success. If the speed of the narrative made difficult the job of transforming Garine from type into human being, it made doubly hard the task of bringing alive these other characters who did not benefit by the direct and continuous attention of the narrator.

Hong, for example, is animated (we are told) by an all-inclusive hatred, bred from the misery he has known. And a killer has his secret: he must see things differently from other men just as a torturer like the policeman Nicolaïeff must have had special experiences which now make him enjoy his cruel profession. Klein, the old hand at revolution who has had all the experiences of torture and imprisonment, and knows at first hand the difference between killing from a distance with a gun and killing intimately with a knife, and who in his deathly fatigue gasps out how hard it is merely to be "ein Mensch . . . a man," also possesses a secret. So does Tcheng-dai, who has sacrificed all his possessions to build his moral prestige, and, in his seeming detachment from everything, is providing for his own immortality ("taking care of his biography"); he can render the Revolution ineffective with a nod, and if he cannot achieve his ends and stay alive, he will achieve them by committing suicide.

There is also Rensky, the collector for museums, whom we see only once but long enough to learn that he has gone to the Temple of Angkor Vat to carve on a wall a smutty inscription in Sanskrit, just for the pleasure of baffling some future, presumably serious, archaeologist. And Gerard, the former high-school principal, who leaves the narrator full of surmises about a curious sexuality that has absolutely nothing to do with anything that will happen or can happen in the rest of the story. There is also Rebecci.

This little Italian anarchist has wasted his life in talk; he now runs a shop in Saigon where he sells "pacotille"—cheap junk like the mechanical birds that are his specialty—and kills time telling impossible yarns to a little circle of Chinese girls. A consuming curiosity makes him an authority on erotic literature, but, like his politics, his eroticism remains theoretical—in this case because of the presence of his alert Chinese wife. His futility seems absolute, and yet this is the man whose teaching has produced Hong.

There is not one of these people who is not interesting to Malraux in his own right. We know this because we know that Malraux will investigate similar types, sometimes at considerable length, in *Man's Fate*. But in *The Conquerors* the unvarying point of view makes it impossible for the reader to see life through their eyes. And the pace leaves no time for us to see them, even as they look to the narrator, for long.

Originally Malraux had written a ten-page scene in which Garine discusses Borodin at length with the narrator. Borodin here sounds much less the typical functionary than he does in the finished book. The propagandist, we learn, is in the Revolution because he enjoys the activity; he wants the Revolution to go on and on. Success is not the object. He lives for his role. The doctrine not only has to be spread, but it must be spread *by him*. This Borodin is far and away more interesting than the one in the finished novel, and there is no doubt, after these ten pages, that Malraux was deeply interested in Borodin as one kind of human being. There is also no doubt that the passage had to be suppressed. These were ten pages in which, because of the requirements of point of view, nothing could happen—and a ten-page stretch with no action is awkwardly long, given the rhythm of the narrative. Coming so late in the action, long after the exposition was finished, this scene would have broken the stride of the story. Technically speaking, Malraux had no choice. The passage was published separately a year after the novel.[2]

And so, two years later, when he is ready to try a second novel, he discards a relatively successful technique. *The Royal Way* will have rapid pace, but attain it by other means; we will not see narration in short scenes again until *Man's Hope*. The impressionistic style will be greatly chastened. He will abandon the political setting and eliminate all the interesting but minor characters, who, in *The Conquerors*, threaten to become major. And yet in spite of all this, he will be telling the same fundamental story and orchestrating the same fundamental theme.

The arresting first page of *The Royal Way* sets the pace and tone for the entire book:

Cette fois, l'obsession de Claude entrait en lutte; il regardait opiniâtrément le visage de cet homme, tentait de distinguer enfin quelque expression dans la pénombre où le laissait l'ampoule allumée derrière lui. Forme aussi indistincte que les feux de la côte somalie perdus dans l'intensité du clair de lune où miroitaient les salines ... Un ton de voix d'une ironie insistante qui lui semblait se perdre aussi dans l'ob-

---

[2] "Les Conquérants, fragment inedit," *Bifur*, No. 4 (December 31, 1929), pp. 5–15.

scurité africaine, y rejoindre la légende que faisaient roder autour de cette silhouette confuse les passagers avides de potins et de manilles, la trame de bavardages,
de romans et de rêveries qui accompagnent les blancs qui ont été mêlés à la vie des
états indépendants d'Asie.

«Les hommes jeunes comprennent mal ... comment dites-vous? ... l'érotisme.»
(P. 13.)

This time Claude's obsession joined the struggle; he peered persistently at the
face of this man, trying to find some expression in the shadow cast by the light
bulb behind him. A form as indistinct as the lights on the Somali coast lost in the
brilliance of the moonlight that sparkled back from the salt ponds . . . A tone of
voice insistently ironical which seemed to him also to get lost in the African darkness, joining the legend, the web of gossip, yarn, and pipe dream such as collects
around the whites who have had a finger in the life of the independent states of Asia,
that the passengers, eager for a game of cards and a bit of scandal, kept spinning
about his vague figure.

"Young men don't quite understand . . . what do you call it . . . ? eroticism."

"*Cette fois*" opens the story abruptly and violently, and again this
time *in medias res*. The fifth word introduces one of the two main figures,
through whose eyes we shall see most of the action. We are already aware
that his vision is likely to be warped. Already the focus is where it will
stay until the last page, on Perken—with the mystery that surrounds him
suggested here by Claude's inability to see his face. Already Malraux is
exploiting his visual imagination; the picture is essentially a movie shot
with Perken's black bulk back-lighted between lamp and lens. And
already Claude feels his effort to see and understand Perken as a
struggle.

Meanwhile the quick reference to the Somali coast places the scene
geographically and reference to moonlight on water has suggested what
the word *passagers* confirms, that we are on a ship. We learn, our attention returning to the figure in the foreground, that Perken is one of those
mysteriously important figures who haunt the fiction of the East (if not
the East itself). From his way of speaking we know that he is not French
and we get a sample of the jerkiness of speech which will regularly identify
what he says. He introduces the dominant theme of eroticism. And at the
bottom of the page we are taken off the ship in a rapid flashback to the
Somali brothel where he and Claude met.

Malraux's technique is inferential and allusive, and the burden on the
reader is accordingly heavy: a moment's inattention means missing some
detail like the allusion to the Somali coast. The technique is also inex-

plicit: Claude has an obsession, for example, but we do not know what it is. Yet in this brief space the chief characters have been introduced; we have had an inkling of the importance of obsession in the psychology of the characters; an atmosphere has been established and a principal theme presented.

From here the story moves rapidly. Before they reach Bangkok, Claude has invited Perken to join him in the search for Khmerian bas-reliefs, and Perken, bound for the same region anyhow and needing money, has accepted. The French colonial authorities turn out to be obdurate about helping the mission, jealous of possible success, and insistent that any discoveries, made at whatever personal risk, be public property. With dubious guides they set out in oxcarts up the Royal Road of Cambodia, find the abandoned temples they want, and after numerous disappointments load the sculptures on the carts. At this point the natives desert the caravan. To return by the way they came would be unthinkable. They would both lose their treasure and fail to satisfy the needs of Perken, who is very anxious to find traces of a rival adventurer named Grabot from whom there has long been no news. Instead of going back, they set out across hostile country toward Siam. At the first native village they enact the ritual of friendship with the Moi tribesmen, but see such unmistakable signs of the presence of a white man that they search the village for him and find Grabot. He has been captured, blinded, and harnessed to a treadmill. Certain that the same thing will happen to them, they retire to their hut and watch the tribesmen prepare to surround it. After a long and terrifying wait, Perken crosses the compound to the threatening warriors and faces down the chiefs. The adventurers are freed to cross to Siam and get the trinkets they promise in exchange for Grabot. But in the excitement, Perken has tripped on an uptilted bamboo spike and gashed his knee. By the time they reach Siam and a doctor the blood poisoning is past cure, and there are no facilities for amputation. Knowing he must die, but anxious to get back to the Northern tribes he has governed, Perken sets out on a litter in a race against death, against the column which has been sent from Siam to punish the natives for the blinding of Grabot, and against the railroad which threatens to bring civilization to the people over whom Perken has reigned for years. Claude abandons the sculptures in Siam and goes with him. They lose their race; at the end of the story Perken is dying in Claude's fraternal embrace.

On the level of meaning of a simple adventure story, *The Royal Way* is exciting, reasonably comprehensible, and rapid. (Where the adventure is hard to follow, the difficulty could be removed by publishing a good

map with the book, to correct Malraux's occasional inattention to geographic detail and the reader's ignorance of the terrain.)

But there are additional levels of meaning, psychological and metaphysical, and, just as in the case of *The Conquerors*, Malraux's technique
turns out somewhat inadequate to the task of conducting the story on the
three levels at once.

Its failure at the psychological level seems to have been caused by a
certain clumsiness in manipulating the point of view. Claude Vannec, to
whom the point of view is entrusted, is too complex a character. He is a
trained archaeologist, and knows Sanskrit; has a taste for adventure, an
active set of nerves, and a tendency to dwell at length on a few fundamental, obsessive ideas. He is an intellectual who has refused to choose
"between eating in bargain restaurants and selling autos." His trip to
Cambodia is a gamble on making a quick fortune. When we first see him
he is in a state of intense anxiety because the slowness of the ship is de-
laying the moment when he can "turn dream to action." He is also fascinated by Perken, in whom he recognizes immediately one who has
"refused to live in the community of men now that he is growing old and
he is alone in the world." Perken reminds him of his own grandfather:
the same hostility toward accepted values, the same taste for action combined with awareness of its vanity, the "same unwillingness to accept."
In other words, he sees a man not unlike Garine, one "with a deep-set will
which he [Claude] often sensed without being fully able to grasp it"
(p. 21). Eventually he comes to realize that what makes Perken appeal
to him so much is the obsession with death that tortures them both.

Obviously, point of view is a much more complicated problem here
than in *The Conquerors*. The anonymous narrator of the first novel has at
most a lightly defined personality. He is there to see and interpret the
action for the reader, and the reader has no reason to fear that the action
will be distorted in passing through the mind of the narrator. This ob-
viates the sore problem of twisted refraction. *The Royal Way*, on the other
hand, is Claude's story as well as Perken's. Claude's constant anxiety and
his screaming nerves are always palpably present, and in Parts Two and
Three they dominate the narrative. If we see the novel as the account of
the passion and death of the hero, we must also see it as the account of a
neophyte's special initiation, during which he has been present at a mystery
and from which he emerges—we are specifically told—a different person:
at the end of the book he is represented to be just as attached to the life
he detests as he is fascinated by death, his nerves have quieted, and his

great anxiety has at last dropped away in what may be taken to be an enlightened acceptance of his predicament.

But previously we have been as much occupied with Claude's nerves as with the destiny of Perken. From the moment they enter the jungle until they emerge in Siam the young man is never far from the verge of hysteria. The jungle is a nightmare of putrescence and of things that breed in slime. And his revulsion runs headlong into his obsessed insistence upon beating his way through to the temples, on finding the bas-reliefs, and ultimately winning fortune. Of the three moments in the story when tension is highest, one is Perken's walk across the compound, to be sure, but the other two involve not Perken but Claude: the one where he crawls along the façade of the temple on hands and knees, in deathly fear of stinging insects, and the other where he is so exasperated by his failure to crack the stone and detach a piece of sculpture that he picks up a hammer and pounds in wild fury on the stone with its claw. To make so positive a character the "central intelligence" would be hazardous, technically, in any case, even if Malraux maintained his original arrangement through the length of the story. He does not maintain it. After seventy-nine pages in which the point of view has been Claude's, Malraux comes to the scene where Claude is so occupied with breaking the stones that he could not plausibly be made to observe his companion, and we are allowed a direct glimpse, instead, into Perken's mind—he is converting the value of the sculptures into machine guns. Having broken with his original method, from here on Malraux adopts a strategy of convenience. Perken's actions will be reported as Claude sees them, but his states of mind, instead of being betrayed by revealing actions, will be revealed by direct statement. The technique thus becomes similar to the familiar movie one where one camera is used to supplement the other: when Perken takes his crucial walk across the compound, one lens—corresponding to Claude's eye—watches him go, but another moves with the hero—corresponding to *his* eye and mind—and the first film is frequently cut so that portions of the second can be spliced in. Such an expedient, obviously, runs quite counter to the precepts of Henry James and Percy Lubbock and the other exponents of carefully arranged, consistent optics. We know from *The Conquerors* that Malraux was quite capable of disciplining his point of view if he wanted to. But in *The Royal Way* other problems pre-empted his attention.

Chief among these was obviously the desire to exhibit Perken's mentality. Perken's ambition has been, in the past, to "put a scar on the map." He now wants a curious "peace." His attempts to influence the savage Northern tribes have given him an intimate satisfaction, but an incomplete one. He realizes that it will always remain incomplete, but still he has joined with Claude because he needs money to buy arms so that he can go on protecting his domain against civilization. He has, as he says, given up hope, but he has not renounced the hopeless effort.

This man has rejected society and cast himself in the role of one against the world. His feeling of rupture is so strong that he sees his own eroticism as an expression of this hatred. (There is great satisfaction, he explains, in saying to oneself, "That makes one [woman] more. . . .") This eroticism is an intellectualization of sex. Perken regards the sexual partner as nothing more than a complex of sexual responses. His aim is such complete possession that the protagonist knows the sensual experience of the partner as well as he knows his own. By its nature such sexuality is doomed to eternal disappointment: Perken realizes clearly that its satisfactions must always be smaller than those the imagination conjures up, and remarks that his eroticism, since it is a determined reduction of the physical function to the idea, is not only *a* perversion but possibly *the only* real perversion. In any case, its insistence upon complete domination marks his eroticism as one of the expressions of the Will to Power. Perken displays the same exacerbated individualism as Garine, the same intolerance of law and discipline, and like Garine he sees his action in Asia less as an attempt to establish a new order than as an expression of his rupture with the old.

He is also obsessed by his own mortality, and has equated death with any decline of the physical powers; a man begins to die, he thinks, from his first momentary sexual impotence. Every choice he makes is ruled by his fear of his own weakness; he invariably elects the course which will let him show that his decline has not yet begun. And yet he is always aware that the choices are hollow and the victories empty, that his destiny must inevitably catch up with him. "What weighs upon me," he cries out, "is my humanity" (p. 106). The essential absurdity of life itself he finds a basic value: awareness of it adds intensity to everything one does. Keeping death eternally present is part of living well. In other words, he is the blood brother of the Garine who declares that the fact that life is absurd does not mean that one must live absurdly, and of "A.D." defying the Absurd at the end of *La Tentation de l'occident*.

The gist of his story is that his efforts fail as they were bound to. He refuses to accept the ignominious death that would follow capture by the Moi savages. But the wound he receives, quite by chance, kills him anyhow. When the doctors condemn him, he turns to eroticism, but his experience with the woman is, as always, a defeat. Then he tries to get

back to his own tribes and help them ward off the encroachments of "civilization," and is defeated for a third time. Meanwhile he has seen his
decline written in the eyes of a native chief whom once he could have
dominated easily but who now is mainly interested in getting Perken
and Claude to move on lest they bring trouble to his village.

There would be no doubt that Malraux intended Perken to be a tragic
figure lodged in the familiar tragic impasse—such that the hero can bring
himself to live only in a situation which must eventually destroy him—
even if he did not make his hero talk about his *condition d'homme* and even
if the note on the title page did not refer to this novel as an *initiation
tragique*. At times the heroic figure bulks somewhat larger than life size,
in a way that is normal and acceptable when the tragic mood is functioning. What is less acceptable is that the perspective varies within the story
so that Perken looms much larger at times than at others.

This is the price that Malraux pays for not having adopted a strictly
disciplined point of view. For it is when we are seeing Perken as Claude
sees him that Perken assumes his fullest stature. Claude has obviously
read Nietzsche. He has at least a vague intention of making his life conform to an *Übermensch* pattern. Like Perken, he has accepted the "can-
cerous" vanity of life, and, like Perken, he feels that he should make his
awareness a condition of existence, and live the more intensely for living
always in the presence of death. He sees adventure as a means of liberation from the imprisonment of life. To him, Perken is a sort of precursor,
who has lived by these ideas which Claude is determined to test; in his
mysterious way, he already knows the answers. It is hard to imagine this
Perken, the one Claude sees, as being anything but impervious to the
disasters of ordinary men. But at those junctures where the point of view
shifts and we see the world as Perken sees it, he is as vulnerable as anyone
else. The mystery is swept away. He is first a frightened man forcing
himself to do something he does not want to do, then a hurt one, finally
a weak and wretched one—and never at any point so big as he has seemed
to Claude. Consequently the reader never believes in him as he believes
in Garine. Psychologically the book is at least mildly incoherent, as if it
had been necessary to reduce Perken's stature in mid-course so that the
story could reach its outcome plausibly.

Meanwhile Malraux contrives to add a third level of meaning—and
puts a third burden on his reader—by using symbols to reveal a metaphysical significance both in the story and in the picture of his hero.
There is too much of the symbolism for it to be unintentional and it is

far too obvious for one to mistake its import. From the moment their expedition enters the jungle the adventurers are uncomfortably aware of their surroundings as a morass of slime and subhuman life. Six days after departure, Claude can no longer distinguish between "life that wiggles and life that merely oozes." They are in a domain where man is not master, where even the human mind seems to decompose, and where their acts have no human significance. Everything Claude succeeds in doing presents itself to him as a victory over crawling things. His hideous climb along the top of the temple façade is one long paroxysm of revulsion at the life that slithers over his fingers. And he comes to a point where to control his chattering nerves is a real triumph. Bugs crawl on every page: leeches, earwigs, "beasts of the ruins," stinging ants. The opening in the temple gives on a "court of earwigs." When finally the men find the stone they want, loosen it, and turn it over, insects go scuttling down the underside, and since they are in retreat we gather that there has been a serious human victory—although since the direct reward of loosening the stone is to confirm the omnipresence of the insects, the victory seems somewhat ambiguous.

The symbol becomes more explicit in the chapter immediately preceding the entry into the Moi village where the adventure comes to a climax. During a conversation in which he re-establishes the whole context of obsessions that will form the background of his magnificent act of courage, Perken cries out: "All these nasty insects crawl on our lamp, enslaved by the light. Those termites live in their hill, subjected to the hill. I refuse to be enslaved." He means, of course, that he will live by no law but his own. Here is the *non serviam* which all of Malraux's heroes pronounce, sooner or later, phrased in the language of the insect symbol. Now the insects have assumed the full burden of symbolizing the nonhuman. They become so important in translating Malraux's meaning that every obstacle Perken and Claude meet will be assimilated to them. The assembly of Moi warriors who wait to burn the hut where the adventurers have taken refuge is equated with a swarm of bugs, in a metaphor which is periodically revived for several pages; they are like ants and wasps. In an anguished urge to kill as many as possible before they kill him, Claude sees a mass of leeches writhing over a flame. Consequently, when Perken goes out across the compound toward the savages, he is no more a man going to meet hostile men than a human going to test the quality of his humanity against the nonhuman.

This reading of the symbol is confirmed by the state in which Claude and Perken have just found the adventurer Grabot. This man has been brought recurrently to the reader's attention since the opening pages of the book. Perken refers to him repeatedly, as an example of diverted sexuality, as an example of will power, as one at once enslaved by the jungle and master of it. Then, bit by bit, the reader learns why Grabot is very much on Perken's mind; no one knows where Grabot has gone, and Perken is extremely anxious to find him. His existence comes to have a bearing on the success of the expedition; Grabot may be a guarantor of their safety among the unsubdued tribes, or he may, on the other hand, have turned savage himself. One gathers that Perken thinks of Grabot as the one man who is his equal, and, perhaps, since Grabot's freedom of action is uninhibited by fear of pain or death (during his military service Grabot is said to have blinded one eye with gonorrheal pus in order to square accounts with an army doctor who has touched his pride by suspecting him of malingering) Perken may even recognize him as his superior. In any event, the reader is fully prepared to meet another impressively Nietzschean, *Übermensch* character, the complete incarnation of those qualities which, in the view which pervades the novel, characterize the superior human. By the time the meeting is at hand, talk of Grabot has occupied so much space, becoming more and more frequent as the story progresses, that it is perhaps a fundamental weakness of the book (judging it according to the standards which define a "well-made" novel) that we should have heard so much about him while seeing him so little.

But when they find Grabot, this apotheosis of the human has become unrecognizable. The Mois have blinded his other eye and locked him in a hut where he has been harnessed so long to a treadmill that he is now capable of no movement except his circular plodding. He is unable to answer their questions or to tell his rescuers who he is.

The questions show how fully Perken and Claude realize that Grabot has been emptied of his humanity. When he cannot reply to the question, "Who?" one of them unconsciously changes it: "*What* are you?" To this Grabot manages a reply which picks up the syntactical distinction, "nothing."

His rescuers free him and take him to the hut where they expect to stand off the savages. He is completely indifferent to the danger: when Claude's anxiety has reached its peak, he suddenly realizes that Grabot has taken to plodding around the room, as if he were back in his treadmill. The blinded derelict has become proof of the jungle's power to dehumanize the human, and of the vanity of courage.

Consequently the symbols assign an extraordinary value to Perken's subsequent act of bravery: he performs it in full awareness of the vanity of

pitting the human against the invincible nonhuman. In this sense he is the
true tragic figure, the hero whose defeat comes in a manner which affirms
his humanity. The insects defeat him, but Perken could well declare here
that he has done what no insect could have done. He has refused *not* to be
human.

His wound infects and the universal decomposition of the jungle sets
in. As he lies dying the insects swarm about him, and Claude, watching
him die, sees his face "cease imperceptibly to be human." Perken's victory
has been swallowed up in defeat. All the struggle is for nothing, after all.
In the last analysis there is no more point in being human than in being an
insect. No point, that is, unless there is something inherently better and
nobler that somehow takes the sting out of the defeat.[3]

Clearly *The Royal Way* is a less successful novel than *The Conquerors*.
In eliminating the minor characters and the minor themes, Malraux had
also eliminated no little of the primary stuff of which any novel is built, the
texture and the feel of life. In taking his story out of the political setting
he has sacrificed much of the interest by which, in the twentieth century,
a political novel naturally and quite legitimately benefits. Perken is not
only a less imposing hero than Garine because the shifting point of view in
The Royal Way blurs the picture of him, but also because his situation in
life is nearer that of the nineteenth-century outposts-of-empire man than
to man in our own time or to Man in general. Garine, on the other hand,
is potentially either a picture of ourselves or of Man as we know him.

And even more clearly than in *The Conquerors*, we see that Malraux's
troubles are related to the size of the job he has set himself. At bottom,
part of *The Royal Way* is an adventure not greatly different from "The
Heart of Darkness." (In fact, the similarity seems more than accidental.
In one story men go up a river into a jungle to look for a man whom they
find ruined by the experience he has gone through; in the other we substitute a jungle road for a jungle river, and the name Grabot for the name
Kurtz.) But the difference between Malraux's story and Conrad's is not
merely that Malraux's people have two objects in view instead of one and
that his story continues after the finding of the jungle-rotted white man.
Conrad's aim is to tell a story most effectively whereas Malraux's is to load
a story with oblique comment and accreted significances. In *The Conquerors* Malraux had succeeded better with the actual task of narration
and like Conrad left the accretion of meanings more to chance. In the sec-

[3] For a longer treatment see my "Notes on Malraux's Symbols," *Romantic Review*, XLII
(December 1951), 274–81.

ond, concern for the meanings interferes with the exercise of the novelist's art. The result is incoherence.

Actually Malraux's two books have even more in common than has been said so far. In addition to displaying heroes whose lineaments are extremely similar, who have the same feeling of rupture from the world that produced them, who are equally aware of the invincible power of the Absurd, and who live through fundamentally similar experiences, the two also present the peculiarities which will gradually become the hallmarks of a Malraux novel: the atmosphere of violence, the scene in which the hero affirms his intention to maintain his hero's status, and the noble picture in which Malraux seems himself to affirm what the logic of the narrative denies.

The Conquerors literally drips with blood. Murder is an accepted political technique. The book is full of relentless men who without a qualm send other men to death by the knife, by the bullet, and by cyanide. They are also men who have risked death themselves and undergone torture. Hong has made killing a way of life. Garine executes a man with his own gun. Tcheng-dai's death is as calmly planned as a banquet. Torture is an instrument of persuasion. Garine is wounded and the narrator just escapes being shot. Klein and his murdered companions are repulsively mutilated. The background of the whole story is a military action.

In *The Royal Way*, violence is imminent when not actually present. Perken has the marks of an old torture on his body. The adventurers know from the start that they risk sudden and painful deaths. When they find Grabot, he has had the humanity tortured out of him. While they are surrounded in the hut the choice they face appears to lie between being burned where they are and being tortured if they come out. Perken's death comes from a wound inflicted by a primitive weapon of war.

Malraux has never written a book in which violence has not been an element of man's fate. His novels need it so that whatever acts the hero is forced to perform will have the necessary quality of decisiveness: what he does must be irremediable. For most of his protagonists a life of violence is the only satisfactory one. Violence provides them a field where action is possible despite their feeling of rupture and separation from their fellows. Both Garine and Perken resort to an act of violence as a symbol of their refusal to accept their ultimate destinies.

At Canton, when Garine learns that his jig is up and that he will have either to leave or die of his malaria on the spot, he shoots the well-poisoner who refuses to—or perhaps cannot—reply to his questions. According to revolutionary discipline the execution is indefensible, since such cases should be tried by the People's Tribunal. But Garine is not acting as a revolutionary. The shooting, performed in a paroxysm of anger and nervous exasperation, marks his personal refusal to be defied: Garine the man has not yet abdicated. This is the final gesture of the Conqueror. For precisely the same reason Perken kills two savages. He has just read in the eyes of their chief the yellow man's recognition of the white man's failing powers. Two other natives present at the palaver, also reading the eyes of their chief, raise their rifles. Perken calls out as though to someone behind them and when they turn their heads, shoots them down. He has lost strength, but he too has refused to abdicate. The hero, in both instances, has refused to accept the lesser status that his personal destiny is forcing upon him.

These acts of violence are closely associated with the technique of ellipsis which is a permanent aspect of Malraux's writing. They form a part of the corrective picture in which he juxtaposes to the evidence of man's weakness the poetic proof of his tragic stature. Perken's story is an illustration of man's defeat by the Absurd, but he is not defeated until after he has stalked across the empty commons of the native village toward his potential murderers and until he has killed the two natives. Garine comes out of his fever in the hospital to tell his friend that he refuses to allow the absurdity of life to make him live absurdly, and proves his point later by shooting the well-poisoner. In both cases the scenes are charged with emotion. But as of 1930 Malraux has not begun to capitalize upon the dramatic possibilities offered. In both early novels the scenes which contradict the logic of events are not situated for maximum dramatic effect. In *Man's Fate* and *Man's Hope* the corresponding scenes will be placed at the last high point of the action. But nevertheless the characteristic juxtaposition, although not yet fully exploited, is already present.

In 1930, then, Malraux had two novels, of considerable importance, already behind him. They allowed him to gain a considerable experience of technique, and to gather up his fundamental themes. By themselves they would not have made his lasting reputation as a novelist, but they cleared the way and readied him for the book that would do so. In early 1933 he finished *Man's Fate*.

CHAPTER FOUR

The Power and the Glory

> "... One of the secret and highest forms of the
> Power and the Glory of being a man."
> —THE CREATIVE ACT, p. 216

FOR MANY READERS the quintessence of Malraux is summed up in the scene at the beginning of *Man's Fate*. Tchen stands in the hotel room by the bed of the sleeping man he has been sent to murder and debates with himself whether to lift the mosquito netting or to drive his blade through the material into the receptive flesh. This is an act of irreparable violence; we are in the presence of death; the atmosphere is unbearably tense; the motive of the murder is political and yet the motives of the murderer transcend politics; politics has committed an intellectual to a career of action (or possibly vice versa); the action fails to satisfy either the demands of his intellect or those of his emotions; and we are trying to understand the psychology of the killer and fathom the great loneliness which overwhelms him as it will overwhelm so many other characters in the story. The action is full of despair, anguish, loneliness, violence, and sudden death. We are plunged into a dynamic situation; events already in motion here on the first page are of such import that a hundred pages later we shall still be struggling to catch up.

Tchen tenterait-il de lever la moustiquaire? Frapperait-il au travers? L'angoisse lui tordait l'estomac; il connaissait sa propre fermeté, mais n'était capable en cet instant que d'y songer avec hébétude, fasciné par ce tas de mousseline blanche qui tombait du plafond sur un corps moins visible qu'une ombre, et d'où sortait seulement ce pied à demi incliné par le sommeil, vivant quand même—de la chair d'homme. La seule lumière venait du building voisin: un grand rectangle d'électricité pâle, coupé par les barreaux de la fenêtre dont l'un rayait le lit juste au-dessous du pied comme pour en accentuer le volume et la vie. Quatre ou cinq klaxons grincèrent à la fois. Découvert? Combattre, combattre des ennemis qui se défendent, des ennemis éveillés, quelle délivrance!

La vague de vacarme retomba: quelque embarras de voitures (il y avait encore des embarras de voitures, là-bas, dans le monde des hommes ...). Il se retrouva en face de la grande tache molle de la mousseline et du rectangle de lumière, immobiles dans cette nuit où le temps n'existait plus. (P. 15.)

Should Tchen try to raise the netting? Or strike through it? Anxiety twisted his stomach. He knew his own determination, but could think of it now only

through a daze, fascinated by the white shape of the muslin that fell from the ceiling over a body less visible than the shadow, out of which came a single foot,
turned half-slantwise in sleep, but alive—human flesh. The only light came from
the next building, a great rectangle of pale electric light, cut by the bars of the
window, one of which cut a line across the bed just below the foot as if to accen-
tuate its volume and life. Four or five auto horns screeched at once. Discovered?
To fight, fight waking enemies who defend themselves, what a relief!

The wave of racket fell back: some traffic jam (there were still traffic jams off
there, in the world of men . . .). He came to himself before the great soft white
streak of the muslin and the rectangle of light, unmoving in this night when time
did not exist.

The two questions state the immediate psychological problem and introduce a single visual element, the netting. The declarative sentence following goes from the physical effect of Tchen's nervous tension, through
the reason for it, back to the object of his fascination, adds a topographical
element (since the netting hangs from the ceiling the scene must be a
room), moves Tchen's eye from the net to the body just barely visible
under it, fastens his glance on the foot, and ends with a leap from the
concrete physical detail to the abstract, almost metaphysical consideration
of its qualities, life and humanity—thus returning from the exterior detail
to the mind behind the eye. The next sentence first adds more topographical information (the room is in a city since there is a building close by),
adds the visual image of the light falling on the bed, under which the foot
of the sleeper stands out, and returns to the renewed consideration of the
abstraction, life. Now comes the sudden impingement of the world outside the drama, the racket of the auto horns, followed by the question
asked by the alerted consciousness, now aware of something outside its
own preoccupations; the question is followed in its turn again by the re-
version of the consciousness to its own problem—of which the hesitation
about the mosquito bar is only a symptom—of inflicting death. After this
the consciousness turns once more to the exterior and identifies the cause
of the commotion, and then twists back to contemplate its own condition
in the realization that there are now two worlds, distinct from each other,
which it must simultaneously inhabit. And the final sentence returns
Tchen to the scene in the room but ends in another abstraction: the suspension of time.

Thus the style involves a constant shuttling of the consciousness between the mind and the world outside, frequently within the confines of
the same sentence. Exposition—the actual furnishing of the scene—and
the establishment of Tchen's mental state are accomplished in alternate

touches, with the alternations taking place so rapidly that they seem simultaneous to the reader, much as the successive stills in a movie film create the illusion of motion. Malraux has now dropped the dramatic present tense of *The Conquerors*, trusting the rapidity of the images and the immense tension of Tchen's nerves to give the illusion of immediacy.

Meanwhile, as the passage progresses, a picture emerges which is essentially baroque: the contrast of the deep shadow with the harsh highlight on the bed matches the equally violent contrast between the inherent potential violence of Tchen's act and his complete physical quiescence. But the picture becomes completely visible only late in the passage, through the presentation of one detail at a time, and the order in which the detail is arranged in itself adds to the significance of the picture. For the man on the bed possesses a paper, with which the revolutionists can obtain the arms they need to set off the revolt of Shanghai. The paper must be obtained secretly; it must not be missed; there must be no outcry. The weapon must be the silent knife. Tchen must kill by stealth, take the paper, return to Headquarters, and set off a chain of momentous events. But the reader at this point does not know who Tchen is, or why he is here, or where "here" may be, or the identity of the man on the bed. Malraux thus opens his story with a picture which shows one human figure identified only by name, another who is nameless, an act of decisive violence, and a more detailed presentation of the torture of the figure to whom the performance is entrusted. By a curious paradox, a method which at least in part consists of exploiting only the most immediately relevant, specific, and above all concrete detail achieves a great deal of generality. The creature on the bed, thanks to the completely dominant detail of the highlighted foot, has but one characteristic, the fact that he is alive. Presently this life will be extinguished, and the important fact will be not that this unknown has died but that a life has been taken—to have the full meaning that the passage confers upon it, the verb "kill" must have no object. Thus the movement of feeling in the passage, as opposed to the movement of the style between alternate visual images and mental states, here goes from concrete statement toward metaphysics.

For Malraux is dealing with his favorite and perhaps only subject, "one man and his destiny." We are already in the presence of the great themes of *Man's Fate*. "A man," Kyo Gisors will remark later in the story, "resembles his suffering" (p. 48). The causes of Tchen's suffering will be double: a fascination with death such that he will eventually die by his own choice, for the relief of his own *Angst*, and in circumstances such that he is practically a suicide; at the same time the experience of having killed which will shut him away in that private world he is discovering in this passage, as he stands with knife in hand, preparing to strike. Meanwhile, the paragraph also introduces the fundamental problem of the relation of the individual revolutionist to the revolutionary action in which, as an individual, he expects satisfactions entirely distinct from the ends of the revolution itself—thus joining at the start of *Man's Fate* the presiding theme of *The Royal Way* with the presiding theme of *The Conquerors*. These themes are already visible as the story opens. In its first twenty pages, Malraux's investigation of man's destiny is thus well under way.

Primarily, *Man's Fate* is a sequence of events. Tchen kills his man and gets the paper, goes back to party Headquarters; Kyo takes the paper to the go-between who can arrange to get the Communist raiders aboard the steamer lying in the harbor laden with arms; holding up the crew, loading the launch with arms, and distributing them case by case to the headquarters of the neighborhood groups is a matter of a few hours. And events follow each other at this rate throughout the novel. But action itself is not all—the shortness of time forces the events into a special pattern, and in the pattern itself, the rhythm of the events, we see the outlines of tragedy. And recognition of the tragic nature of the pattern and rhythm is further impressed upon us by the great episode of Katow's death—Malraux's habitual contradiction of the logic of the events themselves. Meanwhile, there are other important figures on the edges of the tragic action, who have their own lives and their own suffering: Tchen the terrorist, Clappique the mythomaniac, Ferral the man in search of power, Kyo's old father Gisors, and Hemmelrich the phonograph merchant. Malraux's exploration of the human lot is no longer concerned with a single representative individual but with a number. And yet, finally, it is the central tragedy of the novel which reveals the full meaning of these other lives: and to the tragedy, and the figures of Kyo and Katow, one must at length return for the final summing up.

All of these aspects of the novel must concern us: the action, its compression in time, the resulting pattern and rhythm, the tragic emotion which emerges from them, the effect of Katow's death, the plights of the ancillary characters and *their* significance, and their relation to the central tragedy.

After Tchen has murdered the sleeper and made off with the precious paper, events move rapidly through a night crowded with action. From Headquarters, after Tchen's return, Kyo Gisors and Katow set off together, the first to find Baron Clappique, who will negotiate for the delivery of the arms, and the second to check on preparations for the insurrection. Kyo finds his man entertaining two trollops in a night club called the Black Cat and sends him off on the errand, then returns to his father's house to await word of Clappique's success. He spends some time talking with his father about Clappique's curious mentality, and is plunged into bitterness by learning from his wife, May, that during the afternoon she has been unfaithful to him. Clappique now returns to report gaily that all is well and Kyo goes out to dispatch Katow with the raiding party who will take the arms off the S.S. *Shantung* by force. As he leaves, Tchen arrives to talk with old Gisors about the psychic aspects of murder. After this conversation we pick up the raiders, board the *Shantung*, hijack the arms, and finish distributing them to the local insurrection groups, who even now are preparing their attack.

The next morning, Ferral is busy buying off Chiang Kai-shek. We learn his background and history, hear him interview the head of the European police about countermeasures against the strike, then go out with him in his car; toward noon we see him surrounded by the crowd that has poured into the streets with the start of the general strike, his car stopped and the chauffeur deserting him.

The scene shifts. We are with Tchen in the first violent fighting. The action is the bloodiest in the book. And all over Shanghai similar fights are going on. By the end of the afternoon, the insurrection clearly has the upper hand.

Again the scene shifts back to Ferral's office, where he negotiates further with a Chinese colonel to bribe Chiang. Ferral promises the decisive fifty million. Then afterward, he joins his mistress, Valérie, and we witness a curious erotic episode involving a light switch.

Another change of scene and we pick up Kyo, Katow, and Tchen as they wait for Chiang's artillery to come and finish off the government's armored train. They have heard of the order to turn over their arms to Chiang. At this point, Tchen proposes the murder of the renegade general. Without arms, the Communists will be completely at Chiang's mercy.

Now there is a five-day break for Kyo and Tchen to go to Hankow. They interview Vologuine, the delegate from the Moscow International, and also talk to Kyo's old friend Possoz. The answer is categorical: it is not expedient for the party to support the Shanghai insurrectionists. The latter are free, at most, to work out their own salvation when and as they can. Tchen departs for Shanghai determined to kill Chiang, and Kyo fol-

lows him, choosing the forlorn hope of organizing some sort of local resistance in preference to seeking his own safety.

There is a break of another two weeks before we open on Clappique
learning from the policeman Chpilewski that his part in getting the arms
has been discovered and that he will do well to be out of Shanghai in
forty-eight hours. Learning also that the police want Kyo, Clappique
starts for Gisors' house to pass the word.

From him we pick up Tchen, striding along the street in European
clothes with a bomb in his brief case. He meets the old clergyman who
brought him up and they walk together for a way discussing Tchen's
anxieties. Then Tchen posts his two confederates and himself takes up a
stand in an antique shop in the street where Chiang's car must pass. Un-
fortunately the dealer, seeing a sale lost when Tchen starts for the door,
seizes Tchen's arm and by the time Tchen has freed himself the car has
disappeared. The confederates also miss their chance. They now retire
to Hemmelrich's phonograph shop, where the latter has to refuse them
shelter because of the danger to his wife and child. Tchen reveals a new
plan to his colleagues: he will throw himself, with the bomb, under Chiang's
car.

We return to Clappique, who is at Gisors' house on a double errand:
to warn Kyo and to borrow the money to ship out of Shanghai. He buys
a few water colors for Ferral from Kyo's uncle, the Japanese painter Kama,
and they discuss, briefly, the difference between Eastern and Western art.
Kyo refuses to leave Shanghai and promises to meet Clappique between
eleven and eleven-thirty at the Black Cat club with some money. We learn
that now, much too late, word has come from Hankow for the insurrection
to keep its arms. As Kyo leaves the house May asks to come with him;
he first refuses because of the danger, then relents and allows her to
share it.

We switch back to Hemmelrich's shop and Katow. Both men know
that a showdown has come. Hemmelrich berates Katow violently because he, Hemmelrich, is not free to join the others in their last stand.

We switch to Ferral, going to join his mistress. He discovers that she
has played him a trick: another man is also waiting for her; she has gone
off with still another admirer, leaving each of the disappointed men a note
saying that the other will explain. Ferral buys out a pet shop and releases
the birds and animals in her room. Then, in a bar, he meets old Gisors,
who has come out to gather what news he can, and they have a quiet conversation in which the old man tells him what is meant by *la condition
humaine*. Still enraged by the way Valérie has humiliated him, Ferral goes

away completely exasperated, picks up a courtesan, and, to relieve his own anguish, purposely humiliates her.

Tchen is now waiting with his bomb. Chiang's auto approaches. Tchen throws himself beneath the wheels. In a moment he recovers consciousness, horribly mangled, and has just strength enough to put the barrel of his pistol in his mouth and pull the trigger. He never knows that Chiang was not in the car.

A few minutes later we are in the Black Cat with Clappique, who has learned that all the party headquarters are now surrounded by police. A bit early for his rendezvous with Kyo, he goes upstairs and loses himself in a game of roulette. When he comes out the hour of meeting is long past and he wanders off to find a prostitute.

Thus unwarned, Kyo and May leave the Black Cat. Near Headquarters they are caught by the police. May is left unconscious on the sidewalk. Kyo is taken off to jail.

Now we pick up Hemmelrich, who has come back to his shop at midnight to find it wrecked by a bomb and his wife and child killed. Free at last to act as he wants, he goes off to join Katow and the others in the last fight against the Nationalists.

Again we rejoin Clappique, who has just met Gisors. Gisors asks him to go to König, the chief of Chiang's police, to plead for Kyo. Gisors goes, but gets a bitter refusal.

Following this we move to party Headquarters. The Communists have exhausted their ammunition and are being wiped out. Katow is wounded and made prisoner. Hemmelrich slips out the back way, kills an enemy almost with his bare hands, and escapes to freedom.

From here we go to the prison where Kyo is confined with the political prisoners. A guard beats him when he protests the maltreatment of a madman, but Kyo succeeds with a few dollars in bribing him to stop. Kyo is taken to König, who offers him freedom if he will inform on his fellows. Kyo refuses and is returned to prison.

Now we follow Clappique again. With no money and nearly insane with fear, he disguises himself as a sailor carrying a set of new brooms, goes aboard a steamer, and makes good his escape. Ferral leaves for Europe by the same ship.

We return to Kyo, who is in the recreation shed of a school where the prisoners are gathered for execution. With him are Hemmelrich's partner Lou, Tchen's confederate Souen, and others. By ones and twos the men are taken out to be shot, or, if important personages in the insurrection, burned alive. Kyo takes the cyanide he has been carrying. Katow gives his pellet to two comrades whose nerve has failed them and accepts death by fire for himself.

Fade out, now, to the next day at Gisors' house. The old man and May have recovered Kyo's body. Gisors, temporarily as it turns out, has given up smoking opium.

Next, after a break of some months, Ferral is in Paris pleading with a group of bankers and the finance minister for help to keep his great enterprise afloat. Various piddling objections are raised. Ferral is helpless. We do not know definitely that aid is refused, but we see clearly that he has become an absurd suppliant, absurdly frustrated.

The last scene is in Kobe, where Gisors is now living with Kama the painter. May invites him to go with her to Moscow, where she can go on with medicine and where there is a teaching job for him. He has no heart for the trip and prefers to stay here with his opium. We learn from May that Hemmelrich is happy, working in a generator plant under the Five-Year Plan, and that Pei, Tchen's other confederate, is there as a fellow-traveling revolutionary writer. Then in farewell she tells the old man that she has almost ceased to weep.

Certainly Malraux's account, thus summarized, is the account of a defeat. Taken at greater length, however, it is something else. The difference is precisely the difference between prose and poetry—especially Malraux's poetry. And what makes the difference is, first, the way the action is compressed in time and, second, the pattern and rhythm resulting from the compression.

At half after midnight of March 21 Tchen kills his man. At one he is back in the phonograph shop. At two Kyo is in the Black Cat looking for Clappique. In the next two hours Clappique does his errand and reports; Gisors has his conversation with Kyo; Kyo learns of May's infidelity. At four he leaves and Tchen arrives. At four-thirty the raiders put out to the *Shantung*. At eleven the same morning, after a break of no more than five hours, we join Ferral. By one we are with Tchen and in the thick of the fighting. At five Ferral is interviewing the Chinese colonel and we know both that the insurrection has won its first battle and that the rest will not be so easy. This is the end of the first rush of action, and there is a break of about six hours before we follow Ferral to the bedroom of his mistress. And here we pass into the next day; at four in the morning Kyo, Tchen, and Katow are watching the last gasp of the armored train and already have the bad news from Chiang. The entire first segment of the action, comprising Parts One and Two of the novel, occupies twenty-eight hours, in twelve of which nothing happens.

For the interlude at Hankow, no time, but merely the date, is indicated.

But back in Shanghai, on April 11, events acquire momentum again and Malraux returns to his detailed timetable. At twelve-thirty after noon Clappique has his talk with Chpilewski. Tchen's walk with the clergyman Smithson and his subsequent, bobbled attempt on Chiang, start at one. At three Clappique visits Gisors and Kyo to borrow money and warn the latter of developments. The conversation between Katow and the bitter Hemmelrich comes a quarter-hour later. At six Ferral discovers that he has been baited by Valérie. Tchen dives under the auto at, or shortly after, ten-fifteen. An hour later, Clappique is upstairs at the Black Cat. At eleven-thirty Kyo and May tire of waiting and are caught by the police. At midnight Hemmelrich finds his shop wrecked. At one-thirty in the morning Clappique meets Gisors and they go off to appeal to König. At five the Communist Headquarters is overrun and Hemmelrich makes his escape.

Now there is another break. At ten in the morning, when Kyo confronts König, he has already been beaten by the guard "some hours" earlier. After the interview there is another break until four, when Clappique makes good his stowing away on the steamer. At six we return to the school to witness the deaths of Katow and Kyo.

Thus the second segment of intense action is over in eighteen hours, and even so is slowed considerably by the breaks in the last day. The rest of the events, like the Hankow part, are vaguely labeled, "The next day," "Paris—July," "Kobe—Spring."

Such is the timetable of the novel. Rhythm and pattern are implicit in it. First there is the burst of frenetic action of the opening insurrection, full of rush and tension. Then the slow, unhurried, ominous trip to Hankow and back. Next the renewed rush in which the insurrection is crushed. And finally comes the part where again time is unimportant and where nothing really occurs, where reader and characters alike *learn* something rather than *witness* something.

The first burst of action, from the murder in the hotel to the success of the insurrection, presents itself as an apparently successful effort toward achieving the first purpose of the protagonists. They seem on the point of victory. But with the receipt of the order from Chiang to give up the arms, it begins to dawn on us, as well as on the characters, that the purpose toward which the action has progressed is not the true purpose at all, that this victory is not a victory, and that the situation of these people is very different from what it has up to now appeared to be. The suspicion deepens to conviction during the more or less timeless visit to Hankow where Tchen and Kyo learn that Moscow has abandoned them. And in the light of this new revelation we embark upon a second rush of action in which the victory turns inexorably into defeat and the central characters come, each according to the rule of his private nature, to catastrophe.

At this point the rhythm again changes. After the capture of Kyo and the reduction of the last Communist forces under Katow the pace again slackens. Between dawn and dark of this day there are only three episodes: Kyo's facing his captors, Clappique's abject departure, and the scene of execution at the school. We are allowed time to contemplate Kyo, who at Hankow determined to return and face what was in store for him, now accepting his fate with the quiet gesture of taking poison, and Katow accepting a last cup of suffering for the sake of two comrades. We are invited to dwell upon the greatness of two human beings who comport themselves so in defeat that out of the defeat rises a kind of victory—a victory whose lineaments are clearer for the contrast with the abjection of Clappique.

The closing events of the story, after the death of Kyo, may even seem to be something like the final lament which, in Sophocles, seems designed to soothe the spectator and send him out of the theater somberly happy to be a man. In any event, we can surely identify the arrangement and design of what happens in *Man's Fate* as tragic.[1] Malraux's account of what took place at Shanghai is the account of a victory.

The effect of victory is greatly enhanced by the quality of the picture which Malraux manages to juxtapose to the obvious and inescapable logic of events, and which reduces the logic to relative unimportance. Discursively, what happens to Kyo and Katow demonstrates that revolution is something for the prudent to avoid, just as the *Oedipus* demonstrates that the prudent will not find it good to kill one's father or sleep with one's mother. But at this point, in both tragic poem and tragic novel, discursive logic has to yield to the sheer magnificence of poetry.

Katow's gesture is both an act performed in the name of human dignity and a proof of human solidarity. After Kyo's death he has felt a horrible loneliness: ". . . alone, alone between the body of his dead friend and of

---

[1] Bert M.-P. Leefmans, in an unpublished essay, "Malraux and Tragedy: the Structure of *La Condition humaine*," finds that this novel follows very closely the pattern of tragedy outlined by Francis Fergusson in his *Idea of the Theater*. Fergusson, in turn, builds upon Kenneth Burke's statement of the tragic rhythm which makes the protagonist move "from Passion, through Purpose, to Perception." I am heavily indebted to Mr. Leefmans, and less directly so to his predecessors.

his two frightened companions, alone between this wall and that whistle lost in the night." But a man can be stronger than his feeling of solitude. He gives the man next to him the cyanide and presently submerges in a new anguish when the man drops the pellet. Then, when they find it, he is in a paroxysm lest the poison have decomposed and lost its virtue. He holds the man's hand tightly while they wait for the cyanide to work. The man dies, and Katow once more feels abandoned. But then the guards come and find the bodies.

> "Isolate the six nearest prisoners."
> "No need," replied Katow, "I'm the one that gave them the cyanide."
> The officer hesitated:
> "And what about yourself?"
> "There was just enough for two," Katow answered with deep joy. (P. 288.)

But *Man's Fate* uses a canvas broader than the canvas of tragedy and broader than Katow and Kyo can occupy by themselves; it involves other destinies than theirs; it has intentions additional to the tragic ones. Tchen, Ferral, and Clappique take turns absorbing the attention of the reader. In a sense they are secondary characters—that is, their roles are subordinate in the development of the story as a piece of fiction. But with respect to the exposition of the book's essential subject they loom large and one hesitates to affirm that they are any less important than Katow and Kyo. If Malraux had chosen to continue writing fictions on the scale of *The Conquerors* and *The Royal Way*, each of their destinies could easily have been made the matter of a separate novel.

Tchen's act of killing establishes his essential status in the world and condemns him to a special kind of anguish. The falling knife sets off his old latent obsession with death, and renews his feeling of fundamental isolation. In the midst of life, death will come to seem the safest, most final refuge and the abode of peace. From a shadow in a room he changes to a type, the Terrorist, and from type to man, and as he does so he comes to accept both his obsession with death and his estrangement. By the time he leaves the hotel and is on his way back to the party council at the phonograph shop he is taking a certain solace in the fact that he has killed. "There was a world of murder and he was staying in it as if in a warm place" (p. 21). We see him still more clearly when his problem becomes one of living simultaneously in two worlds. Among his companions he manages a social gesture, asking for and eating a handful of candy from Katow's bag; and the gesture reveals the anguished man.

But even his old teacher, Gisors, is unable to help him. After their inter-

view, later on the night of the murder, the old man knows that the death
of the young one is now inevitable. "Capable of victory, but not of living
in victory, on what could he call except on death" (p. 63). He sees Tchen's
predicament as not greatly different from the plight of the Conqueror type:
once more it is the predicament of the man equal to conquest but not equal
to enjoying its fruits. For Gisors, Tchen is a man who has thrown himself
into terrorism as if into a prison from which he cannot emerge alive. He
has always known that this adolescent can never live by an idea unless the
idea is translated immediately into act. The feeling of estrangement antedates Tchen's first murder. Revolution has given this solitude a sense and
meaning, but only temporarily. Murder has given it another, also temporary.

Tchen's counterpart in *The Conquerors*, the terrorist Hong, is motivated by a hatred which is the product of the human wretchedness he has
lived in. His behavior is explicable in almost completely material terms.
Tchen is more complicated. Beneath the disposition to murder lies the pre-
disposition, the twist of the urge to destruction, Thanatos, gradually dominating the personality and condemning it at last. If from one angle Tchen's
suffering seems metaphysical in nature, in that it reflects the suffering of a
man condemned as all men are, to live in isolation, it is also something
buried in his subconscious. We merely see Hong. We see *into* the tortured
Tchen.

His solitude hangs heavy on him, even in battle. And when he is one
of a chain of men on the roof of the police station—the top man holding
the chimney and the bottom one hanging over the eaves whence he can
toss his grenades through the window into the room below—even here
where every man is dependent on every other and none is stronger than
the weakest, Tchen is still alone. "In spite of the closeness of death, in spite
of the fraternal weight tugging at his arms, he was not one with them"
(p. 101).

The order for the insurgents to turn over their arms makes Tchen's
fate certain. Learning at Hankow that the order is irrevocable, he announces his revolt against the party discipline: he will take upon himself
the murder of Chiang Kai-shek. (Now the opportunism of the Communist
bureaucrats becomes clear. They will not approve and back Tchen, but
they will not prevent him; if he fails the failure will be his own, but if he
succeeds . . .) The failure of the first attempt is bitterly ironical. But
the irony disappears when he reaches his new decision, to throw himself
under the car with the bomb. Everything now becomes simple. He attains
the euphoria of complete certitude.

Since Hankow, Kyo has known that this is how Tchen will end. Tchen has tried to explain the attraction of terrorism:

"I want a stronger word than joy. There isn't any. Even in Chinese. A . . . total peace. A sort of . . . what do you say? Of . . . I don't know. There's only one thing deeper. Further from man, nearer . . . Are you familiar with opium?"

"Hardly at all."

"Then it's going to be hard to explain. Nearer what you might call ecstasy. Yes. But thick. Deep. Not light. An ecstasy toward . . . downward."

"And it's an idea that gives you that?"

"Yes: my own death." (P. 142.)

And he dies with the feeling of complete possession of himself, in total, absolute knowledge. For an hour and more before his death he has felt nothing of the old weight that hung upon him.

Much can be made, if one reads *Man's Fate* as a sort of political parable, of the fact that Tchen does not kill Chiang. It is even possible to treat his death, as Mr. E. B. Burgum[2] does, as retribution for having rejected the discipline of the party. And certainly Malraux is haunted by the political problem of the man who wants to be a revolutionist but cannot abide the discipline, whose particular destiny it is that he must take direct action. Hong, Garine, Tchen, and Hernandez (in *Man's Hope*) end in revolt, and one way to read *Man's Hope* is to take it as the account of the conflict between the individualists whose ideal is *being* something and the Communists, whose ideal is *doing*. But as a final reading of Tchen's story, this purely political one seems inadequate.

Tchen's motives are only superficially political. When he kills the man at the hotel he forgets why he is killing him, and when he dashes himself under Chiang's empty car, there is no shadow of feeling in his heart that thanks to his sacrifice the revolution may now succeed. He is at last bursting the gates of his prison, destroying his solitude, freeing himself from the bonds of man's predicament. Dostoevski speaks somewhere of how man is the only animal bent upon his own destruction. For Tchen, at least, self-destruction is man's fate, and like Kyo and Katow he ends by accepting his fatality.

Tchen is so interesting in himself that he threatens the unity of the book

---

[2] In *The Novel and the World's Dilemma*, of which the chapter on Malraux gives an extreme example of the not uncommon habit of reducing Malraux's novels to mere political fables. The author assumes that Malraux is an orthodox Marxist, engaged in dealing out rewards and punishments to his characters according to their observance of the party line. Signs of Marxist orthodoxy in Malraux's work are, as a matter of fact, extremely rare—as is also any evidence of direct knowledge of Marx's writings.

as a whole; the reader becomes so absorbed in him as almost to forget the main plot. The same is even truer of Clappique. When Kyo first sees him at the Black Cat, Clappique is entertaining a brace of de luxe prostitutes with a wonderful account of his maternal grandfather's life, loves, and fantastic burial—upright on his horse like Attila. One girl is too drunk to listen, the other too dull to follow, but Clappique hardly needs a listener. He is his own audience. One part of his personality listens while the other performs, lost in its role. The more fantastic the role the better. His voice changes with the needs of the story. He assumes character after character, entirely different with the girls from what he is with the waiter or with Kyo when Kyo finally gets his attention. His narrative is accompanied by a wealth of gesture, some of it as strongly pantomimic as the gestures of Rameau's nephew.

Le baron pelotait la Philippine, mais il continuait de parler au visage mince, tout en yeux, de la Russe:

— ... le malheur, chère amie, c'est qu'il n'y a plus de fantaisie. De temps en temps,

l'index pointé:

«... un ministre européen envoie à sa femme un pp'etit colis postal, elle l'ouvre—pas un mot ...

l'index sur la bouche:

«... c'est la tête de son amant. On en parle encore trois ans après!

Eploré:

«Lamentable, chère amie, l-lamentable! Regardez-moi! Vous voyez ma tête? Voila où mènent vingt ans de fantaisie héréditaire. Ça ressemble à la syphilis.—Pas un mot!

Plein d'autorité:

«Garçon! du champagne pour ces deux dames, et pour moi ...

de nouveau confidentiel:

«... un pp'etit Martini ...

sévère:

«trrès sec.» (P. 34.)

The Baron was fondling the Filipino girl, but went on talking to the thin-faced, wide-eyed Russian one.

"It's a sad thing, my dear, but there's no fantasy any more. From time to time . . ." (He points his finger.)

"A European cabinet minister mails his wife a l-little parcel. She opens it . . . Not a word . . .

(The finger goes to his mouth.)

"It's her lover's head. Three years after, people are still talking of it!

(On the verge of tears.)

"Lamentable, my dear, l-lamentable. Look at me. You see my face? That's what twenty years of congenital fantasy gets you. It's like syphilis . . . Not a word . . .

(All authority.)

"Waiter! Champagne for the ladies, and, for me . . .

(secretively again.)

"A l-little Martini . . .

(Sternly.)

"Very dry."

One suspects this scene of being carefully, almost lovingly, worked over, just as one suspects that Clappique was copied from life.[3] From the start, although his part in the action is minor, he is treated as a major char-acter.

When at length he pays his check, he pockets only ten dollars of the change from a hundred-dollar bill and hands the rest to the Russian girl. Here at last is something she can understand; she rises to take him up-stairs. He refuses. He would prefer it to be some other night, preferably when he has no money. For the moment, his mythomania has given him all the satisfaction he needs and its attractions have proved stronger than those of sex.

But Clappique is not merely a mythomaniac; he is also a buffoon. The two things need not go hand in hand: in *The Royal Way* we had the word of the ship's captain that there is a necessary element of mythomania in every adventurer. Clappique is a mythomaniac who is *also* a buffoon. There is very small doubt that the personage of Clappique invites Malraux not only because mythomania is one form of man's condition, but also because the buffoonery offers possibilities for the shaping of the novel itself, through "comic relief," of course—the at once funny and extremely horrid behavior of the Gravediggers' scene—but even more through the possibilities of contrast. Between the scene where Kyo rejects König's proposal, in the name of human dignity, and the scene where the pro-tagonists die, Malraux sandwiches the episode of Clappique's last day.

---

[3] In general I have avoided discussing the possible prototypes of Malraux's characters, partly because I am persuaded that the question of who sat for what portrait is rarely more significant in literature than it is in painting, and partly because such discussions might involve libeling living persons who are entitled to privacy. The case of Clappique is in point. Literary gossip makes him a composite of two actual people, one the husband of a close friend of Mme Clara Malraux, the other a traveling companion of one of Malraux's journeys. The fact, if it is a fact, adds less to our understanding of Clappique than does the consideration that to these models should be added Malraux himself, at least to the extent that the mythomaniac character has an inevitable interest for any novelist whose fictions closely parallel, and rectify imagina-tively, his own experiences.

Insane with fear, and hounded by his mythomaniac reveries, the Baron finally disguises himself and sneaks aboard the steamer. The effect is to raise the tone of the master scene of the whole novel.

Clappique is the creation of a writer who has learned much from Dostoevski. His ability to drop into a role is very reminiscent of the accomplishment Fyodor Karamazov demonstrates in the scene at Zossima's cell. His inability *not* to tell a lie makes him sound like old General Epanchin in *The Idiot*. (Malraux refers frequently to both these books, incidentally, in later writings.) Clappique also has the facility of getting out of touch with reality that we marvel at in the hero of *Notes from Underground* when the latter harangues the prostitute in the name of morality. And doubtless Malraux's reading of Dostoevski was as influential in the formation of Clappique as any direct observation of characters he may have met in his travels. But Clappique remains quite different from Dostoevski's buffoons even so: he is much better bred; there is small evidence that he takes direct pleasure in self-laceration; he is not so colossally capable of limitless self-abasement; the roles in which his imagination casts him are not an escape from a social situation—an intolerable feeling of inferiority in the presence of others. His mythomania is a denial of life, old Gisors tells us. Like opium, action, eroticism, or the creation of empires, it lifts, temporarily, the weight of human servitude. Clappique is absent from the story from the completion of his errand in Part One to the beginning of Part Four, but from the latter point he commands a constantly increasing share of Malraux's attention. We watch him in the bar with Chpilewski, learning that his jig is up; we meet him again at Gisors' house where he warns Kyo a first time and also wangles a loan; we pick him up again at the Black Cat and follow him up to the roulette table where he fritters away both his money and Kyo's life.

In the earlier episodes we watch him as he appears to some other character, but in these later scenes the point of view shifts so that we can look out from inside him and see the world as he sees it. Alternate gains and losses pin him to the table. He does not forget the passage of time and the plight of Kyo: his inability to move his left hand, which he holds in such a position that the face of his wrist watch is always turned down, betrays a determination to deny time, not an unawareness of it. He manages to confuse reality and unreality, and to relegate Kyo to the realm of the unreal; reality is here in front of him, this brightly lighted table, this agile, demonic little ball. Momentarily he contrives to reconcile the two personalities within himself: the Clappique who, like Tchen, wants to be destroyed and the Clappique almost frantically eager to live. The roulette ball becomes alive and seems so capable of liberating him from his own anguish that he wants to go on winning, not for the money but so that he will never have to stop playing. One part of him—the part that is the actor in his eternal charade—even identifies itself with the ball. And so he lets Kyo get away unwarned.

Now, Kyo's fate has already been decided, long before this evening, back in Hankow, and by Kyo himself. Clappique's feckless conduct is decisive only in that it determines the time and the manner in which that decision to continue the fight in Shanghai results in Kyo's undoing. Clappique is under the spotlight here no more because of his effect on the other characters than because his conduct is, itself, of great human significance. He has, for the moment, found a refuge from life. For the next few hours he will do his utmost to stay in the refuge, until at last life, with its anguish, crowds in upon him again. He comes out of the gaming house and goes off to find a prostitute with whom to continue his feverish make-believe. After this encounter, he tells her, without believing it himself, he is going to commit suicide. Actually he is going on into ever thickening guilt and fear.

There is potent testimony that, in writing the novel, Malraux became so fascinated with his Clappique that the latter threatened to run away with the story. In *Marianne*, December 13, 1933, there appeared a Malraux item entitled, "Un chapitre inédit de la Condition humaine." The page is ornamented with photographs of two naked women, one clearly Oriental and smoking what is probably opium. The accompanying legend runs: "Dans l'hôtel des sensations inédites." An editorial note offers supplementary information:

This chapter, lifted out of the final version of the work, was placed between the scene where Clappique, fascinated by the game, allows Kyo to be captured and the one where he joins the latter's father, Gisors. The text was taken out, not at all because of the kind of scene it contains, but because it gave too great an importance to the secondary character of Clappique. When the chapter begins, Clappique, exhausted by his night of gambling during which he has betrayed his friend, by the fascination that he has just discovered in the pleasure of losing, uses his last remaining strength to escape and gets back to his hotel in a state of chaotic frenzy.[4]

The material not included in the final text turns out to be what the presentation in *Marianne* suggests. Clappique is lured by a nude woman

---

[4] For further details see "Note for a Malraux Bibliography," *Modern Language Notes*, LXV (June 1950), 392–95. I have to thank my colleague Jean-Albert Bédé for assistance in preparing the article.

into her darkened room, where, in the midst of the erotic episode, he discovers that he is performing for the benefit of a group of *voyeurs* hidden in the darkness. The plot departs from scatological folklore only in that Clappique, whose anxiety state has been so intense all that night, connects his audience with Chiang Kai-shek and the Kuomintang, feels himself in vague but great danger, bolts for the door but finds it locked, manages finally to reach and twist the key, and emerges in such disarray as to provoke the mirth of a passing *boy*.

Why did Malraux suppress the episode?—The theme of eroticism, already copiously exploited in the scenes between Ferral and Valérie, had possibly become an aesthetic problem. Moreover, the tone of an episode in which Clappique appears with no more dignity than the victim of a particularly lurid farce, may provide too much contrast with the serious tone of the episodes that precede and follow it. But it is also evident that as a fictional character Clappique is becoming an embarrassment. The momentum of the story is forcing events toward their conclusion. The destinies of May, Kyo, Gisors, Katow, Ferral, and a number of others have yet to be dealt with. This consideration calls for the curbing of Clappique. Actually, the suppressed episode, if left in the book, would have raised hob with the timetable. He leaves the gaming house at one o'clock. The narrative requires him to be joined by Gisors by half after one or shortly thereafter. If the chapter printed in *Marianne* had not been taken out of the book, simple arithmetic reveals that Clappique would have been placed in the necessity of having had carnal knowledge of three different women in three different places in little more than half an hour. Malraux suppressed the episode so that Clappique would not run away with the story.

Like the protagonists of the main, tragic, story, Clappique has his little moment of seeming victory, there at the gaming table where for a short time he succeeds, or almost succeeds, in denying life. But at the end he simply crawls away. His victory is turned into defeat, just as the defeat of Kyo and Katow has been turned into victory.

Like Clappique, Ferral seems to grow as the novel progresses, after a beginning where he seems to be no more than the official bad man. In the economy of the novel he seems the least necessary of the characters. Two of his four big scenes—those which he shares with Valérie Serge—are certainly marginal and could easily be omitted without affecting the course of the action. As the representative of foreign, imperialistic capitalism busy at an office telephone, energetically organizing the reaction, squeezing money out of the Chinese conservatives, directing the efforts of the police, and arranging to bribe Chiang Kai-shek, he sets in motion the forces that eventually crush the insurrection; he is interesting less as a human being than as a source of harm. He is the Antagonist, necessarily an unsympathetic figure.

But just as *Man's Fate* is not just a novel about an insurrection, so Ferral is not merely a convenient substitute for the devil. When he appears in his new role of unassuaged lover, he is far less antipathetic, much less the mere tycoon industriously defending the fortune he has built. The Consortium is the expression of human drives which identify him with the earlier heroes of Malraux. Socially he is on the other side of the barricades, but in other respects he is in the same predicament as they. The Consortium expresses his lust for power, and is his means of "leaving a scar on the map." Money is less important to him than his ability to impose his will on other people. The geography has changed and we have come out of the jungle, but this exploiter is still recognizably the same type as Perken, the man who, though not walled off in an inaccessible hinterland, is still one who would be king. Further, he has the same anarchic temperament as Garine, like him has no use for law except such law as he can turn to his own ends, like him has attached himself to a "great action" (his Consortium is comparable to Mitsubishi and Standard Oil), and like him has committed himself to these things in order to satisfy his own personal and private needs.

Critics who look everywhere in Malraux's novels for portraits of the Adventurer should give Ferral more attention. Much more clearly than either Kyo or Tchen, he is cut to the adventurer pattern; he is a member of a prominent middle-class family; a brilliant career as an intellectual is already behind him (like Vincent Berger in *Les Noyers de l'Altenburg* he is an ex-professor); after a try at politics, he has now placed himself where such types are happiest, in a situation where a man is what he does. In Ferral we once more have Malraux's version of the *Übermensch*, though an *Übermensch* in a sack suit who frequents the best hotels.

It is in a hotel that his full identity is revealed—he is incapable of assuagement, a *grand inassouvi*. Merely to possess a beautiful woman does not satisfy him. He must share her private experience. And so while the sporadic gunfire in the background marks the agony of the armored train, Ferral denies Valérie the privacy of darkness. She protests and turns off the light. He turns it on again. She capitulates. But like the victories of men who escape man's fate through opium or through mythomania, this one also is illusory.

For when the insurrection has been put down and its leaders are on the eve of their final passion, Valérie not only makes a fool of Ferral, but says in the letter she leaves him that she has done it to show him that she does not accept his domination. After he has loosed the birds and animals in her room, he has his moment of conversation with Gisors in the bar and then goes off to find a courtesan and take her home with him. Such women are not mere trollops. They are trained in social accomplishments, and custom dictates that they entertain their clients. This one offers to sing for Ferral. "No," he replies brutally, "take off your clothes." The affront to her dignity is fully intentional. Ferral is finding relief from his frustration. The only consolation for the blow he has taken from Valérie is to humiliate some other human being, even the most defenseless. A few hours earlier than Kyo and Katow, he has found *his* victory changed to defeat, thus recapitulating the experience pattern so common in the book, just as did Clappique. And like Clappique, Ferral will have no moment of reconciliation with fate.

Ferral is certainly not a winning character, but the fact that the novel does not drop him at this point attests Malraux's persistent interest in him. The scene where Ferral reappears, in Paris, actually reveals nothing explicit about the Consortium Ferral is there to defend. What is revealed very clearly indeed is that whether he retains the nominal chairmanship of the Consortium or not, Ferral is no longer dominant; he is at the mercy of a group of sedentary nonentities who sit sucking on caramels as they listen to his arguments. Given Ferral's temperament and the drives which have determined his career, this situation is the embodiment of the Absurd. To have this character end in complete absurdity was clearly important to Malraux, for to risk an eighteen-page return to the fortunes of Ferral, just after the passage on the death of Katow, was to make a heavy wager: if it failed it could easily dull the intense tragic emotion of the finest pages in the novel.

Where Ferral is a victim of his inner urge to dominate, old Gisors— Kyo's father—is a victim of his own apathy. He is also superbly intelligent, and endowed with that understanding of life that Malraux tends to attribute to those who, like Gisors, are lifelong students of art. Possibly we should take him merely as an example of the human type whose action is inhibited by the unrestrained play of the intelligence. But this reading seems inadequate, after all. Gisors is also a father, and the specific source of his anguish is his fatherhood. He loves Kyo so deeply that he is tortured by the separation caused by Kyo's commitment to a life of action in which the father cannot participate. This kind of human relationship is something new for Malraux. The recent death of his own father, for whom

Malraux seems to have had both great affection and intellectual respect, may have turned his attention to the latent poignancy of a father's feelings about his son. At the same time, he had been intimately friendly with Bernard Groethuysen, who was old enough to have been his father and who appears to have combined Gisors' magnificent gift of understanding with an innate ineptitude and distaste for action very like his. And in addition, Malraux was writing his book just before the birth of his daughter Florence, his first child, and we know from Gide's *Journal*[5] that Malraux feared paternity as a deterrent to action.

Gisors is thus wise as a father should be wise. In addition to his own special wretchedness he knows all the other forms of anguish. Much of our understanding of Tchen, Kyo, Ferral, and Clappique derives from our knowing what they look like to him. But this man whose teaching at the University of Peking helped form a revolutionary generation is powerless against his own paralysis. The physician cannot save himself. He owes his famous serenity to opium.

For a moment after Kyo's death he gives up his pipe and pellets and accepts the fullness of his suffering. But at Kobe he is smoking again and with the help of opium has fallen back into apathy. He no longer feels the burden of life and the awareness of death which, we now learn, have always plagued him, but he has joined those like Clappique and Tchen, those who have tried to escape man's fate by denying life. In the end, nothing is real to him but the vanity of everything. His presence and his mood dominate the last pages of the book and quite outweigh the happiness— which we do not see but only hear about—of the people who have escaped to Moscow.

Gisors' escape from his anguish has at least the merit of harming no one but himself. A type like König, on the other hand, finds relief only in inflicting pain. Like Tchen, he is psychically condemned to shed blood. Like Ferral, he is driven by the need to humiliate. He is happy, he tells Clappique, only when killing. It seems that years ago he was serving in Seminoff's White army and was taken prisoner by the Reds. They beat him unconscious, and while he was unconscious tore the insignia off his shoulders and replaced it with red stars fastened by nails driven deep into the flesh. In his pain he wept like a woman. The traumata of his experience are indelible. He takes a perverted pleasure in recalling the details of his humiliation, and heats his fury with it each time he has an opportunity to torture or to execute. For Malraux, some such experience is necessary to

---

[5] Entry for September 4, 1936. Gide learns that Malraux, momentarily in Paris between battles, feels remarkably freer to lead a life of action since his separation from his family.

explain the otherwise inexplicable mentality of the Policeman, not merely in Asia but everywhere; not merely the jailer who serves the enemy but (witness Nicolaïeff in *The Conquerors* with his smiling statement that there is no courage that will survive a ten-minute private conference with an experienced interrogator) the policeman who is one's own ally. The police mentality, we shall learn in *Days of Wrath*, is everywhere alike; the work requires a special human type. Such men exist to preside over prisons and the prison is so completely assimilated to the idea of humiliation that as Malraux's novels follow each other the prison achieves the status of a symbol: Garine leaves Europe to escape a prison sentence after the absurdity of his trial; Kyo's ultimate ordeal of humiliation—from which he emerges victorious—comes when he is whipped on the hands by his Chinese jailer; for Kassner in *Days of Wrath* the time of his imprisonment is another name for the Days of Scorn; in *Man's Hope* the liberated proletariat is equated, in a striking medical metaphor, with men newly released from jails; the great novelists listed by the debaters at the Altenburg Priory, Defoe, Dostoevski, Cervantes, are all men who have served time. (One can only speculate as to the relation between the persistence of the symbol in the novels and the fact of Malraux's early, and absurd, detention in Indochina.) For a König the need to humiliate is so powerful that it unseats the normal need of the individual: he has been a year without going to bed with his wife. Clappique, who has come to him to plead for Kyo's life, immediately senses the hopelessness of his errand; he recognizes in König one of those men whose anguish can be assuaged, *like his own*, only by a sweeping, universal negation of the world. The difference is that Clappique's instrument of negation is his mythomania.

Meanwhile, humiliation is also at issue in the case of the wretched little Hemmelrich, the complete victim of circumstance. Hemmelrich's humiliation does not come out of one horrible incident, as does König's. His whole life has been a traumatic experience. He has never been able to earn a living that would let him respect himself. The source of his present misery is that now that the opportunity offers to strike back at his anonymous humiliators, he is not free to do so. He has married a Chinese woman out of pity for someone even more wretched than he. She is ill. Their child has mastoiditis. For him to take an active part in the revolution is to expose them; he has to begrudge the use of his little shop, and deny it entirely to Tchen when Tchen needs a refuge. He does not even have the dignity of being free to die as he likes. Every call to volunteer for a dangerous mission renews his anguish, and the torture is so great that in anger he lashes out at the only man who really understands him. Then at last a bomb relieves him of his responsibilities and he leaves the mangled bodies of his wife and child to run to Communist headquarters and share in the ultimate battle. It is one of the unexplained ironies of *Man's Fate* that Hemmelrich should be one of the few characters to emerge not only unscathed but happy, learning for the first time in Russia that human labor can be a sign of dignity as well as one of humiliation.

Man's Fate is clearly intended to do what tempted Malraux when he was writing *The Conquerors*—to surround his protagonists by a number of other characters who illustrate the variety of forms man's destiny can take. The later novel not only brings to life the population of *The Conquerors* and *The Royal Way*; it even adds types like Hemmelrich to their number. To do so, Malraux has had to find a new technique. He has adopted a shifting point of view.

Limiting the point of view by the use of a central intelligence had cramped Malraux considerably in the first two novels. In *The Royal Way* he had been forced to discard it occasionally because there were essential things in the story that Claude Vannec could not possibly know. In *The Conquerors*, where he expended an inordinate effort to put the whole narrative in the mouth of one character, his method inhibited his exploring many areas which obviously interested him, for the relentless focus upon Garine made investigation of the other characters look digressive. The limitation of point of view had advantages, most particularly the advantage of heightening the dramatic intensity of the novels, but it also implied the neglect of many other tempting dramatic possibilities.

In *Man's Fate* the reader sees the reputedly "secondary" characters as clearly as he sees Kyo and Katow, and perhaps understands them better, precisely because of this change in optics. Of Hong, Rensky, and Rebecci —and much of the time Perken and Garine—we saw only the exteriors, and fathomed their conduct only as some intermediary character between us and them fathomed it; in the case of Hong, we did not get even that close, since the narrating character saw him only once and reported most of Hong's activity as it was reported to him, at second remove. But now the reader sees the world, from time to time, as Tchen, Clappique, and Ferral see it. Sharing their vision does much to erase the difference between primary and secondary character.

The method permits an extremely useful variation in emphasis. While we are seeing the action with Tchen, for example, Clappique and Ferral are minor people. We are admitted to Clappique's mind only in the second half of the story, *after* we have already watched him through the puzzled eyes of Kyo and the somewhat amused ones of Gisors. And we begin seeing as Ferral sees, only when he appears as the unassuaged erotic, the humiliated man bent on vengeance, the man who has staked all on an enterprise that has come to a dead end. The change in optics as the story progresses may mean merely that Malraux's interest in these characters increased as he went along. But it occurs at those places where we become aware that these people, as well as the protagonist, mirror the universal fate of man. We no longer feel them to be minor figures. The change naturally enlists not only the interest of the reader but also his sympathy. It is infinitely harder to remain aloof and not identify oneself somewhat with a character, however unpleasant, when one sees the world as he sees it. The identification and resultant sympathy does much to persuade us that the condition of these individuals, even though they may need the psychiatrist more than we, is part and parcel of our own.

The new technique makes Malraux give up one signal advantage. Since there is no longer a surrogate for the author whose opinions are privileged, critics have tended to take the utterance of any character, so long as it suits their book, to be the utterance of Malraux himself. For an author like Malraux, whose books are combed for political opinions, the disadvantage is doubtless considerable, but it is certainly outweighed by the *literary* advantages of the method. For it permits him to probe his characters more deeply, and not only this but to show them from various angles, as they appear to various fellow characters, thus rounding them and obviating the danger, grave in the early novels, of creating personae rather than men. When necessary, he assumes the omniscient and omnipresent author. Like Flaubert's "God in creation," he is everywhere present and never visible. Or hardly ever: he makes in cold fact a number of interventions, but they are always unostentatious and subdued in tone; one is hardly aware of them. Most of the time the action is presented from the point of view of the character best placed to see it; more rarely, for lack of an available character, it is seen as it would be seen by a well-informed but rather uninvolved bystander. The reader's credulity is not strained and the presence of so many important characters is rendered possible.

Meanwhile, in adopting the broader canvas and the ramified action, so that the reader's interest would extend to a half-dozen characters at once, Malraux has assumed the burden of keeping the reader aware of the continuity of the action and the structural relations between episodes. The care he has expended in this respect is evident. He links various separated episodes by repetition of detail whose significance bridges the gaps between: Ferral in Valérie's room hears the drumfire of the armored train which is the government's last resource and which Kyo, Katow, and Tchen will shortly watch expire. And when Kyo needs money to bribe the prison guard who beats the madman, he has ready in his pocket the money which he would have handed Clappique the night before if Clappique had kept the rendezvous. Such details are not forced upon the reader, but are present by the dozen to testify to Malraux's awareness of the complexity of his task.

The intention behind Malraux's technique, then, is to permit him to juxtapose a number of individual human destinies with the destinies of the heroes of his central tragedy. So the meaning of the novel must be looked for in the relation of these ancillary stories to the main one—not in the main story alone, not in the ancillary stories alone, but in all together. Too exclusive interrogation of the ancillary gives . . . chaos. Too exclusive attention to the fate of Kyo and Katow gives back an answer too simplistic because too exclusively political.

For, politically, *Man's Fate* is a very ambiguous book. Official Communist critics have been right, from their point of view, in approaching it warily; for them it is tainted by an individualism such as Trotsky had already denounced in *The Conquerors*, and this individualism is one which no few readers, including the brilliant and non-Communist Sartre,[6] have felt to be extremely middle class. To be sure, since in the end Kyo and Katow enjoy a human dignity and a feeling of fraternity which is denied to the other characters, revolution appears to be at least an instrumental good. But beyond this? Kyo and Katow may not be identifiable with the "Conqueror" type, like Garine (who would like to find in revolution a Good-in-itself); but they are no more imaginable as "curés de la révolution," the custodians of progress who take over when the fighting has finished; their place in the classless society of the Marxist future is hard to see. And much of the pathos of the book emerges from the inevitable conflict between the legitimate interests of the individual and those of the grand revolutionary enterprise.

Considering what happens to the protagonists, the revolution looks like a very immoral thing; Kyo and Katow die because of no fatal defect in their characters, but because the International lets them down, because it is more expedient for brave men to die than for the International to come into open conflict with Chiang Kai-shek. They die, moreover, as a result of bureaucratic fecklessness and incompetence, for the order they have asked for, authorizing them to keep or hide their arms, is finally issued too

---

[6] In "Etude," published as preface to Roger Stéphane, *Portrait de l'aventurier*.

late to be anything but an additional irony. Thus, if we are to be guided by the most emotionally compelling part of the story, we may conclude that the situation of Kyo and Katow in the revolution merely illustrates another of the various blind alleys which make up man's lot. For if revolution is the only acceptable form of human activity, it is one that leads straight to disaster. One participates at the cost of one's eventual destruction. In fact, if the book were first and foremost a political fable, and if its import were to be judged by the fates of its principals, it could easily be understood to condemn revolution.

But in the last section of the book we learn that Pei, Tchen's second in the attack on Chiang, is happy in Russia, writing propaganda. Hemmelrich, we know, is there also. In fact, all those "who could escape" from Shanghai are back in revolutionary work. May is on her way back to Moscow, because to take up her medicine there is the best way to "avenge" Kyo. As she sits there in Kobe, waiting to leave, she thinks: "The Revolution had just been through a terrible malady, but it had not died" (p. 308). Does she mean, by "malady," the failure of the Shanghai insurrection, or is she thinking of a weakness nearer the heart, at Moscow? In any case, she takes satisfaction from the thought and is willing to continue her part in the struggle.

Why not dismiss the ambiguity by insisting upon a distinction? There is Revolution, with a capital letter, and opposed to it there is the specific revolution, owned and operated by a group of men in Moscow. Why not say that Revolution in general is good, but that the Communist revolution kills those who serve it, is fallible, opportunistic, sooner an evil than a good? There is a hint of such a distinction in Pei's remark that while he is glad to be a revolutionary writer, he will never be a "pure" Communist. Possibly it is also suggested in the contrast between May's desire to avenge Kyo and her lack of enthusiasm for the return to Moscow. But the real reason for not making such a distinction is that Malraux's novel does not make it, and to insist upon it would be to insist upon clearing away an ambiguity which the novelist prefers to maintain.

The dialectic of the novel is too complicated to permit such simplifications. The pages in which we see men made happy by the revolution are in an obscure position. They occur where there is no dramatic tension. They convey information from off stage; what we *see* in these same pages is a saddened young woman, about to try to make what she can of a life from which the animating force, her love for Kyo, has been removed, talking with a pathetic old man. His suffering is what dominates these last pages.

Légers, très élevés, les nuages passaient au-dessus des pins sombres et se résorbaient peu à peu dans le ciel; et il lui sembla qu'un de leurs groupes, celui-là précisément, exprimaient les hommes qu'il avait connus et aimés, et qui étaient morts. L'humanité était épaisse et lourde, lourde de chair, de sang, de souffrance, éternellement collée à elle-même comme tout ce qui meurt; mais même le sang, même la chair, même la douleur, même la mort se résorbaient là-haut dans la lumière comme la musique dans la nuit silencieuse: il pensa à celle de Kama, et la douleur humaine lui sembla monter et se perdre comme le chant même de la terre; sur la délivrance frémissante et cachée en lui comme son coeur, la douleur possédée refermait lentement ses bras inhumains. (P. 313.)

Light and very high the clouds went by above the dark pines and were absorbed again into the sky; and it seemed to him that one of their groups—that very one— expressed the men he had known and loved, and who were dead. Humanity was thick and heavy, heavy with flesh, with blood, with suffering, eternally clinging to itself, like everything that dies: but even blood, even flesh, even suffering, even death was reabsorbed up there in the light like music absorbed by the night's silence: he thought of Kama's music, and human sorrow seemed to rise and be lost like the song of the earth itself; over his relief, trembling and hidden inside him like his heart, once more sorrow slowly closed its inhuman arms.

The slowness and insistence of the rhythm is inescapable. So is the effect of repeating the important words: *lourde, même, sang, mort, résorbait, douleur.* The enumerations, slowed down and emphasized by the repetitions of *même,* in the parallel constructions, form something like a procession. This passage is of course an extreme example, but an extreme example of the feeling which presides over the closing of the book, and the fact that we learn in the same pages that for some men the revolution is proving beneficent is dwarfed by the unhappiness of the old man.

This is one of the many places in Malraux's work where the discursive logic is overwhelmed by the picture. We may be in doubt about the political argument; there can be no doubt about what has happened to Gisors. Nothing is real now but his suffering, and since life is nothing but vanity, the suffering is meaningless and irremediable. Gisors is conquered by the Absurd.

The Absurd is mentioned explicitly only once in *Man's Fate* and then, curiously enough, by Katow, who never appears at all worried by such metaphysical considerations. No character is directly motivated, as Garine is, by the consciousness of the vanity of what he does. But negatively the old worry about the Absurd is still with us. And since, in Malraux's earlier novels, man's fate was defined in terms of the Absurd, we do well—having abandoned the political interpretation as incomplete and unclear—to re-examine what happens to the other characters in *Man's Fate.*

During that last moment of calm before the catastrophe, in the bar where Ferral joins him after releasing the animals and birds in Valérie's room, Gisors tries to put into words that will mean something to Ferral the essence of the human predicament. ". . . Man does not merely want to govern. He wants to constrain other men to his will, as you say. To be more than human in a human world; not just powerful—all-powerful. The chimera called the will to power is just an intellectual justification. It's the will to Godhead; every man dreams of being a God. . . . A god can possess but can't conquer. . . . The dream of a god would be to become man but keep all his power. The dream of man is to become god but keep his personality. . . ." (P. 213.)   ₁86

Gisors is talking to a man who has just defined intelligence as "the means of making other people obey," and is picking up the words Ferral has used. Clearly he means that the "will to constrain" is only a symptom. But wanting to be a god, or to be at once man and god, applies to every character in the book, for to be a god in this sense implies at once the enjoyment of the benefits of being human and the escape from all the servitudes which are the badges of the human condition. *Man's Fate* could conceivably have been called *Of Human Bondage.* Out of the gulf which separates what we are from what imagination makes us want to be flows the anguish that plagues us.

The badge of this generally shared condition is man's loneliness. Each of the characters in turn suffers from solitude. Malraux freights this suffering with significance by multiplying symbols: Kyo's phonograph record, the whistles which shrill throughout the early parts of the book to remind the characters (particularly Tchen) of the world from which they are cut off, and the armored train which Mme Magny makes a presiding symbol of the novel and of Malraux's work as a whole. On the morning of the second day of the insurrection, when Kyo, Katow, and Tchen watch the train expire, there comes a new burst of firing. The officers, helpless at their telephones, have passed the word to fire at will; as death approaches, the attempt to maintain communication is useless. Each man is on his own in his last hour. The approach of Chiang Kai-shek's army becomes audible. "Behind each turret, each man in the train heard the sound as if it were the voice of death itself" (p. 124). The symbol will turn up twice in later novels (the planes of the Spanish Republicans, the tank in *Les Noyers*) but will be less explicit in meaning and even ambivalent, since these later armored vehicles are also scenes of fraternity. But for *Man's Fate* one may easily accept the reading of Mme Magny.

But not in all the extension she gives it. It is true that when the revolt of Shanghai expires, each of the central characters is overwhelmed by a feeling of essential separation from the rest of mankind. But it is also true that, in two of them at least, the feeling proves weaker than a feeling of essential human fraternity. Kyo and Katow come the nearest to finding, if not escape from, at least a way of transcending, man's fate.

In the crucial scene where König offers Kyo the opportunity to betray his friends and then threatens him with torture for refusing, Kyo defines his own motives with luminous clarity. "I think that Communism will make dignity possible for those I am fighting for. What is opposed to it, anyhow, is what keeps them from having any—unless they have a wisdom that's as rare among them as among others; perhaps they would have to have even more, because they are poor and their labor separates them from their lives" (p. 269). König challenges impatiently: "What do you call dignity?" Kyo replies: "The opposite of humiliation."

Certain of Malraux's characteristic themes are compulsive drives that determine conduct. Human dignity does not belong among these, even though its opposite, humiliation, certainly does. Dignity is a moral value. It does not drive men to die; when they die for it they die by choice. In a purely negative way a concern for it underlay the conduct of Hong in *The Conquerors*: his hatred was directed at those who respect themselves and he could not imagine such people respecting themselves without scorning someone else. But he was less intent on relieving the burden of social injustice than on exterminating those who profit by it or even those who simply do not object to it.

Kyo sees the great problem to be one of turning human pack-animals into men. He has worked with the laborers on the docks, shared their life, speaks with authority of their predicament. At Hankow he is present when a group of seven dock workers is brought in, handcuffed, for having set upon the Red Guard and tried to make off with rations meant for the troops. Why did they do it?

"Before," says one of them, "we could eat."

"No," Kyo contradicts, "before we didn't eat. I know. I worked on the docks. And if we have to starve anyhow, we can at least do it so that we can be men" (p. 145).

Kyo and Katow are obviously something new among Malraux's heroes. Neither is a case of exacerbated individualism seeking in action (revolutionary or other) the relief of a private anguish. Kyo is protected from some forms of anguish by his sense of the heroic. He is subject like other men to the feeling of solitude (note that it is *before* he has learned of May's infidelity that he is so bothered by the phonograph recording) but his loneliness has been largely relieved by his love for his wife. What anguish Katow may have known belongs apparently to the past. As we see him in the novel, except at the end, where, after all, he has every right to feel for a moment that he has been abandoned, he seems even less concerned than Kyo about escapes. These certainly do not figure among his present motives. And possibly this is why, until the book comes to its climax, Kyo and Katow attract the reader's attention less than do Tchen, Ferral, and Clappique; they are both reasonably well adapted to the lives they have chosen and thoroughly devoted to the revolution. Consequently they are less picturesque as psychological cases.

Kyo's devotion to human dignity is what liberates him, in the last moments of his life, both from the feeling of solitude and from the "metallic realm" of the Absurd. Lying there in the school hall among all these men who are about to die, he realizes that his death, as much as his life, has meaning.

Partout où les hommes travaillent dans la peine, dans l'absurdité, dans l'humiliation [note the repetition of the prepositional phrases, a rhetorical device on which Malraux falls back almost invariably when he wants an intense and solemn emotion], on pensait à des condamnés semblables, à ceux-là comme les croyants prient; et, dans la ville, on commençait à aimer ces mourants comme s'ils eussent été déjà morts ... Entre tout ce que cette dernière nuit couvrait de la terre, ce lieu de râles était sans doute le plus lourd d'amour viril. ... Il mourait, comme chacun de ces hommes couchés, pour avoir donné un sens à sa vie. (P. 283.)

Everywhere where men worked in suffering, in absurdity, in humiliation, they were thinking of condemned men like him—thinking as believers would pray—and in the city they were beginning to love these dying as they would the dead. . . . Out of everything that this last night covered on the earth, this place of death was probably the richest in virile love. . . . He was dying, like each of those lying there, for having given meaning to his life.

For Kyo, death is not the final monstrous ignominy, the ultimate monstrous defeat. He can face it; dying is easy, he thinks at one moment, in these circumstances. With death's horror he has also escaped the victory of the Absurd and the torture of loneliness. The best commentary is to put the passage above beside the dying words of Perken in *The Royal Way*: "There is no death . . . There is just *me* . . . *me* . . . going to die" (p. 178).

And what is true of the death of Kyo is even truer of the death of Katow. Here is the latter's exit from the story:

«Les petits auront eu de la veine, pensa-t-il. Allons! supposons que je sois mort dans une incendie.» Il commença à marcher. Le silence retomba, comme une trappe, malgré les gémissements. Comme naguère sur le mur blanc, le fanal projeta l'ombre maintenant très noire de Katow sur les grandes fenêtres nocturnes; il marchait pesamment, d'une jambe sur l'autre, arrêté par ses blessures; lorsque son balancement se rapprochait du fanal, la silhouette de sa tête se perdait au plafond. Toute l'obscurité de la salle était vivante, et le suivait du regard pas à pas. Le silence était devenu tel que le sol résonnait chaque fois qu'il touchait lourdement du pied; toutes les têtes, battant de haut en bas, suivaient le rythme de sa marche, avec amour, avec effroi, avec résignation, comme si, malgré les mouvements semblables, chacun se fût dévoilé en suivant ce départ cahotant. Tous restèrent la tête levée: la porte se refermait. (P. 288.)

"The kids must have been lucky, he thought. Come on! Let's suppose I died in a fire." He began to move. Silence fell again, like a trapdoor, in spite of the moaning. As before, against the white wall, the spotlight projected Katow's shadow, now very black, against the great night-darkened windows; he walked heavily, dragging his legs, slowed by his wounds: when his swaying brought him up to the light, the shadow of his head was lost against the ceiling. All the darkness of the room was alive, and eyes followed him step by step. The silence had become so complete that the ground echoed each step; every head, nodding up and down, took up the rhythm of his stride, with love, with fright, with resignation, as if, though all were doing the same thing, each had revealed himself as he followed that clumsy exit. Then the raised heads stopped; the door was closing behind him.

Here again the rhythm is slow, and solemn, although the slowness and solemnity are not so reinforced by rhetorical devices (there is only one instance of the repetition of the preposition: *avec amour, avec effroi, avec résignation*) as the passage about Gisors' despair. Its unevenness may be Malraux's instinctive response to Katow's heavy limp. A certain note of simplicity is set by the slightly vulgar *les petits*, the slangy *auront eu de la veine*, the familiar *allons*, and these are a further guaranty against the intrusion of unwelcome rhetoric. The next sentence, which shifts the point of view from Katow's mind to the observer's, is stripped of everything but fact. And then, in the silence, one watches not the figure of Katow but the black shadow of the man (once again Malraux's basically cinematographic imagination) climbing the dark window. We are not completely sure whether our attention is on the man or on the shadow, since the *il* of the following phrase cannot grammatically stand for *ombre*, but certainly one is as fully aware, in this sentence, of the shadow as of the flesh. In the next, with the phrase which begins *lorsque son balancement*, it is the shadow that one is most aware of, and the awareness confers upon the hero the stature of the shadow, greater than life size. Then the head is lopped off by the ceiling, in prefiguration of the imminent execution, and we become aware of the other men in the room who as they watch Katow's exit are living through what will shortly be the experience of each, so that the departing man represents to each of the others his own fate. And at the same time the reader realizes that he has himself been watching through the eyes of, sharing the experience of, identifying himself with, the condemned. But now one no longer sees Katow; one retires into one's own identity and watches the heads move slightly to the rhythm of Katow's limp, conscious of him *through* these persons from whom one is separated. Then there is the interpolated comment that in the unanimous movement each man reveals himself, the door closes, and Katow is gone.

This picture is what turns defeat into tragic victory and in a sense orients and orders all the values in the book. The destiny of the man whom the International has abandoned is so much more brilliant than the destinies of those who survive the insurrection that the political import of the novel pales before the more broadly human import. Revolution now seems to be not the subject but the setting in which the qualities and defects, the strengths and weaknesses of human character stand clearly out.

Just before the deaths of the heroes we watched Clappique sneak aboard the steamer in disguise. Shortly after, we move to Paris and see Ferral sit frustrate while a group of candy-chewing financiers decide whether or not they will let him go on being a great man. Then we pick up old Gisors, waiting in Kobe for death to end meaningless suffering. From their destinies we know the power of the Absurd. But at the same time we have also seen Katow go out to die, and we know that there inheres in man's fate, in spite of all the possibilities of defeat, the possibility of the power and glory of being a man.

CHAPTER FIVE

The Will to Prove

"It is not passion that destroys the work of art, but the will to prove."
—DAYS OF WRATH, p. 12

Fʀᴏᴍ 1925 to 1933 Malraux had wrestled steadily with the problem of how to state man's basic predicament. But now *Man's Fate* had been published first as a serial in the *Nouvelle Revue Française* during the spring of 1933 and then as a book in June, and in December it had won the Goncourt prize. Critics were, by and large, enthusiastic. Malraux could, if he accepted their judgment, conclude that he had finished the task that had preoccupied him for so long. The catch was, of course, that in succeeding with *Man's Fate* he had deprived himself of a subject.

History was taking a hand, however, in finding him, if not a truly new subject, at least a new and challenging literary problem. Most opportunely for Malraux's development, Europe's time was running out. Hitler's star had risen; Mussolini was departing on his career of conquest in Ethiopia; two more short years would see Franco emerging in Spain and Malraux flying with the Republican air force. The time had come for men of good will to take sides. For a man of good will like Malraux, it was also time to find out how to remain true to himself as creative artist and yet write—to call the thing by its name—propaganda.

It is surprising, really, how little propaganda there had been in *The Conquerors* and *Man's Fate*. The hortatory tone is not noticeable in these books. Their import is less political than metaphysical. And so is the import of the incidental criticism Malraux had written during the years before 1933.

His reviews reveal a critic unable to discuss another writer's work without indirectly discussing his own. When he reviewed Georges Bernanos' *L'Imposture* in 1928, Malraux let drop the remark that Bernanos was one of those novelists whose crucial scenes take shape long before they imagine the characters to populate the books. We know now what Malraux could not have known in 1928, that Bernanos' characters were ready long before the scenes. His correspondence shows very clearly that he had many of them in mind for years before he found an action in which they could take part; he dropped novel after novel twenty pages from the start, simply because he had characters but nothing for them to do. Malraux's insight is really not an insight into Bernanos at all.

But it is an excellent insight into Malraux. *His* themes and situations (inseparable in his case) were ready at hand several years before he found his characters and made them come clear. (In cold truth, his characters never do come clear in the way that the characters of Bernanos do. Close the covers of a Malraux book and the characters stay inside; Bernanos' people have a life of their own, almost independent of the stories in which they figure.) In his review, Malraux was talking about himself and about a problem that continued to occupy him, actually, as recently as 1949. He comes back to it, with reference to the novels of Dostoevski, in *The Psychology of Art*.[1]

Similarly a review of his friend Marcel Arland's *Où le coeur se partage* expresses pleasure that Arland had avoided "technical problems" and gone straight to what Malraux calls the "problem of destiny." Arland's book, he says, grows out of meditations on "the sentiment of death." Anyone who has dwelt long on such a subject, he adds, cannot but be obsessed by the spectacle of human suffering—it is impossible to observe a large number of "useless and lamentable lives," such as men cling to only through a fundamental cowardliness, without becoming conscious of "death's absolute reality." This leads him to make the remark that writers who find a certain strange pleasure in writing about death are careful not to think about their own as they write, and that when one becomes convinced of the profound reality of death one passes out of the domain of art into the realm of action—action conditioned by one's feeling about death. Such remarks may or may not be apposite to Arland's forgotten novel, but they are apposite beyond challenge to the first three novels of his reviewer, as anyone who has ever opened them knows. Once again Malraux is talking about himself.

A book of Keyserling's furnishes him the pretext for saying that the tendency to conceive philosophy under its dramatic aspects "is increasing in importance throughout the Occident and will perhaps result in "a profound transformation in fiction." An important function of the novelist is "to translate into myth the thoughts of men essentially different from us and to make these myths a . . . means of discovering our possibilities, of our most unformed and elementary tendencies, of everything in us that may take form and become a part of our inner life." Still another review hints at his interest in writing as a possible means of "liberation," and,

---

[1] "The Creative Act," p. 147; and *Les Voix du silence*, p. 333. In recent years Dostoevski has come to represent to Malraux the archetype of the novelist.

knowing him as we do, we read Malraux to mean liberation from the oppression of man's inevitable destiny. His Preface to the French version of *Lady Chatterley's Lover* studies Lawrence as one who has tried to make eroticism—which Malraux assumes to be centrally important not only in *Lady Chatterley* but everywhere else in Lawrence's writing—a means of achieving a maximum "intensity of being" and a possible escape from the bondage of being human. He concludes, as the author of *The Royal Way* and of *Man's Fate* would be obliged to conclude, that to his mind the escape gives upon another blind alley. His frequently quoted Preface to the Gallimard edition of *Sanctuary* puts an infallible finger upon the points where Faulkner's novels are most like his own. With the modern detective story, Malraux asserts, Faulkner has managed to combine much of the feeling of Greek tragedy, and, especially, has captured the feeling that each of his characters is rushing headlong toward his destiny. "Fate . . . [writes the author of *Man's Fate*] stands behind each of these beings like death in a ward of incurables." Malraux is also intensely interested in the obsessions which shape the conduct of Faulkner's people, and is even more interested in the role of obsession in determining the relation of the author himself to his book. "One can see how completely *The Brothers Karamazov* and *Lost Illusions* dominated Dostoevski and Balzac, when we read these books after the beautiful, paralyzed novels of Flaubert. And the point is not merely that the artist is dominated but that *more and more for the past fifty years* he has been choosing what should dominate him, and that he organizes the resources of his art in relation to that." The italics are mine, but the invitation to apply the insight to his own novels is Malraux's. What else had he done during the decade of his trips to Asia and of his first three novels than seek out what would obsess him and what at the same time would be his subject as well as his master?

The criticism, in brief, is interesting and revealing. But it does not, any more than the novels, reveal the least concern with making propaganda.

After 1933, however, Malraux had to face the fact that he was one of the spokesmen of the Left.

His position as a Leftist was not, as it happened, entirely clear. Neither *The Conquerors* nor *Man's Fate* had convinced the Russians that he was simon-pure. There was too much unorthodoxy, individualism, and adventure about such books. He had never, according to his own report, held a card in the Communist party. At the Moscow Writers' Congress of 1934, when he had found himself plunged into the controversy with Karl Radek over the role of the writer as individual, Malraux's theme had been that to the bourgeois writer's insistence upon the individual, the Communist must reply with an insistence upon Man. At the Congress in Paris the next year, Malraux was still probing the problem of the Leftist writer without abandoning the view that had displeased Radek. Speaking of the mechanism of artistic creation, he had explained to his hearers that every artist begins by imitating, and that if he is to find his own form, he has to take his departure not from life itself but from the form of some other artist: only later can he hope to be able to express his own vision of the world.[2] But when he attains this ability, each new discovery is for him the discovery of a difference, and he acquires a new and personal form, itself different from the forms he has inherited from earlier artists. Hence, Malraux had concluded, the writer who is to create his own style has to destroy the borrowed form with which he begins his career. So much insistence upon the individual form, upon originality, and upon the concern of the individual artist, hints at a certain reluctance to accept the submergence of the individual artist which is required by collectivist aesthetics. What Malraux was saying was that whereas as citizen the poet must not be an individualist, as a creator he is inevitably forced to be one, and the opposition he sees between artist and citizen suggests that the Leftist artist has by definition to become something of a split personality.

And in the Preface to *Days of Wrath* published in the same year, he continues to wrestle with the same angel. The theme of human fraternity has disappeared from recent literature—according to Malraux—because writers have been possessed by the "fanatic desire to be different" (p. 12). The writer's individualism has thus shut him off from the collectivity which nourishes him. To be truly fertile, the individual must at once cultivate his difference and maintain his communion with the group. "It is difficult to be a man. But no more so to become one in broadening one's communion than in cultivating one's different-ness—and the first nourishes, as much as the second, whatever it is that makes a man a man . . ." (p. 13).

The task of the artist, he says, is to create. And the enemy of art is "the will to prove" (p. 12). In other words, the function of the artist is not primarily to produce propaganda. And yet, Malraux adds, a work of art has both quality (a function of the harmony of what is expressed and the means employed) and action. The action operates by what he calls "a deplacement of the values of the sensibility" (p. 12). The phrase is cryptic, but presumably Malraux is talking of the sensibility of the reader, and

[2] See Bibliography. The articles in *Commune* (1934–35) reproduce the content of his speeches.

saying that the public effect of a book is to cause some change in the reader's affective attitudes. In the case of the *Days of Wrath*, the public effect would be to operate a change with regard to individualism and its opposite.

Whether or not Malraux comes very near settling the question of the writer in a collective society is obviously open to debate. Is he saying any more than that the way to produce propaganda in literature is not to aim directly at writing propaganda but to write well and trust the emotional bias of the work to dispose the emotions of the reader in the desired manner? And has he said more about individualism than that the writer must both cultivate his individual differences and his relations with his group? In any case he satisfied the Russians: *Days of Wrath* is the only one of Malraux's books to have circulated freely in the Soviet Union, and thus the least "corrupted" of his fictions by concerns which Communists consider "bourgeois." Picon has called it the least characteristic of his novels.

Malraux himself seems to have found it the least satisfactory. The handful of galley and page proof that has been preserved shows him making a fantastic number of changes in his text between manuscript and magazine publication. Collation of the magazine text with the book shows some two hundred more.[3] He had found a theme which fitted beautifully with his desire to write what would be literature and still have the force of propaganda, and thus be appropriate to his role as a leader of the Left. But he still had to find a way to treat it. The *Days of Wrath* is another dry run, a trying out of the new theme of Brotherhood, the feeling of "Virile Fraternity" which rewards the active revolutionary. It stands in relation to *Man's Hope* as a book like *The Royal Way* stands to *Man's Fate*.

In *Days of Wrath* a Malraux fable finally attains complete simplicity: there is only one plot and everything conspires to focus the attention on one character, who fills the stage. The feeling is as close to being theatrical as a prose fiction can come. Time is reduced to the status of an illusion. Ordinary narrative elements are suppressed as much as possible. We are in the presence, as Malraux says in his Preface, of one man and his destiny.

A Communist named Kassner is standing in a Nazi office while the prisoner ahead of him is being interrogated. The other man is taken away and Kassner steps forward. The official at the desk tries to identify him from photographs and fails. Flashback now to the shop which is the local revolutionary headquarters, when someone reports that the police have surrounded Wolfe's house and Wolfe remembers that he has left at home

---

[3] The proofs are preserved in the Fonds Doucet, Bibliothèque Sainte-Geneviève, Paris.

an incriminating list of names. Change of scene to Wolfe's apartment, where Kassner begs a light from an S.A. man, lets himself in, chews up and swallows the list, and comes out to be arrested. Now back to the interrogation and we get Kassner's history from the notes on the Nazi's desk—son of a miner, scholarship man at the University, founder of a proletarian theater, prisoner in Russia who went over to the Partisans and then to the Red Army, delegate in China and Mongolia, writer, back in Germany in 1932 organizing strikes, organizer of the underground Information Service . . . (The device is familiar: we got Garine's background in the same rapid fashion from the British Secret Service report.) But the Nazi does not recognize him and he is taken to a cell: the cell wall is covered by inscriptions left by previous occupants. Flashback to the union-organizing Kassner has been doing just before his arrest. But now he hears steps. Six guards come to his cell and beat him. Gradually consciousness returns. The beating has been less awful than the anxiety state in which he has fallen. He realizes that he may go insane.

Later. Kassner is worried about his wife, whom he imagines dead. When a guard goes by humming a tune, Kassner picks up the music. The music fights a battle to keep off a great vulture. Kassner realizes that to stay sane he must organize his fantasy. Gradually the fantasy becomes wilder and more confused and Kassner realizes that he is losing ground. But at this point someone in an adjoining cell taps on the wall. Clearly the tapping is a code, but before Kassner can grasp what it is about, the tapping stops.

He drops back into his fantasy again. The images are wilder now and completely irrational. Finally the fantasy breaks and Kassner returns to himself, realizing that his insane babbling endangers many of his comrades. He knows that he should kill himself. But he has no way to commit suicide: even his fingernails are too short to open a vein.

A guard comes now and gives him a piece of rope to unravel: madman's work. But after the guard has gone the tapping begins again. This time Kassner discovers the code and slowly spells out the message: COMRADE TAKE COURAGE ONE CAN . . . Then a door slams and Kassner hears the guard beating, perhaps killing, the man in the next cell.

The message has given Kassner strength. He works endlessly on a long speech he will someday make—perhaps—of exhortation to his comrades. No danger of going insane now. The speech is completely rational, firm, pathetic, eloquent. Then suddenly he is taken by two guards and put in an auto. Almost in a dream he learns that they have caught the "real" Kassner: i.e., some comrade has identified himself as Kassner and accepted almost certain death by surrendering to the Nazis. He is free. Presently he is talking to the pilot of a small airplane.

There is a storm over the Carpathians. Commercial airline planes are grounded. But the pilot is willing to take the three-against-one chance. The storm catches them above the mountains, ices the controls, blows them in circles, but the pilot desperately dives his ship through the clouds into clear weather. Shortly they are in Prague.

His wife is not at their apartment. He follows her to an enormous mass meeting held to protest the Nazi terror. He does not find her there either, but he does find the feeling of community which emanates from this horde of people come together in the common cause.

And then, at last, back at his apartment, he finds his wife and child.

This is all that happens: a Communist agent is taken by the Nazis, imprisoned and beaten and kept for eight days in a cell waiting to be killed and fighting to keep his sanity; then on the ninth day he is released because someone has surrendered in his place, is flown out of Germany into Czechoslovakia, and after some search is reunited with his wife.

And these are the only people we see. The only names used, except his wife's, are those of people who do not appear in the story—for example, Wolfe, whose fecklessness causes the original trouble. The man who risks his life to fly Kassner through the storm is known to us merely as "the Aviator." The Comrade in the next cell who is killed, perhaps, for tapping the message of hope, is unknown to Kassner and the reader. So is the other who gives up his life so that Kassner can be freed. Even Anna, until the very end of the story, is more a fragment of Kassner's consciousness than a person, and even then she is also the voice of her husband's fate. Thus the single figure of Kassner has to fill the stage.

He is a student and writer—thus an intellectual—committed to a life of revolutionary action. His origins are nearer those of the working class than those of Garine or Kyo, but by his education he is outside the working class just as by sympathy he is with it. Like Kyo, he is the son of a man whose excellent qualities are paralyzed; Kassner's father had been a militant until, after the death of his wife, he had taken to drink. Like all of the heroes (except Perken) he has followed the Revolution to the Far East. Like all of them he is the prey of his own anxieties.

How completely Malraux feels his work as theater is clear from the way he subordinates everything else to this central dramatic figure. The settings are mere backdrops: a glimpse of an apartment where he is trapped, a Nazi office, a prison cell, the car in which he rides when he is being released, the cabin of the plane, the meeting hall in Prague, his apartment. The spectator-reader is aware of the settings *only* as something *behind* the character. The traditional narrative form's preoccupation with the scene of the action is missing here.

Time is also a negligible factor. The significant action can even be said to take place outside of time. When Kassner is told that he has been nine days in prison he can neither believe nor disbelieve. And in the plane he again loses his notion of time as well as his orientation in space. His hours in the airplane seem nearly as long as his days in prison; he is asking the pilot whether the ground below is not Czechoslovakia almost before the plane has entered the storm. In other words, we not only have one man occupying the stage, he is also very close to being a figure on whom time has no significant bearing: the eternal tragic figure of man.

Malraux's desire to exclude all purely narrative episodic elements is so very marked that we are not really permitted to witness the beating Kassner receives from the Nazi torturers. We scarcely see the men who beat him. Their lantern, set on the cell floor, throws its light obliquely on their chins and cheekbones. (This is the only instance in the book of the type of picture of which Malraux is elsewhere so fond, and this is the only one of his books in which such a picture does not occupy a place of considerable structural importance.) Here their blows come at him out of the darkness. And the beating is sketched only briefly, in terms of increasing pain and loss of consciousness. Quite possibly the motive for toning down the beating may have been discretion: in his admiration for T. E. Lawrence, Malraux may have wished to avoid competition with the beating given Lawrence by the Turkish soldiers in the *Seven Pillars*. But at the same time it is true that too much attention to the beating might lead, or drive, our eyes away from the very lone and very central figure.

Now such earmarks as this attempt to focus entirely on one figure to the exclusion of the others, to keep the others almost anonymous, to foreshorten and distort time, to minimize the physical décor, to remove the emphasis from physical action, and to avoid subplots—not to mention the imminence (and occasional presence) of violence, the intense feeling of dread, and the presence of an unnamed but either infra- or suprahuman evil—testify that Malraux's intention in *Days of Wrath* is to do in prose something that approaches what the ancient Greeks did in verse. We hereby confirm the assertion of his Preface:

> The world of a work like this, the world of tragedy, is always the ancient one: the man, the mob, the elements, the woman, fate. It is reduced to two characters, the hero and his sense of life; the individual antagonisms which permit the complexity of the novel have no place. (P. 11.)

But when he has purposely limited himself to a single central figure, how does Malraux maintain the tension necessary to tragedy? To make his hero motionless, or nearly so, for those nine days in the prison cell, is a little like the situation in which Aeschylus places himself by chaining his hero to the Caucasian rock: very little can happen and the hero has no choice but to be passive. Obviously Malraux has purposely placed himself in an artistic predicament such that he can extricate himself only by employing the resources of a very intricate craftsmanship. How he does so is best revealed by following in detail the employment of a modern fantasy technique for a purpose which is as old as the tragic theater.

Kassner has just been beaten by his captors, and returns to consciousness with the feeling of *intimité trouble* which he remembers having experienced in childhood. This is replaced by the sensation of being crushed by the walls of his cell. He looks gratefully at the air vent in the stone wall, thanks to which the crushing weight becomes his own carapace. His mind turns to his wife, whom he has left behind in Prague. She is dead . . .

. . . but if he can circle his cell ten times before the guard passes on his next round, she will turn out to be alive. He fails; the guard returns too soon. So now if he can count a hundred before the guard passes again . . . and this time he wins—and having counted to a hundred in time, he emerges from the fantasy abruptly, realizing that this is the way to insanity.

Insanity?—Merely the mind seeking escape from what it cannot endure face to face interminably. Three times in the preceding movement it has looked for a refuge in childhood, first in the comfort of infantile well-being, then in two of the games which are universally an element of the lore of make-believe. But Kassner cannot afford to risk losing his grip on reality; insane babbling would endanger too many besides himself. He is resolved to fight off the fantasy.

But the appeal of the refuge is too strong. He starts to sing, noiselessly, what he imagines to be a song. And he hears the music as though it were coming from outside him. This music has the virtue of driving off a huge vulture—how it came and how long it has been in the cell with him we do not know—and as the vulture disappears, the audible music changes into music that Kassner can *see*, a series of events out of his own experience, the first of which is a frost over Gelsenkirchen and the shouts of miners engaged in a strike there. Since we know that Kassner grew up in Gelsenkirchen and that his father was a miner, we conclude that the flashback to Gelsenkirchen and the shouts are another attempt to escape into childhood again. But the escape is momentary; the flashes of visible music continue.

He sees flashes of sunflowers ripped by Partisan bullets, of winter in

Mongolia, hears frogs on a rainy morning with the noise of trucks in the background. Then Chinese merchants are running from the Red Lances; there is a flood of the Yangtze and corpses are being washed up against trees that have fallen in the current . . .

Kassner's mind is still racing through his past, not childhood now but the episodes of an earlier period of the Revolution—one in which Kassner has been free to act, unimpeded by stone walls. We note that the reminiscences are logical, orderly, perfectly coherent, a reconstruction but not a distortion of real events. The comfort, however, is again temporary. The sequence of flashes moves into a faster rhythm.

And all these faces against the cold, insect-ravaged ground, listening for the thunder of the White Army on the horizon of the Steppes, the Mongol plain, and his youth and his suffering and his very will itself were all lost and tumbling according to the rhythm of the "motionless movement" of a constellation. (P. 34.)

Here the music, after being visible so long, becomes audible again as a cascade of funeral song . . .

This part is much harder to interpret. Obviously the effect of the music is the one so often experienced in the movies when the musical background emerges from behind the photographed events and forces itself upon the consciousness of the audience. The feeling of falling, which is introduced as soon as something suggestive of his present predicament invades the fantasy, and is accompanied by the fall of the music, is also accompanied here by a reference to the "motionless, moving" stars and is apparently caused by it. It is plausible, at least, that the stars somehow stand for—or at least the inexorable course of astronomical movement represents—inevitability, and the feeling of inevitability acts to shatter the fantasy. At any rate, the fantasy has now collapsed; Kassner is back in his cell again; and the vulture has returned. In the presence of the vulture the music has become audible, and will remain so until the bird has again been driven off.

The music has the effect of keeping the vulture at a distance. And shortly the music seems to bear Kassner away, into a feeling of "inexhaustible communion which perpetuated the past by delivering it from time" (p. 34). But eventually the music picks up the melody of a Gobi Tartar song which has been a favorite of Kassner's wife and the reminder of his actual predicament throws him so violently out of his fantasy that not even the vulture, or the feeling of being crushed, remains. He is completely himself and he gets up and walks about his cell.

After a moment he is drawn back into the fantasy again. The music once more becomes visible and this time there flashes back at him another area of his experience, and the music itself comes to represent Red Fraternity. Fraternity of all sorts—then, more specifically, it is the singing of the "International" by the wounded Communists at Essen. Their song lifts Kassner into a state of exaltation and, as happened previously, comes in conflict with a symbol of the stars. "And forever these prisoner stars would turn through immensity, like the prisoners in the prison yard, like him in his cell" (p. 36). Immediately the firmament of the stars is torn apart and all its tatters draw back into the form of the vulture . . .

Once more the fantasy collapses. Kassner has a shot of himself transformed into an earwig (from an animal with a carapace he has become an insect which lives in the damp under stones) and then sinks into hebetude as the music, audible now that the vulture has re-entered the fantasy, runs on in long phrases of plain chant. Momentarily his mind wanders back to the bric-a-brac of the ecclesiastical antique shop which, before he was arrested, was being used by the local Communists as a rendezvous.

Here the fantasy is interrupted by the tapping of the prisoner in the neighboring cell. Kassner does not recognize the message, but the sound forces him for the moment to focus completely on what is happening around him.

Into the void that follows the tapping, however, there comes a rush of new images. The music has ceased now for good, and everything from here on is purely visual. Kassner sees a smear of oil on water; it turns first iridescent and then rose, and then the surface is broken by caret-shaped marks. This scene he recognizes as some river where the shells of the Whites have killed the fish, as he once saw it in a cold dawn. Presently the dawn turns golden and the water gives off flashes—and these are the flashes of church vestments, in the light of icon lamps . . .

This is a new development, since up to this point the elements of experience picked up in the fantasy have been coherent and unmixed. Now two distinct areas of his experience have been confused: his earlier fighting against the White Russians has telescoped with the events of his most recent period of freedom. For it was just after he left the ecclesiastical antique shop that he was arrested by the Nazis.

Now he realizes again that he must impose some sort of order upon the fantasy. But the compulsion to make images is too strong for him. The shiftings of the images come faster. A flash of the antique shop is followed by one of St. Basil's Church, now decorated all about with baubles from the shop; and St. Basil's in turn takes the shape of a fortified monastery. Below it is a counterrevolutionary town under attack by the Communist Foreign Battalion. And in the monastery there is a cell. And in the cell a prisoner. He will presently escape and run down endless corridors where he will at length find an airplane. The prisoner's wife is in Prague . . .

And now comes a turning point in Kassner's struggle. By a conscious act of the will he pulls his imagination away from Anna and from his own predicament, and plunges back into the part of the fantasy where the town is being invested by the revolutionaries. At last he is accepting the refuge, choosing to dwell in the part where he will be most comfortable. Previously, when the fantasy touched his wife, the effect was to snap him completely out of his dreamworld and back into his cell. The dream reference to her has now lost its power. He wills to continue to invest the town rather than return to his cell.

Back with the attackers he is now watching a procession of orthodox crosses from the town. A Pope appears on a hillock. There is a great silence. He wonders if he has become deaf.

Only when a guard looks into his cell does Kassner realize that he, Kassner, has just screamed aloud.

Now a succession of Popes advance from the hillock toward him, wearing on their bodies all the baubles of the antique shop. He hears a dog howl.

In a moment (the effect here being one of the alternate waking and dozing of very fitful sleep) Kassner realizes that the howl has come not from a dog in the fantasy but from a prisoner in an adjoining cell.

Straightway Kassner re-enters his fantasy. He is watching a dog, or perhaps a ferret, move toward the Popes. The Popes are motionless. Smoke rises in the censers they hold . . .

How long, he asks himself, since he has had a smoke?

The wind now brings the smoky church-smell toward him and he hears the cry of a tortured peasant.

No, not a peasant but again the prisoner . . .

Next, rifle fire is coming from the Whites. One of the Popes fires. Kassner is tending the same machine gun he once tended in the Caucasus. The gunner beside him is the one who was with him there. The Popes retire. The abandoned bodies on the field form a great white vulture with its wings torn off.

Immediately Kassner becomes conscious of his cell again, but a voice from the fantasy is saying to him, "They are all dead." It repeats, "Anna is dead" (p. 44). The walls move in on him once more.

The dramatic movement of the fantasy seems clear enough. Ever since Kassner returned to this psychic refuge after the first tapping on the cell by the prisoner next to him, the fantasy events have increased in turbulence, the association of events remote from each other in various periods of Kassner's experience has become more arbitrary, the falsification of waking reality more outlandish, the similarity to a dream state more marked. Kassner has tended more and more to capitulate to the fantasy; each invitation to remain in the cell has been rejected—the first misinterpretation of the prisoner's scream, the appetite for tobacco, the misinterpretation of the second cry, and so forth. And now, when the fantasy has collapsed and the vulture is back with him, Kassner, who started out by fighting off the fantasy, is in a paroxysm of desire to get back to it.

"Back to the town!" (p. 44).

In the besieged town a man is sitting in front of a wall, catching snowflakes in his vodka, while, behind and above the wall, hanged men dangle. There follows a witches' Sabbath—peasants of the town, wearing robes they have taken from the Popes, race through the streets among furniture pulled out of the houses of the wealthy; the peasants duck back indoors and thousands of riderless white cavalry horses thunder through the streets, followed by horses which have broken loose from the peasants' barns. Yet this stampede, somehow, may not be horses at all but the great Russian cold. . . .

Here the fantasy ends for good. The man drinking, the corpses, the *Walpurgisnacht* of the peasants, the racing beasts, and the cold render the fantasy no longer even a crude parody of reality. Kassner has lost his battle. He knows that the moment has come to choose between madness and suicide. But before the decision to kill himself can be carried out, the tapping on the wall begins again and this time he catches enough of the message to know that beyond the wall is a friend. His passion is consummated.

Nicola Chiaromonte[4] contends that in this part of *Days of Wrath* Kassner, like Garine in *The Conquerors*, is struggling against the force of the Absurd. In part, at least, his idea is based upon the similarity of the play of Kassner's imagination in the fantasy with the play of Malraux's imagination in *Lunes en papier*. To the extent that both stories exploit the kind of irresponsible imagination which might characterize fever or troubled sleep, the identification itself is proper. But there is no question of the Absurd in Kassner's predicament. He is fighting to keep his sanity and the stake is the safety of any number of his colleagues whose identity he may reveal. What we watch in the fantasy is a struggle for several lives. Hence the tension.

    [4] "Malraux and the Demons of Action," *Partisan Review*, XV (July 1948), 776–89, and XV (August 1948), 912–23.

Actually, the theme of the Absurd, however dear it may have been to Malraux in the past, has to be absent from *Days of Wrath* for the story to make sense. For the one reading which accounts for all the materials and techniques is this one: a man is thrown into a predicament from which, if he must depend upon his own strength alone, he can extricate himself only through death or insanity; he struggles against insanity and realizes that he has failed; he accepts the alternative, but before he can kill himself he receives help from an unknown comrade; then another unknown elects to lay down his own life in the hero's place, and still a third is willing to run horrible risk to fly him out of danger. In its strict unity, *Days of Wrath* is limited not merely to one fable and one hero, but to the orchestration of one theme, and this theme is not the Absurd but Virile Fraternity. Never, not even in the horror of solitary confinement, is Kassner completely alone. He experiences in all its plenitude the feeling of communion which Kyo and Katow know only at the end of their lives and at the briefest of moments.

Within the data of the story, the opposite of Virile Fraternity is less human loneliness than human indignity. Thus, the feeling of communion is a reward for a victory over humiliation. It is no small victory. *Days of Wrath* is, as a matter of fact, the only one of Malraux's fictions in which the hero comes out the winner and the only one in which Malraux is not forced to contradict the logic of the outcome of events by the juxtaposition of the corrective picture. For the moment the familiar note of interrogation is absent: there is no questioning the values to which Kassner is consecrated. They also are assumed to be essential data.

Kassner's victory is no less a tragic one. He has escaped the present danger, but it is clear at the end of the story that he will remain in Prague only long enough to assume a new identity and then return to the hazardous fight against the Nazis, and that he will go on fighting until at last he is caught and killed. "Even your next departure . . ." his wife says to him brokenly. She means to add, "I can accept even that." The modern reader, intently concerned with Kassner's present safety, suddenly realizes with a shock that he has been somewhat like a spectator at the *Oedipus* who innocently hopes that this time nothing unpleasant will happen and that for once things will go well with Thebes.

It is as if Malraux had attempted to bring together once and for all, within the form of fiction, all the elements of tragedy. All the stripping down, all the concentration of focus upon a single figure, the subordination of all else to the plight of the human being, the unremitting tension, these all work to the same end. Characters and spectators are never permitted to relax. Here is a man fighting against the evil that wants to beat him down; and next a man beaten about by Nature; and finally the same man searching for the woman; and when the tension is at last relieved the story is finished. The Preface leaves no doubt that this search for a narrative form which can accommodate a tragic mood was intentional. If *Days of Wrath* attracts less attention from his critics than do the other novels, the reason is doubtless that Malraux made good his intention.

Whether result was worth the effort is another question. One does not finish the story with the satisfaction one feels at the end of *Man's Fate*, the feeling of complete fulfillment that comes at the end of the successful tragedy. Possibly admiration for a technical success is as much as one can be expected to feel. More likely, one's very awareness of the technical success itself supplants the appropriate tragic emotion. But in any case, Malraux had now exhausted the possibilities of the tragic novel. After the great effort of concentration that *Days of Wrath* is, there was no going further in that direction.

In *Days of Wrath* he had a novel that perhaps conformed with his notions about the proper way to make propaganda. He did not, apparently, have one that realized his aspirations regarding propagandistic fiction. Two years later, *Man's Hope* would differ, except that it would keep the essential theme of fraternity and the intention to make propaganda, in every possible way. This time, however, the intention of the literary artist would conflict directly with the intention of the propagandist.

The fundamental unit of narrative in *Man's Hope* is the brief, vivid scene, rarely longer than three pages and much of the time far shorter, set off on the page from the other scenes by wide breaks, each containing a fragment of action or a bit of dialogue. Scenes may shade into each other, as in the series of telephone conversations with which the book opens, or they may suspend abruptly at a very high point of excitement as when, with his bombing accomplished, the pilot turns away from his target and sees the enemy fighters appear—at which point the scene is cut and we do not see the plane again until, after an intervening scene, we watch it limp into its home field, badly shot up. A series of scenes, grouped, makes a chapter, chapters are grouped in subsections under Roman numerals; the subsections are joined into sections which bear titles; and the sections are brought together in parts, of which the book has three.

The function of the breaks varies considerably. They may correspond to a shift in interest from one character to another, or indicate a brief lapse of time, or, somewhat more rarely, show a change of place within a rather restricted area. For example, Manuel is talking with some soldiers in a village street when an auto-load of civil guards, thinking the place safely in the hands of the Fascists, come riding in giving the Fascist salute. They are arrested and taken to the town hall. From there Manuel telephones for orders. Now the scene breaks and we cut in again at the court-martial, later on the same day. In the new scene the focus stays fixed on the captives; if Manuel is present we do not see him. Then the scene is cut again, just as one of the captives is shouting, "I am on your side." When we cut in once more Manuel is coming from the town hall and the execution has already been carried out. Together the three scenes make up a complete incident which could, though it does not, have a title of its own, and the breaks have merely done the work of a transitional paragraph. But in certain chapters, some of the breaks are reinforced by asterisks. These occur when the time elapsed between scenes is greater than usual or else when the juxtaposed scenes take place in settings more distant than usual from each other. In at least two of these cases—the Descent from the Mountain sequence after the crash of the Republican bomber and the description of the early fighting at Barcelona—the asterisks seem to imply that except for Malraux's concern about unity a new chapter would be in order. This suggests that the chapters are ordinarily intended to group together not only scenes that form one complete incident but also scenes that take place in rapid succession.

Such a method fits admirably Malraux's familiar reluctance to furnish transitions and his willingness to leave the logical relations between the various sections of any discourse to the ingenuity and good will of the reader. The general effect is very similar to that of the rather typical Malraux sentence which abounds in the text: "Les balles piquaient l'air autour de Barca avec leur bruit de guêpes; il courait vers les fusils, entouré de bourdonnements pointus, invulnérable." (*Il courrait vers les fusils* is stated as objective fact. *Entouré de bourdonnements pointus* is his private feeling about his situation. *Invulnérable* is his feeling about himself. The punctuation has the same force as the breaks between the scenes as the sentence shifts from one area of consciousness to another.) In either case, sentence or chapter, the technique remains one of radical illipsis. Malraux's technical problem is thus double. He has to create scenes and to juxtapose them for proper effect. There are one hundred forty-six scene-units in the novel, grouped in fifty-eight chapters, and these again, according to an intricate and not always clear plan, into the larger divisions.

There is no doubt about the nature or source of Malraux's material. The story follows the historical development of the war in Spain from the beginning to the battle of Teruel. Many of the pages could have been lifted, almost without change, from a combat diary. Certain episodes, like the one of the aviator who proposed the "Italian fashion" to some patriotic prostitutes and got turned in to the MP's for a Fascist sympathizer, are obviously included in the book merely because they are the kind of thing that actually does happen, and doubtless did happen. They provide a note of authenticity in the military history. Much narrative effort is expended on such subjects as how the crew of a bomber feels when sent out on a mission without enough fighter cover. Malraux even makes one of the characters an American journalist, lets us see fragments of the action through his eyes. Relatively few of the action scenes sound like novelistic invention; we are aware of the presence of the novelist mostly in the conversation pieces and a few sequences like the execution of Captain Hernandez.

In his Preface to Andrée Viollis' *Indochine S.O.S.* he had remarked that many novelists have felt the temptation of a "new form" of novel which would combine journalism and fiction, had added that they have been disillusioned on trying it, but had further added that, even so, one of the important aspects of the novel in France "from Balzac to Zola" has been the intrusion of the characters into a world which they reveal to us simultaneously with the revelation of themselves. Reporting, he goes on, has the appeal of "permitting both the intelligence and the sensibility to possess the real." He has seen this kind of writing in the Soviet Union.

This Preface was written in 1935, a year before he went to fight in Spain. In 1937, Malraux still has the Russians firmly in mind. He is in fact reporting—which is doubtless why the passages on conversations and on fighting in airplanes sound so much more authentic than do the scenes of infantry fighting: conversation and aerial combat were what the combatant Malraux knew best and at first hand. (The ground fighting sounds strangely like fighting in World War I; one day of this murderous kind of battle would surely have decimated the Republican army.) *Man's Hope* must consequently be taken to lie on the borderland between journalism and fiction.

But if the guiding intention which dominates the creation of the actual scene-units is clear, the intentions determining the juxtaposition of scenes and their grouping into larger divisions seem to be multiple and conflicting. It is here that the clash between art and propaganda reveals itself.

One motive, and possibly the most consistently evident, is a preoccupation with the rhythmic, patterned rise and fall of emotional excitement.

In Part One, Section I, the first chapter is cut into extremely brief scenes, in an effect as chaotic as the first disorganized night of revolution in Madrid. The second chapter, though somewhat less broken up, is still full of rapidly shifting scenes, roughly corresponding to the disruption of life in Barcelona. The third, dated later, contains only two scenes; these are closely related to each other and built around one event, the breaking down of the Montagne barracks door. The fourth is a single scene largely devoted to conversation. The progression of the chapters, then, is from intense action to talk and from excitement to calm. Between them the first two chapters use up twenty-two pages, and the second, calmer, pair, only ten and a half.

The second subsection again has longer and more broken chapters at the beginning, the last two occupying only five and three-quarters pages out of a total of twenty-six. Again we progress from action at the beginning toward a conversation piece at the end. The third subsection has a first chapter, with no breaks at all, devoted entirely to a conversation, then a longer one (eight pages and a half as against four and a half) which narrates the action of a combat bombing in eight brief scenes, and closes with a six-page chapter, in only two scenes, given over to conversation. Clearly, in this part of the book, broken chapters and rapidly shifting scenes go with action. Length and unbroken scenes go with relative quietude. And just as clearly, the pattern of this section as a whole moves from the excitement of action in the first two subsections toward a dominantly reflective, conversational third, just as both the first two subsections reproduce a similar movement on a smaller scale.

The pattern of the second section seems determined by a somewhat different principle. There are two subsections instead of three. The first is almost entirely action, with frequent shifts of place. The ten-page first chapter is full of action *and* talk, and is followed by Scali's interview with a Fascist aviator, the bombing of the Toledo Alcazar, a brief chapter of events at the Jefatura, and a chapter on the return on Marcellino's plane. But the second of the two subsections has relatively little shift of scene. The place, except for the three and a half pages in which Leclerc bombs the gasworks, is always Toledo. Attention is focused more and more on the figure of Hernandez until at last, after the capture of Toledo by the Fascists, he dominates the stage for three consecutive chapters. Thus chapters where there is as much or more talk than action come at the beginning, and the movement is one from less to greater tension as Hernandez' doom approaches—as if a camera lens, having moved about a great deal in the earlier subsection, had now selected its subject and come to rest upon it.

The organization of Part Two seems at first glance less complicated, since there are two divisions instead of three and the sections are not divided into subsections. The first four chapters of the first section, having to do mainly with Manuel's stopping the rout on the road to Madrid after the defeat at Toledo, and the corresponding effort of Magnin and Scali to restore discipline among the aviators, group a total of thirteen scenes. But after this series the setting changes to Madrid. From here to the end of the second section the subject is the ordeal of the city. Place shifts only between the center of the city and the outskirts. And of these last twenty-two chapters, only two, the final one in each section—in each case a battle piece —contain more than two scenes; three contain two scenes each. All the rest consist of a single scene each. The effect is to slow down and emphasize each scene, and to present each episode in the suffering of the city at a slower, heavier, more accented pace. The two chapters which are broken up into more than two scenes are the ones in which the Republicans triumph (although in the first case the triumph is only temporary) and Franco's troops are pushed back. Thus each section ends on a note of victory and of excitement; the tension does not drop away at the end.

Part Three stands as an epilogue to the other parts. It returns to the basic rhythmic pattern of Part One. The first four of the six chapters are full of action and consist of multiple scenes—seven in chapter i, five in chapter ii, fourteen in chapter iii, but then four in chapter iv, and one each in chapters v and vi; it is hardly necessary to add that the last two chapters are conversation pieces.

Obviously there are other factors than rhythm which have a part in determining the arrangement of scenes and chapters in the organization of the book. A battle scene naturally requires more shifts of perspective than does a conversation scene, and there is no battle sequence in the novel in which the scene does not change repeatedly, to show the action from the angle of various individuals in the front of the fighting or back at the command post. There is a corresponding frequency of scene shift in the air fighting: no one sees the fight completely, there being no more isolated individual in the world than the specialist at air combat crouched at his post in the plane. The perspective has to go from eye to eye. The account of every battle in the book is composed of these converging perspectives, and the chapters are broken accordingly.

Yet, even so, and quite in spite of the natural law that seems to be at work here, the novelist has the final say in what order scenes of fighting and of conversation will follow each other; he is free to decide where he will narrate and where he will dramatize. The scenes of fighting and triumph in Part Two come at the ends of the sections and not elsewhere because Malraux elects to have them come there, where excitement is appropriate. So the importance of the rhythm remains great and there is small doubt that much of the "meaning" of the book is derivable from it.

But at this point the intention of the propagandist conflicts with the intention of the artist. For the meaning of the book is further affirmed directly to the reader's intellect by the titles of the parts and sections. The title of Part One is in no way mysterious: "The Lyric Illusion" refers to the early victory brought about by the fervor of the Republicans when they throw back the Fascist legions with little more than their enthusiasm and their bare hands. Then this unsupported fervor turns out to be too small a foundation for building an army capable of fighting a protracted war; after a first section called (confusingly) by the title of the whole part, there comes the section called "Operation Apocalypse," covering the decline and fall of the first phase of the Revolution up to the loss of Toledo and the death of Hernandez. Politically, the inability of the Republicans to fight off their enemy with fervor alone, and the eventual collapse of the Anarchists, is followed by the rise to responsibility of the Communists, who set their own price.

There is nothing new in this idea for Malraux. In *The Conquerors* Garine joins the Communists rather than the Anarchists because the former are technicians of action while the latter are talkers. The Communist wants to *do* something, the Anarchist to *be* something. He is actually little better than the captive of his desire. In *Man's Hope* the Anarchists are capable of great courage and sacrifice, but less interested in the success of the Revolution as an enterprise than in their own individual satisfaction: one of them says that he had rather be a certain kind of revolutionary than win the Revolution. And when they are unable to bring the Revolution off, they are dangerously ready to settle for martyrdom. By definition, the Anarchist is the complete individualist and entirely incapable of conceiving the necessity of discipline. The Communist knows that fervor stops few tanks. Puig's courage is magnificent, but it gets him killed on the first day of the war; Sils, called the "Negus," a brave hand-to-hand fighter and a good man with dynamite, loses much of his value when the war outlasts his enthusiasm. Meanwhile the undisciplined horde must become an army that wins battles. The Apocalypse has to be organized.

Part Two, "The Manzanares," belongs to the Communists and includes the course of fighting from the disastrous retreat from Toledo to the first successful defense of Madrid; the Manzanares is the river back across which the Republicans finally push Franco's legions. Within the part, however, the intention behind breaking it into sections is less clear. "Blood of the Left," for the section on the passion of the people of Madrid would be eloquently appropriate for the *second* section if only the tribulations of Madrid had not begun in chapter v of the *first* section, called, for obvious reasons, "To Be and To Do." Before chapter v the general subject is the disintegration of the leaderless Republicans. After it the subject is the defense of the city. The division is made, as it happens, at the point where, for the first time, the Republican infantry stalls Franco's advance and the latter is forced to fall back on bombing the helpless inhabitants of the city. The section ends, thus, in the excitement of a brief victory. The end comes where it does because of the needs of Malraux's rhythmic pattern; the needs of the artist have prevailed over the needs of propaganda as represented by the titles.

Part Three goes on to what, within the scope of the book, is the final victory of the Republicans. The peasants, for whom the part is named, are now revealed standing shoulder to shoulder with the combatants. There is one last agony of effort, at Teruel, with the peasants in the foreground much of the time. And the novel ends with the Fascists in full retreat. Following the guidance of the titles, then, the reader may conclude that *Man's Hope* contains an unmistakable propaganda lesson: the Revolution must succeed; it can succeed only if organized; the only competent organizers are the Communists; thus the leadership must be handed over to the Communists at any cost.

But it is already clear that the rhythmic pattern and the thesis of the propaganda interfere with each other. And it is true, further, that the thesis suggested by the titles does not coincide with the scenes of heightened emotional effect which Malraux is clearly out to obtain, whereas the rhythmic pattern is designed to set these themes in great relief.

Like *Man's Fate* and the earlier novels, *Man's Hope* is constructed with a view to highlighting these quintessential scenes—extremely intense, richly pathetic, and so placed with respect to the general rhythm of the book as to assure a maximum aesthetic effect. As in the case of the scenes involving Tchen and Katow in the other novel, their force is to place in question the whole issue of the meaning of victory and defeat. For there are certain characters in *Man's Hope* whom the rise of the Communists places in a very uncomfortable predicament. They are in the Revolution because they believe in it, because they have ideals, because what they want in the way of human decency and dignity is available only through the defeat of the Fascists. Such is Captain Hernandez. There are others who sustain the tragic human losses of Revolution without having the consoling belief that only in Revolution lies the real answer to the most burningly immediate human problems. Such is old Alvear, the teacher and art dealer. And there are still others who, having seen the bankruptcy of the "Revolution of Fraternity" in Part One, discover later that, even so, the value of fraternity is the one great and abiding value available in Revolution. Such is Magnin.

With respect to the rhythm, the scenes in question occur at junctures which add to their residual poignancy. Hernandez goes through his personal calvary just after it becomes clear, through the fall of Toledo, that only by accepting the conditions of the Communists can the Revolution be saved: his death terminates the second and final section of Part One. The scene that presents the passion of old Alvear, questioning the value of Revolution itself, follows close upon the final picture of the disintegration of the Republican air force in the confrontation of Scali and Leclerc, and leads into the story of the defense of Madrid. Magnin's experience of fraternity in the famous scene of the descent of the mountain is the climax of Part Three and of the novel.

How powerfully these scenes contradict the propaganda thesis is clear when one realizes the power of the scenes themselves.

Hernandez is a soldier by profession—which in the circumstance means that he is a man of convictions strong enough to put him outside the Toledo Alcazar with the Republicans when all his atavisms should have been working to put him inside with his brother officers. At the same time, he is an outstanding victim of the situation, for he cannot command without the backing of an army organization. The men theoretically under his command look for orders not to him but to their syndicates. When he gives an order to change a barricade the man in charge challenges his authority.

"Captain Hernandez, commanding the Zodocover section."
"So then you're not from the C.N.T.? So just what do you have to do with my barricade?" (P. 132.)

The situation is discouraging in itself, but this is not the worst: Hernandez is also caught between his own ideals and the dynamics of political war. He is a Republican because he wants justice. But the week before, one of his anarchist acquaintances has been brought up before a court-martial for misappropriation of funds, although actually all he has done is displease the Communist faction. Refusing to let an innocent man suffer when he knows him guiltless, Hernandez has testified in his behalf and thereby fallen into the worst graces of the Communists. Hernandez wants the Revolution won and knows as well as anyone that only the Communists have the force and cohesion to weld together a winning army. He thus lives in the midst of a fundamental contradiction: to win the war he will have to sacrifice the ideals for which he is in the war. Like the Anarchists, he wants to *be* something. When the Fascist commander of the Alcazar sends out letters to be forwarded to his wife, Hernandez orders the letters forwarded, even though the action stirs considerable speculation about his motives, because he wants to *be* the magnanimous man whom the Fascists cannot disdain.

The siege of the Alcazar fails inevitably, through sheer lack of organization. An hour after the Fascist relief column arrives there is not an ounce of hope of holding the city. The Republicans simply desert their arms and run. Hernandez, with a few other determined men, stays behind to hold out as long as possible and so is captured by the Fascists.

Now in the logical economy of the novel Hernandez is wrong, as are the others who insist on wanting to "be" rather than to "do." He is merely one of those waste pieces, rejected when they are no longer useful, the expendables. The Revolution, as Garcia tells Scali in another context, is no place for the tortured mind to find peace, or for the delicate conscience to be at ease. Once a man has committed himself to the Revolution the choice is made, and "in certain cases it is a tragic choice, and for the intellectual nearly always so, and especially so for the artist." No man need think, Garcia adds, that the Revolution can liberate him from his private tragedy.

Possibly Hernandez also welcomes death as a solution of his difficulties, just as certain Anarchists prefer death to surviving their own revolutionary fervor. He is obsessed with death during his long talk with Garcia, in which Garcia tells him that perhaps he is fated to meet his destiny here and now. And when they are marching away to be executed and the man next to him produces a hidden razor blade and cuts the ropes on Hernandez' wrists, the latter does not follow when the other man makes a break for it. Facing certain death, Hernandez simply is not up to making a bid for freedom. Immediately one thinks of Tchen and the euphoria he attains when finally he decides to die under Chiang Kai-shek's car. Hernandez is another in the line of Malraux characters who find death easier to accept than life.

But he is not reminiscent of Tchen alone. As one who has entered the Revolution to satisfy his own private ends he evokes the figure of Garine—even though his ideal of justice is hardly Garine's ideal of personal power. He also has something in common with Kyo Gisors, since Kyo chooses to return to Shanghai and almost certain death rather than abandon the enterprise that Hankow and the Communists have jettisoned. They are all of the types who can serve the Revolution only at the cost of being destroyed by it.

It could of course be argued that in making the flaw in Hernandez' character so obvious, Malraux betrays a change in his own sympathies and an evolution away from the early incarnation of his hero. The argument has the merit of being simple and rectilinear but the disadvantage of failing to account for such pertinent facts as the prominence which Malraux gives the Hernandez episode in his novel. "Operation Apocalypse" occupies more than a quarter of the whole story, and the figure of Hernandez not only dominates it but is almost constantly before the reader. The grouping of scenes is so arranged that as the section progresses attention is increasingly confined to him. At the beginning he is the commander of a bad situation and, as such, part of the situation. At the end, waiting for his turn to face the firing squad, he is entirely alone, so far as the reader is concerned, and occupies the entire stage. No other character, not even Manuel, who is Hernandez' opposite number—the man who is made more of a man by the Revolution instead of being destroyed by it—is the object of such long-sustained and attentive treatment. In other words, Malraux confers upon Hernandez a somewhat special status.

This impression is further heightened by the virtuosity of Malraux's technique. The last chapter of the section in particular abounds in the kind of sharp visual imagery Malraux's readers have come to expect of him at his best.

Trois fascistes viennent prendre trois prisonniers. Ils les mènent devant la fosse, reculent.

—En joue!

—Le prisonnier de gauche a les cheveux taillés en rond. Les trois corps, plus longs qu'à l'ordinaire, surplombent ceux qui les regardent et font silhouette sur la célèbre ligne des montagnes du Tage. Que l'histoire est peu de chose en face de la chair vivante—encore vivante ...

Ils font un saut périlleux en arrière. Le peloton tire, mais ils sont déjà dans la fosse. Comment peuvent-ils espérer s'en echapper? Les prisonniers rient nerveusement.

Ils n'auront pas à s'en échapper. Les prisonniers ont vu le saut d'abord, mais le peloton a tiré avant. Les nerfs. (P. 259.)

Three Fascists come and get three prisoners. They bring them up to the ditch, then step away.

"Aim!"

The prisoner on the left has a crew haircut. The three bodies, longer than ordinary, loom above the men watching them and are outlined sharply against the famous mountain range of the Tagus. What does history amount to, compared with living— still living, flesh . . .

They leap backwards. The squad fires, but they are already in the grave. How can they hope to get away? The prisoners laugh nervously.

They won't be getting away. The prisoners had seen the leap, first, but the squad had fired before that. Nerves.

This is the kind of writing to which we have been accustomed by *Man's Fate*, the kind of violently immediate vision characteristic of Tchen's scene in the hotel bedroom, of the scene which Katow drags up from his memories of the White firing squad waiting for the prisoner to stop sneezing, of the picture of the Chinese going out to be executed just before Katow goes and buttoning his vest carefully as he exits. This prose sets the death of Hernandez apart from the rest of a book in which many other men die but never, elsewhere, with so much art.

Further, the arrangement of events in the last chapter of this episode recalls that of a similar one in *Man's Fate*. The capture, the awakening in prison, the interrogation (including the treacherously special treatment of the prisoner), and the final death scene occur in the same order for Hernandez as for Kyo Gisors. And in each, the interrogator is somewhat discomfited by the superior detachment of his victim.

Meanwhile, the same idea about death haunts Hernandez that has haunted earlier Malraux characters. Discussing the subject with his friend Moreno before the fall of the Alcazar, he has heard Moreno testify that the awfulness of death lies in its complete finality; any amount of torture is bearable if the victim can only look on toward a future when the torture will have stopped. What is intolerable is the knowledge that there will be no future. This knowledge confers upon the torture something of death's finality. During his interrogation Hernandez remembers Moreno's words: "The worst of death is that it makes everything irremediable that comes before it, irremediable forever. Torture, rape, followed by death, that's what is truly terrible" (p. 254). The impression that we are reading an earlier Malraux here is inescapable.

In short, the Hernandez episode has the shape and quality of the tragedies in the earlier novels. Here is a man caught in a trap which he has helped create and powerless to extricate himself. The choice that has put him here has been prompted by the best that is in him. Once again we have the man who cannot live in harmony with himself except as a participant in action leading straight to his own destruction. As in *Man's*

Fate the tragic data are ambiguous: there are men, like Garcia, Magnin, and Manuel, who accept the Revolution and tolerate the discipline without going down under its weight, and they are not minor characters like Hemmelrich and Souen in the earlier novel. They are tougher men than Hernandez, more empirical in outlook, less given to introspection and questioning. Magnin is bothered to death by the intransigence of the Communists, and he too is forced to compromise with his own sense of what is right; but he feels the goal is worth the sacrifice. "All action is Manichaean," explains Garcia. "It carries its own evil within it." Even so—the words are still Garcia's—admitting the unpleasant truth, "it is still better to have resisted" (p. 392). But such a view is dubious consolation to a man like Hernandez as he stands by the grave where his fellows already lie and waits his turn to stand before the rifles.

But according to the logic of the propaganda that prompted Malraux to give the divisions of his book such titles as "Operation Apocalypse" and "To Be and To Do," Hernandez is merely an example of the man who is unequal to his historical moment. And right here is the conflict between propaganda and art. For it is profoundly right and in full accord with the tragic mood of the reader that Hernandez should feel as he does and die as he does.

The episode involving old Alvear is equally disturbing. To the veteran Malraux reader the old man has a privileged position from the outset. Because of Jaime's blindness, he is the bereft father; like old Gisors he has long been living vicariously in his son. He also has the special prestige and authority of being a lifelong student of art; it is clear from both *Man's Fate* and *The Psychology of Art* that the study of art conducts the student to superior wisdom and understanding, if not to happiness. Young Scali, himself vastly upset by his failure to handle the drunken aviators, has come at Jaime's request to get the older man to leave Madrid. Alvear refuses and sits quietly sipping brandy, talking to Scali (whose books on art he knows) through the bombardment of the city. He does not know at this point, of course, that the Fascists will be turned back and that Jaime will eventually regain his sight. For all he can tell, his words are his intellectual will and testament. This scene has attracted much critical attention. Gide, for example, copies out much of the dialogue in his *Journal*. Certainly Alvear's words are portentous. "A man commits to action only a limited part of himself, and the more the action claims to be total, the smaller is the part of himself that he commits. You know that it is difficult to be a man, Mr. Scali—more difficult than the politicians think . . ." (p. 322). Malraux has a way of bestowing special importance on certain characters by making them repeat words already spoken in earlier novels by equally interesting people. "It is difficult to be a man," first occurs in *The Conquerors*, where the words are spoken by the revolutionist Klein when, broken by fatigue, he tries incoherently to explain the motives of his own action. The phrase is repeated in the Preface of *Days of Wrath*. Out of context the words mean little, but hearing them a third time from the lips of Alvear, our attention is arrested; they certify the importance of the rest of what he has to say.

A page earlier he has remarked that if each man would apply to himself one-third of the effort he expends in changing the form of government, Spain would become a decent place to live in. A page later he amplifies the remark: "The only hope Spain has of keeping what you are fighting for, you and Jaime and so many others, is that it may maintain the thing that we have been doing our best to teach for so many years . . . the quality of man" (p. 323). Other characters, of course, in the earlier books, have been relatively uninterested in the outcome of Revolution. Garine, the Conqueror type, finds Revolution essentially a way of life and the satisfactions available from the experience suffice him without reference to the outcome. Others, like Kyo, find the promised end-result of dignity and decency a sufficient reason for what they do. Now, for the first time, we are confronted by the thought that neither in the process of Revolution nor in the achievement of its success is the desideratum attainable, because the economic liberation of man does not, itself, contain the promise of a better life. "Economic slavery is heavy, but if we have to make political or religious or military servitude heavier in order to destroy the other, why bother?" (p. 321).

Here, as in the first instance, propaganda and art pull against each other.

The third of these exceptionally powerful scenes, the descent from the mountain of the wounded aviators, reintroduces the theme of fraternity which has been almost entirely submerged since the death of Hernandez. The heroes of the piece are not the aviators but the peasants. The little man who has come through the lines with word of the hidden Fascist airfield cannot read enough to point out the location of the field on Magnin's map, but he has no fear of riding in the plane so that he can show the way, and hardly understands what Magnin is saying when the latter asks if he is not afraid. Other peasants come with their old cars and trucks to light the poorly equipped Republican field with their headlights for Magnin's predawn take-off. Still others bring down the crippled and the dead from the wrecked plane. The whole episode is a solemn picture of human solidarity, and of solidarity not within the Communist party but within the larger fraternity of Man.

The essential scene is placed at the climax of the whole novel. The chapter on the successful defense of Guadalajara which follows it is much briefer and written in a much quieter tone, and is so arranged that it progresses from the excitement of battle down to a quiet, reflective calm. The battle chapter moves from greater tension toward less, and the following chapters are each less tense than the one before it. In other words, tension grades constantly down from the descent of the mountain to the end of the novel.

The eleven scenes of the focal chapter narrate a bombing mission and the disaster of one of the plane crews.

We open with a telephone conversation between Magnin and Operations. Magnin learns that the peasant has come in to report the hidden field. A half-hour passes before

The peasant is brought to Magnin and shows him where the field is. Magnin tells Operations that he will try a dawn bombing if there is cloud cover enough to replace the fighter cover the Republicans do not have. He makes the rounds of the village asking the peasants to come with their cars. Coming back through the first village at the end of the circuit he stops to ask why the long line of peasants is carrying such loads of food and learns that they are volunteers to replace the cars which "have gone to the flying field to help Madrid." This scene is an omnibus, taking up several hours and building to the climax which reveals the effort of the peasants. Cut to

The field, five o'clock. The planes are readied and all three take off by the light from the cars and trucks. Now

In Magnin's plane, air-borne over Teruel, the peasant is lost. From this angle he can no more "read" the ground than he could read Magnin's map. Magnin flies low down the road toward Saragossa so that the peasant can orient himself. Just in time the man points out the field and they go in on a strafing run. Then

They turn immediately back and bomb the field. As they pull up the weather opens and enemy fighters appear.

The Fascist pursuit tries to cut Pujol's bomber out of formation. The Republicans stay together to concentrate their defensive fire. Presently Republican fighters appear and the Fascists turn away, but Pujol's plane is going down. He gets rid of a bomb caught in his bay just in time and makes a crash landing on the side of a mountain. Cut to

Pujol beside his plane. The plane is a wreck and the crew is caught inside.

Here the break is reinforced by an asterisk and we pick up Magnin again, back at his field. He and Moros have brought their planes in, intact. He sets out to return to the fallen plane. Various hospitals can give him no word, until finally he learns that the village of Valdelinares, far up on the slopes, has been trying to get a doctor. He gets a call through to Valde linares, talks to Pujol who has walked to the village from the wreck; they agree that Pujol and the peasants will try to bring down the injured crewmen and the dead machine gunner while Magnin climbs from Linares to meet them. When he reaches Linares he finds more peasants than he can use, ready and anxious to make the ascent. They set out.

Again the break is marked by an asterisk; from here on the story belongs not to Magnin and the fliers in alternation, but to all. Cut to

The group laboring up the mountain, with Magnin riding a stirrupless mule. They meet Pujol and his copilot, Langlois, coming down.

Pujol tells the story briefly—of getting the men out of the plane, of Gardet with his nose cut nearly off staggering to a near-by cabin for a shovel, of the child who comes to see what has happened and runs away when he sees Gardet's wounded face, of the peasants who have come from Valdelinares to help.

And now the rescuers from below turn about and they all move off down the mountain. This is the scene toward which Malraux has been building from the start. The ten preceding scenes occupy approximately twenty-two pages. This one will take up seven by itself. There are no significant events in it. Nothing happens. It is all one continuous picture, slow, rhythmical, minutely detailed—a repeated reviewing of the column, from several angles, by various eyes.

First the column passes Magnin on its way down the path. Individuals stand out; Magnin's eye picks up first the four stretcher bearers followed by four more, empty-handed, waiting to relieve them. On the first stretcher is the bombadier, leg broken, cheeks hollowed with pain, and the "solid infantryman's" face thus taking on a romantic mask. Next the crewman Mireaux; since he was crushed in his turret his injury is not visible under the blankets and his pain gives him merely a childish look. He tosses a remark to Magnin about the snow up above. They clasp hands before the stretcher moves on. Now we have a kind of pattern: the identification of the man on each stretcher . . . the manifestations of his wounds if visible . . . the handclasp, if possible . . . a quick word.

Gardet is next, his face bandaged now, eyes swelled shut; it is impossible for him to shake Magnin's hand. He says that he is not blinded and that he doesn't want the peasant women to try to give him soup.

Now comes Scali; nothing about his wound to attract attention—he has an explosive bullet in his foot. He takes some soup . . .

The focus switches to the old woman who gives it to him. Magnin tells her not to try to give any to "the comrade with the bandaged face." She replies that the village's last chicken went into this soup and that she has a son at the front. . . .

The focus picks up the line of bearers again and the last peasants come by us, carrying the coffin with the body of the dead gunner, an Arab. On top, in lieu of flowers, the peasants have put one of the wracked, twisted guns from the plane. Magnin is now looking down the whole line from the rear.

As the bearers relieve each other, Magnin's eye falls on the women and notes the contrast between their general poverty and the shininess of the thermos bottles they carry. One asks Mireaux's age. Twenty-seven. She has been following the stretcher for minutes, hovering over it for a chance to help. For Magnin she incarnates maternity.

Magnin's eye returns to a broader scene and he becomes aware of the rising mountains, the lowering valley.

Another woman questions him. Who are these men whom she has come to help save? Magnin tells her.

And again we are aware that a pattern has been established; the eye moves from wounded men to villagers, back to the line and the coffin, out to the landscape, and back to a villager.

Magnin now moves back up the line and stops Scali's stretcher. We can look down the zigzag path ahead and the column spread out along it. Langlois standing as a sort of point, far in advance. Pujol between him and the column. The stretchers, one after another, laboring across a frozen brook.

Scali speaks, "I had . . ."

Magnin interrupts, "Look, what a picture!"

And, as though the pitch of emotion had risen dangerously high, we get a relief—the story Scali would have told Magnin if Magnin had not interrupted, about his sister's romance years ago with a Spaniard in Murcia. For years young Scali's Spain has been a land of picturesque backdrops. Now Scali snaps abruptly into the present. Spain is now this coffin and this twisted machine gun.

The contrast of Scali's past and present is parallel to the one in *La Tentation de l'occident*, between the Asia of "A.D.'s" imagining in the Prologue and the Asia of his actual experience.

Now Magnin's eye takes over again, gradually. The spectator, from some privileged vantage point which is not that of any participant, sees him whip his mule forward, ahead of the column, until he comes to the apple tree at the sharp angle of the path. Here he turns to watch Langlois and then the stretchers pass by and we see through his eyes as the wounded men are once more enumerated. For three lines of text he meditates; then the meditation melts into a new enumeration, this time of wounds . . . the broken leg, the dangling arm, the maimed face.

Next another fragment of conversation; one of the women has another question: why had the Arab been in the plane? Magnin does not answer. His eyes are on the great birds wheeling overhead. She asks something else, "Is it true that noses can be repaired nowadays?"

Now the column has gone on and Magnin's eye follows it from behind, as the path widens below him and permits the peasants to group around the coffin; the peasants pick and thread their way, shifting their burdens to avoid shocks. Linares comes in sight. The coffin catches up with Scali. Magnin's eye singles out the machine gun on top, then moves out to where, on the Saragossa road, black smoke is still rising from the charred Fascist planes which will not go to the Guadalajara now or ever and then moves back to the austerely triumphal procession of the peasants.

From Linares the children come running out, stop as the procession nears them, solemnly watch it pass.

All of Linares is out as the column enters the town, watching it from the ramparts. For a third and final time the line passes in review. First the bombadier, then Scali and Mireaux, then Langlois with his bloody bandage and his bare foot—a little like Don Quixote and more impressive to the watchers—next Pujol, more impressive still from all the blood on his jacket, and finally Gardet. The others have smiled in greeting; Gardet's head is turned away. This, to the peasants, is the face of war. Awkwardly they rise and salute, fists closed.

This is all. The procession now vanishes into the mist, leaving the watching peasants behind. Then in two extremely brief scenes, which together occupy hardly more than a half-page—one a quick shot into the ambulance where the wounded lie, each man shut up in the privacy of his own suffering, and one in six lines of a telephone call—the chapter is ended.

There is no other place in his writing where Malraux demands so much of his visual imagination or makes such elaborate use of it. Actually the number of things registered is small: the wounded men, the bearers, the other peasants, Magnin (seen once), the mountain backdrop (also seen only once), the path, the brook, the apple tree, the children, the ramparts of Linares. The whole effect is produced by the alternation of angles of observation and by the choice of rhythms. The review of the column is repeated three times (at the arrival of the rescue party, at the turn by the apple tree, and at the walls of Linares) and the reviews are separated from each other by the two meditations, the snatches of conversation with the peasant women about the chicken, the Arab, and noses. With Magnin we watch the column pass, move up to the front, watch it pass again, move once more to the front, and watch it pass for a third time and disappear. The eye repeatedly moves away from the men on the stretchers, only to be pulled back to them as if by an obsession, to be held there by the slow enumeration and adumbration of detail. No other scene in Malraux's work, not even the final exit of Katow in *Man's Fate*, attains such emotional amplitude.

And yet this scene glorifies the fraternity of men, precisely the fraternity which, according to the propaganda thesis of the novel, will not and cannot win revolutions! Even more in this episode of the descent of the mountain than in the episodes of Hernandez' death and of Alvear's conversation with Scali, the emotional effect upon the reader—that "modification of his sensibility" mentioned in the Preface to *Days of Wrath*—is directly opposed to the conclusions to which, as a propaganda piece, *Man's Hope* should have led him.

Hence an extremely curious situation. *Man's Hope* is a characteristic Malraux novel in that it embodies—not once but three times—the opposition of an emotionally satisfactory picture to the conclusions of the discursive argument of the novel. But in the other novels it is clearly Malraux's intention that the discursive argument should be refuted, whereas in *Man's Hope* this cannot be the case. We are forced by the facts to conclude that the kind of novel his artist's instinct makes him write is not one that can be placed at the service of propaganda. Certainly propaganda found its way in only at the expense of destroying the over-all artistic integrity of the book.

Yet in its parts *Man's Hope* is still a novel of high quality—and extremely interesting in what it reveals about Malraux as writer.

The subject makes certain major differences from the earlier novels obligatory. All Malraux's novels use a historical event for their background, but in the others concern for the destinies of certain individuals is dominant: here, most of the time, the event dominates the private destinies. The figure of the hero, the lone tragic figure looming over the whole book, disappears, and as a result of the disappearance Malraux has to renounce using many of his habitual devices. The workings of one individual *Angst* or another are no longer appropriate as motives of action, and in the whole book there is only one *Angst*-ridden figure whose fate is determined by his *Angst*—Hernandez.

It is true that in one sense the story is built largely around Manuel, who grows in stature from that first night of the war when his usefulness is largely due to his owning a useful automobile, to the last scene when, a colonel now and certain to be a general shortly, he sits alone in the isolation of the hardened commander. He has gained in self-confidence until at last he has thrown away the omnipresent stick, which has been the badge of his feeling of inadequacy, and he has come to accept his increasing solitude. But the reader does not attach himself to Manuel as he does to Kyo Gisors or to Hernandez. Concern for him never becomes great enough to effect the transposition of values like the one in *Man's Fate*, where we are interested in the fate of the Shanghai insurrection, after a while, only because its effect will be decisive on the fate of Kyo. Manuel is an interesting character and his development under the pressure of Communist discipline and under the guidance of the Catholic officer Jimenez is humanly and politically significant, but if he had been killed, like Puig early in the story, he would have been merely another battle casualty. In 1931 it had been possible for Malraux to deny with some force that the Revolution was the "heroine" of *The Conquerors*. He could not have denied in 1937 that the war in Spain was the "heroine" of *Man's Hope*.

There is little need in *Man's Hope* to intensify the action and to concentrate it by the familiar foreshortening of time, or try to sweep the reader along in the illusion that the destiny of the characters will not wait. The characters have time to eat and sleep and do so abundantly; and they talk. *Man's Hope* is full of verbose people, and their conversation is frequently tangential to the concerns of the novel as narrative rather than styled to advance the progress of the book. The pace of events is the historical pace of the early months of the war, and where the narrative leaps across gaps of time, as it does occasionally, there is no implication that the events omitted are insignificant. Rather, the implication is merely that there are enough significant events in the book without adding to the number.

As a war novel, *Man's Hope* confronts Malraux with the standard difficulties, plus a few special ones produced by the duplicity of his intentions. Stendhal's original discovery that the participant in a battle sees little, knows less, and understands less yet, of what is going on immediately about him ("War is no more than this?" cries the surprised hero of *The Charterhouse of Parma*) delineates the classical dilemma. Fabrice del

Dongo sees a lot of smoke, is caught up in a meaningless charge, fails to recognize the famous men he passes in the murk, and is not quite sure just what battle he has fought in. Malraux's dilemma has even more points to its horns, for where Fabrice does not have to understand Waterloo and where Hemingway, in another instance, could avoid the problem by making the meaning of the war equivalent to its effect upon Robert Jordan, Malraux has to concern himself not only with the experience of war but with its political and metaphysical meanings at the same time. The reader must be kept aware of ideas as well as of the feeling of combat and with tactics and with strategy. Malraux cannot risk losing his reader in the consciousness of one individual character whose awareness of war is largely an awareness of being shot at, and at the same time he cannot neglect the fact that the most intense reality of war is precisely this awareness. He cannot afford to adopt an optics which, by assuming too great a distance, would permit the reader to sink back into the role of privileged spectator and abandon the role of participant, because to do so would be to jeopardize that "modification of the sensibility" which would dispose the reader in favor of the anti-Fascist cause. In other words, the reader has to be made to feel the fight as the combatant feels it and at the same time understand it as the participant quite probably does not, to experience war simultaneously on the plane of personal, intimate effort and danger, and on the other planes as above enumerated.

This necessity places the events of the story against a very different scale from the events in the earlier novels. For example, at the beginning of the narrative, the "Negus" passes out revolvers to his companions; and where he got them is the subject of a very brief explanation. "With two friends and a few helpers, he had cleaned out, that night, the armories of two war vessels. He still wore the mechanic's coverall he had put on to get himself on the boats" (p. 26). Two sentences now suffice. But in *Man's Fate* the similar exploit, Katow's raid on the S.S. *Shantung*, occupies five full pages and is presented as the event at which everything that happens previous to it in the novel is pointed, including Tchen's murder. The difference in scale is the difference between insurrection and war.

The great advantage of the narrative technique that Malraux adopts, and which in essence consists of conveying the detail of war in the brief, narrative-unit scenes and of grouping them so that the manner of grouping implies a commentary, is precisely that it meets the multiple problems presented by the subject. The individual scenes permit the play of the visual imagination which is perhaps his most valuable gift, and with their great, keen immediacy of sensation handle the feel of actual participation. Grouping them takes care of the panoramic view and at the same time permits revealing the significance of what has happened. Quite probably the feeling of greater "density" or of richer "texture," which critics find in this book as compared with the others, rises from this.

Meanwhile certain of Malraux's familiar themes and equally familiar character types disappear, and there is considerable rearrangement of the others. Mythomania is gone, and no character plays the role of Clappique. Eroticism is also absent, and there are no counterparts to such erotics as Ferral and Perken. Death, in a story where many men die, has lost much of its importance; and the characters who are most obsessed with it, Moreno and Hernandez, appear in the part which most clearly harks back to the earlier novels. For other sensitive types, Scali for example, the obsession has lost its grip since they began fighting. The people are much less concerned with solitude, estrangement, and "incommunicability" than ever before. (Manuel's solitude is a special condition of the soldier, not part of the predicament of being human.) And the realignment of the values which are the opposite of solitude continues.

In *Days of Wrath*, virile fraternity was already the opposite value both of human solitude and human indignity; in *Man's Hope* it is even more clearly the opposite of indignity or humiliation. The wounded Barca explains that he has been fighting because he does not like other men to disdain him. And the instinct of the besiegers of the Alcazar is to give razor blades and cigarettes to the defenders just to show that they are not the kind of men the besiegers can scorn. The same motive makes Hernandez forward Moscado's letters. In view of Malraux's tendency to equate imprisonment and humiliation, it is highly significant that in an impassioned speech the "Negus" should cry out: "When men come out of prison, nine times out of ten they can't look steadily at anything. In the proletariat, too, there are many eyes that can't fix on anything."

The opposite of humiliation is probably too vague an emotion for Malraux to be able to give it a single, satisfactory name. Certainly he feels it to be an escape from scorn, but he feels it also to be the "harsh, fraternal exaltation" that supports the courage of the dynamiters as they move forward against the Fascist tanks. It comforts Siry and Kogan as they wait in the mud for the Moors to charge and whistle to each other like a pair of birds because they have no common language for a Bulgar and a Frenchman to talk in. It has its apotheosis in the descent from the mountain. Fraternity and release from humiliation do not win wars: "Humiliation," remarks the Russian Pradas, "would not arm a hundred men." "I doubt," says Garcia to Magnin, "that you have built your escadrille upon fraternity alone." Fraternity, we have seen, is even more likely to lose a war than to win it. Yet is a good for which men die.

If only ten years of warfare had not occupied Malraux between 1936 and 1946, we should be able to see to what extent the disappearances and transpositions of the themes in *Man's Hope* were dictated by the needs of that book, and by the technique adopted in consequence of those needs, and to what extent they were victims of an evolution of his attitudes and affections. There is simply not enough of his writing available for one to find an answer to the question. *Les Noyers de l'Altenburg*, coming five years after *Man's Hope*, is too brief to be useful at this point. Yet some themes—death for instance—do resume in it some of the importance they do not have in *Man's Hope* and did have in *Man's Fate*. The Absurd has more importance than it has had since *The Royal Way*. These re-emergences suggest that the demands of the particular book he was doing had much to do with what themes Malraux exploited in *Man's Hope*. But this conclusion must be tentative.

One may well agree with Marcel Savane's judgment, that *Man's Hope* will endure into the twenty-first century as one of the best revelations to later readers of what it meant to live in the twentieth.[5] But if so, it will survive more by its value as a document than as a piece of literature, and by its appeal to the comprehending intellect rather than to the emotions. Its confusions, its loose ends, its diffuseness, may even increase its documentary interest. In its consciousness of what the fighting was about, *Man's Hope* towers above the book that is inevitably compared with it, *For Whom the Bell Tolls*. But Hemingway's book has the tight unity, the coherence, the constant emotional tension, and the finish, that Malraux's does not. The difference is that Hemingway intended a novel while Malraux intended a novel and something more. The books are thus not entirely commensurable. If Malraux's book outlasts Hemingway's, all that will be proved is that novels are not necessarily the most durable of books.

[5] *André Malraux*, p. 95.

CHAPTER SIX

The Age of the Fundamental

> *"We have come back to the Age of the Fundamental,
> Mr. Scali."*
>
> —MAN'S HOPE, p. 323

AFTER defeat in Spain, defeat in France. The Germans had broken through, and France was out of the war. For Malraux there had been the taste of military prison and then the even less tolerable imprisonment of life in a captive country. Out of this time of humiliation comes the last of his novels. His wound was hardly healed when he began *La Lutte avec l'ange.*

The part that was saved from the Gestapo and found its way to the publisher Skira in Switzerland, *Les Noyers de l'Altenburg,* is peopled by characters who are recognizable resurrections of characters in his other novels. The themes are the old, basic ones, familiar to every reader of his work. But the tone is subdued, with none of the old notes of triumph. The mood is interrogative: he is questioning the relevance of the themes, the significance of the acts of the characters. And since now the relations of the characters to their author are clearly established, he is also raising questions about the meaning and value of his own career, asking himself what significance these have retained in the face of recent events.

He also puts forth answers to the questions, though tentatively and more obscurely. They are hidden in the covert meaning of the hero's experience, and revealed only in symbol. A careless reader can miss them entirely. Yet when they are investigated we find that in the dark days of 1941 Malraux was not only raising questions; he was also setting down an affirmation of his beliefs and giving us a key to the fundamental meaning of his experience.

We may overlook the warning in the prefatory note to the Paris edition, which says that the text as presented there is not definitive. There is abundant interior evidence that *Les Noyers* is complete within itself. We can give an account of it which leaves no glaring blanks.

It is a novel only by courtesy and for the sake of convenience. Between its five parts[1] there is little explicit narrative relationship. Characters are exposed to view, not progressively revealed or developed. Nothing gives

---

[1] Of which the first and last, printed in italic, are not numbered in the text. For convenience the parts are referred to here as if numbered consecutively.

the reader the feeling of taking part in events. As a novel it does not stand up; the fiction is disjointed and pointless, even baffling. But if it is taken as a meditation in the form of fiction on Malraux's eternal subject of man's fate, the five parts are completely relevant to each other. Part One raises the question which is the subject of meditation and surrounds it with an atmosphere of urgency such as justifies the anxious tone of the entire book. The second part relates the experience which particularly qualifies Vincent Berger to have an opinion on the subject. Part Three finally puts the question in definite words and subjects it to the discursive reason—and the intellectuals who discuss it fail to find a rational answer. The hero, on the other hand, finds an answer, but—as one would expect, knowing Malraux —rather by intuition than by rational process. In Part Four he tests his intuition empirically and finds it valid, but dies at the end of the test. And the fifth part permits his son to make a similar test, in similar circumstances, and to come to the same conclusion. By inspection, nothing is lacking here. *Les Noyers* is a whole.

The first part, set in the prisoner-of-war camp at Chartres just after the breakthrough of 1940, starts as a picture of the life of the new-made prisoners and gradually modulates into musings on the nature and continuity of man. In the vast patience of the French P.W.'s, in such characteristically human gestures as the writing home of letters they know will not be sent, in the banal but eternal concerns of the letters, in the gesture of staking out individual properties within the camp, and in the very faces themselves as soon as the beards have grown out, the soldier named Berger who is the narrator sees men who are as much Gothic as modern. In them he reads "the immemorial memory of the scourge." This feeling for the men about him turns young Berger to reflecting upon the notes left by his dead father, Vincent, under the general title "My Encounters with Man."

In the second part, the father is teaching philosophy at the university of Constantinople c. 1908. The German Ambassador puts him (Berger is an Alsatian) at the head of the Propaganda Service. This throws Vincent in with Enver Pasha and the Young Turks. His lust for action and his organizing ability, as well as his usefulness in making Enver understand his own role, make him invaluable to the young colonel. Together they raise the Arab tribes and repulse Graziani's Italians. Berger becomes a legend and comes to love being one, but he also becomes suspect to his German employers, who frown upon his caring more about the outcome of the action in the desert than about the interests of the German Empire. So he goes over to the service of the Young Turks and undertakes the difficult mission of reawakening the old Turkish Blood Alliance in Central Asia. He goes all the way to Ghazni, on the Afghan-Indian frontier, visiting khan after khan without success. Then finally, after months of struggle against wild country and illness, he suddenly realizes that the Turan is only a myth of Enver Pasha's imagination. The blood alliance simply does not exist. Defeated, he takes ship for Europe, has a final interview with Enver at Port Said, and eventually disembarks at Marseille. Five days after his arrival in Europe his own father—the narrator's grandfather—commits suicide.

Part Three is the colloquy of intellectuals organized by his father's brother Walter. Its subject—whether the idea of man, constantly and eternally identifiable with himself, is at all tenable—strikes Vincent Berger as extremely significant. His failure in the Orient has been a failure to communicate, to break through the wall which stood between him and the Asiatics; and in his inability to understand his father's motives in killing himself there is a similar blocking of communication. Like the other participants, he is anxious to hear the great German ethnologist Möllberg who is widely reported to be putting the finishing touches on his long-awaited *Civilization as Conquest and Destiny*. Möllberg is expected to offer a convincing case for the unity of man's development and the continuity which links civilization with civilization. But Berger learns on the eve of the colloquy that Möllberg's last trip to Africa has changed the great man's mind, and at the colloquy Möllberg in fact declares for the negative view. Others, including Vincent Berger, argue feebly against him. He refutes them and persists in his argument. To the final intellectualist plea, that man has an eternally divine side which is expressed in his willingness to return to the questioning of first principles, Möllberg replies: "Sisyphus, too, is eternal" (p. 102). At intermission Vincent Berger quits the colloquy, again in defeat, and walks to the top of the near-by hill. And there, suddenly, the perspective of some old and gnarled trees fills him with the intuition that Möllberg is wrong: although the Möllbergs cannot be argued down, the truth remains that man is eternally, recognizably the same.

The fourth part takes Vincent Berger to the Vistula front in the first World War. As an intelligence officer in the German army he has had ample opportunity to see to what inhuman lengths his colleagues will go in questioning prisoners. He meets the extraordinarily Biedermeier chemistry professor who has invented an "effective" poison gas, and is shocked to realize that the man is completely unaware of the inhuman nature of his invention. Next he is present at the first gas attack on the Eastern Front. After the gas has been released on the Russian lines, he watches the German troops move forward for the mop-up. They disappear into the trenches. And then suddenly he realizes that they are coming back. Each is bearing a gassed Russian soldier. Berger himself rushes forward to help them, and is finally disabled by the gas, but not before he has joined the mutiny against the inhuman.

In the fifth part Vincent Berger's son, during the second World War, is one of four men who sweat out a night in a tank that has fallen into a pit. They know that the trap is very probably zeroed by the German guns. They survive, and in the morning find an old peasant couple who have been unable to leave with the refugees, sitting in the sun, waiting. "What else could we do?" asks the old woman. "You're young. When one is old, one just waits for the thing to pass" (p. 195). Young Berger feels that he is perhaps seeing man for the first time.

We are left at the end of Part Five with conclusions which are also the implicit conclusions of Part One, but we do not grasp all the implications of Part One *until* we have finished Part Five. It is so enriched by the meaning of the other parts that we are obliged to read Part One twice: first as prologue and again as epilogue. The structure of the book is thus circular.

So is the time plan. The prison camp episode is dated June 21, 1940. Vincent Berger's career in the East begins in 1908 and ends in 1914. The gas attack on the Russian front happens on June 12, 1915. The tank action of Part Five takes place in 1940 but earlier than June 21. And the required second reading of Part One brings us into the fictional present again. This feeling of circularity is reinforced by the words of the old peasant woman at the end of the book: "When one is old one has nothing but wear"— which are almost the identical words used by one of the prisoners very near the beginning. "I'm just waiting for it to wear itself out"—"What?"— "Everything. I'm just letting it wear itself out" (p. 23).

In his habitual disregard for coherence, Malraux does not set off in any relief the things such as this which bind the parts of the meditation together, but leaves them for the reader to catch as and if he can. The long stretches of conversation, in the fourth part, that Vincent Berger listens to while they all wait for the release of the gas, are almost meaningless unless one realizes that these Germans of 1915 are experiencing the same banal and eternal concerns as do the Frenchmen of 1941 in the prison camp at Chartres. The intention of the book becomes clear only if the reader is alert to possibilities, like this, of unasserted meaning, and unless he keeps in mind also Malraux's habit of appealing to a symbol, generally a symbol presented as a picture—like the timeless faces at Chartres, the prospect of the walnut trees, and the grotesque figures of the Germans carrying the gassed Russians—for support where rational discourse fails.

Les Noyers has relatively little of the rapid flicker of visual images, increasingly characteristic from book to book, of Malraux's earlier writing. Through at least three-fifths of the book at any rate, he drops his trick of placing his reader close up to the action of the drama. The verbs are characteristically retrospective and look back upon the action from the present. The action itself is no longer one close-knit, continuous, violent enterprise: the breaks between the parts cover years. Hence the feeling of rush and of the inevitability of events, so completely achieved in the previous novels, now disappears. *Les Noyers* is, to say it all at once, a leisurely and reflective book—as a predominantly meditative book should be.

The chief characters of the meditation may be identified with unusual assurance. Malraux was a second-class private in the tanks at the time of the breakthrough, was in fact a prisoner of war (though at Sens rather than at Chartres: one may wonder about the substitution of one cathedral town for another), and later served in the resistance under the name of Berger. Young Berger, meanwhile, is a writer by peacetime profession and declares that his subject, "for the last ten years," has been man. He turns to writing, when his moment of action has passed, as a prophylaxis against despair and perhaps insanity. And like Malraux, he has had a father in the first World War and a close relative who commits suicide. He is Malraux, or rather Malraux seen in a certain light—Malraux the contemplative artist.

It is equally clear who Vincent Berger is. He has studied at a School of Oriental Languages, has read and admired Nietzsche, and the course he teaches at Constantinople is on the Philosophy of Action (*La Tentation de l'occident* may very well be considered a treatment of the same subject). He shortly permits action to supersede philosophy and commits himself to a life in which action is everything. His father, like Malraux's, has committed suicide. So far he sounds remarkably like his author. But he is more complicated than this, for he also reincarnates the heroes of Malraux's early novels. His great alacrity to accept the invitation of the German Ambassador to set up a propaganda office, and his quick perception that the propaganda service can become a powerful and immensely effective instrument of direct political action, are completely reminiscent of Garine in *The Conquerors*. Similarly, his choosing to join forces with the Young Turks, rather than with the moribund Empire, is prompted by the knowledge that Enver and his colleagues have begun to study the technique of insurrection in preference to "democratic agitation" and parallels Garine's decision to join the Communists rather than the Anarchists. Like Garine still, Berger "attaches himself to a great action," for the satisfaction of personal needs rather than in the service of ethical conviction. With both Garine and Perken he wants to "leave a scar on the map"—the phrase appears verbatim in this book and in *The Royal Way*—and like Garine and Perken he carries on indomitably in the face of severe physical infirmity. Thus in addition to sounding very like Malraux he sounds as much like those heroes who, if not what Malraux was during his experiences in Asia, were doubtless very much like what he would have liked to be. On top of all this, his career is remarkably like that of T. E. Lawrence. The exploit of turning the Arabs into a cohesive fighting force is Lawrence's exploit in support of Allenby. There are few details of Berger's adventure, even down to such minor ones as the advantage of having even a few inferior armored cars, that do not have counterparts in the *Seven Pillars*. And like Lawrence, Berger decides that he cares more about the future of these Mohammedans with whom he has been living than he does for that of the country of which he is officially a citizen. Berger even becomes, as Lawrence did, a legendary figure both with the tribesmen and with the public at home.

Thus Vincent Berger is a composite of his creator and of certain of his creator's heroes, fictional and otherwise. The traits that make him look like Malraux, however, are those we associate with Malraux the "man of action." And the Lawrence whom Vincent Berger resembles is not the taciturn, unhappy, self-tortured, guilt-hounded English eccentric but the young archaeologist who went to the East to dig and remained to fight: Lawrence of Arabia, not Aircraftsman Shaw. The fictional heroes Berger resembles are the glamorous supermen of the early novels. Thus *Les Noyers* takes on the aspect of an exercise in self-contemplation, with Malraux the writer and thinker scrutinizing Malraux the "Adventurer," the "comrade in arms" of Garine.

That Malraux should incarnate so much of his own public personality in a character who dies before the story is finished is interesting but of undeterminable significance. One could read him to mean that *this* Malraux, the man of action, is of the past and does not survive, and that the survivor is the Malraux represented by the younger Berger of the prison camp. Malraux has said nothing since to support this conclusion, but, on the other hand, he has not resumed the man-of-action role since the end of the second World War.

In any case, it is clear that in *Les Noyers* Malraux is surveying his own past and trying to assess the meaning and value of his own experience—the meaning and value, that is, of Vincent Berger's.

The importance of the subject of the Colloquy of Intellectuals *for Malraux's own lifework* can hardly be overemphasized. If Man, with a capital, is an empty notion, then such ideas as Man's hope and Man's fate are equally vain, the labor and the wounds are for nothing. Man's destiny is no more significant than the destiny of the termite, and a tragic view of the world becomes simply silly. In other words, the fundamental bases of all of Malraux's writing are under attack. As one of the speakers remarks, either the idea of human continuity holds good or the whole idea of man collapses into absurdity. One by one the speakers advance their reasons why human destiny has a meaning, and one by one Möllberg refutes them with the classical, more or less Spenglerian arguments of the German anthropologists: cultures are "closed" cycles; civilizations do not intercommunicate; between European and bushman there is no connection except biological similarity. Vincent Berger joins his word to the others, and with the others is refuted—so thoroughly that critics have taken Möllberg's arguments to be the final, desolate expression of the beliefs of Malraux himself.

In doing so, however, they have been forced to neglect the dramatic movment of the episode as a whole.

After the failure to refute Möllberg comes the intermission, and Vincent Berger, breaking away from the group, wanders off up the old Altenburg hill alone. There on the crest are the tall nut trees—*les noyers de l'Altenburg*—dominating the summit and enframing a perspective down the long hillside to the cathedral of Strasbourg in the distance. And there, from the sight of the old trees, Berger experiences a new flash of enlightenment.

La plénitude des arbres séculaires émanait de leur masse, mais l'effort par quoi sortaient de leurs énormes troncs les branches tordues, l'épanouissement en feuilles sombres de ce bois, si vieux et si lourd qu'il semblait s'enfoncer dans la terre et non s'en arracher, imposaient à la fois l'idée d'une volonté et d'une métamorphose sans fin. Entre eux les collines dévalaient jusqu'au Rhin; ils encadraient la cathédrale de Strasbourg très loin dans le crépuscule heureux, comme tant d'autres troncs encadraient d'autres cathédrales dans les champs d'Occident. Et cette tour dressée dans son oraison d'amputé, toute la patience et le travail humains développés en vagues de vignes jusqu'au fleuve n'étaient qu'un décor du soir autour de la séculaire poussée du bois vivant, des deux jets drus et noueux qui arrachaient les forces de la terre pour les déployer en ramures. Le soleil très bas poussait leur ombre jusqu'à l'autre côté de la vallée, comme deux épais rayons. Mon père pensait aux deux saints, à l'Atlante; le bois convulsé de ces noyers, au lieu de supporter le fardeau du monde, s'épanouissait dans une vie éternelle en leurs feuilles vernies sur le ciel et leurs noix presque mûres, en toute leur masse solennelle au-dessus du large anneau de jeunes pousses et de noix mortes de l'hiver. «Les civilisations ou l'animal, comme les statues ou les bûches ...» Entre les statues et les bûches, il y avait les arbres, et leur dessin obscur comme celui de la vie. Et l'Atlante, et la face de Saint-Marc ravagée de ferveur gothique s'y perdaient comme la culture, comme l'esprit, comme tout ce que mon père venait d'entendre—ensevelis dans l'ombre de

cette statue indulgente que se sculptaient à elles-mêmes les forces de la terre, et que
le soleil au ras des collines étendait sur l'angoisse des hommes jusqu'à l'horizon.
(Pp. 105–6.)

The feeling of plenitude in the immemorial trees came from their mass, but the
effort of the twisted branches straining out from the enormous trunks, and the way
this wood, so old and heavy that it seemed to sink into the ground instead of to rise
from it, spread open its dark leaves, forced on one the ideas of endless will and
endless metamorphosis. Between the trees the slope fell away to the Rhine; they
framed the Strasbourg Cathedral, distant in the pleasant dusk, as so many other
cathedrals stood tree-framed in the fields, all over the Occident. And that spire
rising like the prayer of the maimed, and all the human patience and the human
labor that were the waves of vineyards descending to the river, were only an evening background to the immemorial upsurge of the living wood, for the two thick
clumps that wrested the strength from the earth itself to spread it in their branches.
The low sun sent their shadows across the valley to its other side in two wide
slashes. My father thought of the two saints, and of the Atlas: the tortured wood
of these walnuts, instead of bearing the weight of the world, spread the eternal life
of their shiny leaves, and of their almost ripened fruit, and of all their solemn
massiveness, above the wide ring of young shoots and the dead nuts of the winter.
"Civilization or the animal, like the statues or the chunks of wood . . ." Connect-
ing the statues and the chunks were the trees and their dark design like the dark
design of life. And the Atlas, and the face of St. Mark with the ravages of its Gothic
fervor were lost in it like culture, like mind, like everything my father had just
heard said—buried in the shadow of that indulgent statue that the forces of the
earth had sculpted by themselves and that the sun, from the level of the hilltops,
spread out over the anxieties of men, as far as the horizon.

The symbolic value of the nut trees can be and has been neglected even
though it gives the book its title; it can hardly be misunderstood. Since
the beginning of the colloquy (p. 112) Vincent has been aware of walnut
wood as the one material used in the decoration of his uncle's library, where
the talks are held. He has also been very conscious of a ship's figurehead,
and of two Gothic saints, all prominent in the room and of course sculptured
from the same dark wood. At one point Möllberg's talk is interrupted by
the clatter of workmen dumping a load of logs outside. Vincent Berger
immediately associates them with the idea of continuity: woodsmen like
these had piled similar logs, back in the Middle Ages. Möllberg himself has
mentioned the walnut wood in an analogy which denied, absolutely, Vincent Berger's hope in the eternity of man: Berger has asked anxiously
whether one cannot look for permanence in an idea of "fundamental" man,
changeless beneath shifting appearances. Möllberg replies: "These two
Gothic statues, and that figurehead are made of the same wood. But be-

neath the forms, there isn't any fundamental walnut. There are logs"
(p. 102). Thus the subject of the walnuts and walnut wood has assumed
a definite relation to the subject of the permanence of man before Berger
walks up the hill toward the copse at the crest. Möllberg's remark is the
one picked up between quotation marks in the passage where the symbol
of the nut trees enlightens Vincent Berger.

The passage in which the essential intuition is communicated to him
insists heavily upon the impression of age (*séculaires, si vieux et si lourd,*
séculaire again, and *s'épanouissant dans une vie éternelle*). With this is
linked the feeling, derived from the sight of the trees, of endless effort and
endless change (*l'idée d'une volonté et d'une métamorphose sans fin . . .*
arrachaient les forces de la terre). And with these two is joined the idea
of domination: the trees dwarf the distant cathedral, just as they reduce
the other work of men's hands, the vineyards, to the status of backdrop.

Now, the cathedral has also figured as a symbol during the conversation
in the library. Stieglitz, the same speaker who recasts the whole meaning of
the talk (for veteran readers of Malraux at least) by inserting the idea of
the Absurd, has also invited his listeners to take the difference between a
Gothic cathedral and any given piece of recent neo-Gothic as an index of
the absence of communication between men of the two periods. But to
Vincent Berger, seeing the cathedral through the trees, the cathedral means
just the opposite. The trees simply nullify the differences between the man
looking at the cathedral and the men who built it. Berger's doubts are now
completely dispelled. Man's fate is not a derisively ironic phrase. Man has
his continuity, and consequently he has a destiny, though an obscure one.

A year later, when Berger is standing in a trench somewhere along the
Vistula, waiting for the gas to be released upon the Russians, the soldiers
around him talk not about the imminent "experiment," but about the eternal
things which occupy the minds of common men—their work, their loves,
the fidelity and infidelity of their women, their superstitions, their fears,
their wisdom and their stupidity. When they go over the top, toward the
Russian lines, the wave moves out, hesitates, disappears into the enemy
trenches. Then, through their glasses, the officers who have stayed behind
see the men emerging from the trenches again and stumbling back toward
the German lines, looking taller than life-size because they are carrying
the gassed Russians in their arms.

There is a remarkable similarity between this picture and the picture
of the descent of the mountain at the end of *Man's Hope*. These are common men, ignorant men like the Spanish peasants, men incapable really of
understanding the meaning of what they are doing. Yet the rescue—like

the rescue of the aviators, an instinctive response to physical calamity—is a symbolic gesture. It symbolizes man's fraternity.

The rest of the fourth part of the book is a long series of pictures of German soldiers hurrying back to the dressing stations. Malraux's technique changes completely. Before this he has narrated, summarized long stretches of past action, and broken the summaries rarely with dialogued scene. Visual imagery has been incidental and unimportant. But now, in this end of the fourth part, the aesthetic distance is intentionally shortened; visual imagery is thick; there is a minute reproduction of physical detail; the narrative progresses through a series of close-ups. The confrontations between Berger and the returning soldiers are cut by snatches of dialogue which express the horror of the men at what they have seen and the solidarity of their refusal to do anything but rescue the Russians. The Russians are no longer enemies. They are fellow victims of the inhuman. Like the material, the technique is fundamentally the same as in the last great scene in *Man's Hope*; this is a new Descent from the Mountain.

For Vincent Berger, what he has just seen is the final answer to the question of the Altenburg: "Right up to the shining, blue sky climbed the slope with its now renewed smell of trees, the smell of box and balsam still dripping from the shower. Suddenly the memory of the Altenburg cut through my father's obsession. He was standing before the great copse of walnut trees" (p. 163).

The marked similarity of subject matter, technique, and even of moods between *Les Noyers* and the Descent from the Mountain sequence compels attention to the change which has taken place in Malraux's basic attitudes somewhere along the way. In the books before these one hardly sees the common man. The heroes of *Man's Fate* do not come from the working class. Only one character in *The Conquerors* represents the people for whose good the Revolution is supposed to function: Hong. Elsewhere Malraux's eye is on men whose backgrounds are like his own; the heroic pictures are pictures of bourgeois intellectuals. But the figures of the peasants on the mountain, of the mutinous German infantrymen, and (later in *Les Noyers*) of the men in the tank, all come from the anonymous mass. Malraux seems to have a certain impatience with intellectuals. If Vincent Berger enjoys a kind of privilege and is exempt from Malraux's scorn, the other participants in the colloquy are certainly disparaged. There can be small doubt that, except for its Alsatian setting, the Altenburg assembly is closely modeled upon Pontigny, where for years Paul Desjardins brought together the intellectual elite of Europe for its famous conferences. That the portrait of Walter Berger is a caricature of Desjardins is dubious; there is small benefit, in general, in searching for resemblances between the participants of the Altenburg conversations and such figures as Gide, Groethuysen, Charles Du Bos, Roger Martin du Gard, and the others who frequented Pontigny. What is significant is that the organizer of the Altenburg group, Vincent Berger's uncle, is affected, stagey, and remarkably engaged in self-glorification (the letters from Nietzsche which he preserves so proudly are really recriminations that treat him as if he were a lackey). Each of the other distinguished minds that takes up the cudgels against Möllberg has some disqualifying peculiarity: one man has sacrificed his career for winebibbing, another has spent thirty years of his life trying to look like the pictures of Mallarmé, and so on down the long and distinguished list. "Never," remarks the narrator, "was an idea born there of a fact; always of another idea" (p. 82). The *fact* that Vincent Berger needs is the mutiny of the German infantrymen.

The entire emotional and poetic force of the last part of the book is exerted in this same direction.

The walnut-tree symbol is no longer needed. The connection between Vincent Berger's experience on the Vistula and his son's experience on the Northern Front in France is luminously clear without it. The four men in the tank, pounding forward through the night toward the enemy, are as different from each other as men of the same century can be: Prade, the gap-toothed peasant who drives; Bonneau, the frightful little bluffer of a thug from the slums who runs the motors; Leonard, the nondescript radio operator; Berger, the intellectual. The chapter starts with enough observation of the ways and characters of the first three to identify them with the changelessly human types who, in the preceding part, were to go over and follow up the gas attack. Then the tank crashes down into a trap. They wait through an eternity for the German shells to come. There are no differences between them now. They are merely men, and man is "the only animal who knows that he will die." The shells do not come. They discover that a wall of the pit has crumbled and they get the tank out. And in the freshness of the next morning (as the book ends), young Berger realizes that he has discovered "a simple, sacred secret." Here again, the secret is what the intellectuals of the Altenburg did not know.

What has happened is what invariably happens in a Malraux novel: the prose has once again been overwhelmed by the poetry. At most, Möllberg stands convicted only of having picked up and brandished a metaphor (the "fundamental" wood) without realizing that it is two-edged and can be used against him. His argument has not been refuted rationally. The kind of knowledge Vincent Berger has derived from his view of the old trees is of a different order from the knowledge that has beaten down Möllberg's opponents. Berger's knowledge is intuition and poetry, and Malraux's art remains an art of juxtaposition and ellipsis: verification can come only from the cumulation of further insights of the same poetic order.

Thus *Les Noyers* is a reaffirmation of the significance and relevance of Malraux's old, fundamental themes. Through the interpretation of the experiences of its characters, it also offers Malraux's explanation of his own career. And in the process, it reveals an additional meaning in Malraux's novels, taken as a group, which does not emerge when they are studied individually.

The decisive event in Vincent Berger's experience is his mission to the East. Before it he is a man of action. After it he is a puzzled intellectual embarrassed by his reputation for derring-do. "In Tripolitania my father had been in action; here he merely talked" (p. 53). The mission had ended in complete failure with the discovery that although the chiefs of the Central Asiatic tribes had heard of Enver, and might be persuaded to make a gesture in his behalf provided no risk were entailed, the Turan itself— the community of all Turks—simply did not exist. The hero slowly realized that he was being defeated by Asia itself. Only when he reached Ghazni and was attacked in the bazaar by a madman, against whom he was defenseless because of the Oriental veneration of insanity, did his eyes open to the truth.

If *Les Noyers* were a political allegory one could read this experience as a transposition of Malraux's experience of revolution: he goes to the Orient, full of enthusiasm and optimism, commits himself completely to the Communist cause, willingly undergoes great hardship, and then, one day, awakes to the fundamental emptiness of what he is doing. But nothing else in the book encourages such a reading of Vincent Berger's adventure, and there is much to encourage another which is less restricted to politics.

Very early in Vincent Berger's story, his son reports a conversation with a Russian friend:

"You know what a shaman is?"

"A Siberian medicine man?"

"Something more. Lenin was a great man but no shaman. Trotsky, not so great, *was* a shaman. Pushkin, Robespierre, Goethe? No shaman in them. But Dostoevski, Mirabeau, Hölderlin, Poe—they were great shamans. There are some lesser shamans—Heine. Napoleon wasn't a true shaman; he believed too much in things. You find some shaman in geniuses and also, naturally, in idiots. There are more among us Russians than elsewhere . . . Well, the strength, and the weakness too, of Vincent Berger, comes from his being something of a shaman . . ." (P. 40.)

Now, recent literary criticism has made shamans and shamanism fascinating matter. Mr. Richard Chase, in *The Quest for Myth*, provides an illuminating summary of the meaning of the word:

> The Shaman is distinguished from his fellows by being deeply neurotic and sometimes epileptic. He is capable of the utmost extremes of depression and mania and of enduring great hardships of self-imposed isolation, through which he attains, in the eyes of his tribe, a supernatural sanction. As an initiate of the shaman caste he may retire to a lonely hut where he subjects himself to the greatest rigors of discomfort and starvation; he has trances, and he emerges from his ordeal having attained, as Radin says, "a new normalcy and re-integration." Radin suggests that the many myths concerning the change of seasons, the death and rebirth of nature (of which Frazer makes so much in *The Golden Bough*) are primarily accounts of the religious neurotic and only secondarily nature myths. Is not this psychic ordeal a profoundly human phenomenon which we might consider when thinking of a great variety of mythical themes? . . . these mythical themes have in common the withdrawal of the ego from the objective world and the subsequent return of the ego transfigured and possessed of a new potency. In some primitive societies at least, the Shaman embodied this rhythm of the psyche. Radin says that after the Shaman's ordeal, he was accepted by his fellows as a superhuman being who could change into an animal, travel at will through time and space, go to the spirit world, or be possessed by a spirit. In other words, he could do what the characters of all mythical tales could do. (P. 85.)

Certainly this discussion offers a wealth of possibilities for understanding Vincent Berger. He is not, to be sure, an epileptic; he does not change into an animal; he does not at any point have a specifically religious vision. But in other respects his personality, and more clearly still the pattern of his special experience, closely approximate those of the shaman. As in the case of so many of Malraux's characters, the motives of his conduct—particularly his thirst for power and his desire for action—amount to neuroses, the expressions of irrational desires. Berger has moments of depression and is capable of moods, some of which, like the strange feelings of liberty he experiences upon landing at Marseille and again while discussing his father's suicide, are remarkably trancelike. His experience on being beaten by the madman is presented as the awakening from a long-enduring state of bemusement. In the eyes of his tribe (the intellectuals grouped for the colloquy around his Uncle Walter) he enjoys a special status and is the object of unusual deference, while for the general public the newspapers have surrounded him with an atmosphere of mystery. Clearly this status has been won by self-imposed isolation—from his kind and from men as he has known them—and the ordeal in Central Asia has been one of serious suffering. If he has not returned "with ego inspired and possessed of a new potency," he has at least re-entered Europe in possession of a perception of truth which he did not have when he left. He knows that between his own culture and the one he had visited there exists no visible means of real communication.

But did Malraux intend to reveal so much by his chance remark about Vincent Berger's shamanism? Quite characteristically he leaves the reader to find out from other sources just what a shaman is and in just what way Berger shares the shaman's nature. The meaning of the phrase in his passage that promises the most enlightenment turns out to be elusive. Is Napoleon not a shaman because of a great capacity for *belief* "in things" (in which case "shaman" acquires a strong flavor of "charlatan") or because he believed too much in *things* (and was therefore too much a materialist)? In the pages closely following the passage, young Berger, commenting on the remark, seems to understand it to involve charlatanry: "Perhaps," he remarks. "But this shaman was also the man who once said to me, 'I want you to know that a man's strength comes from his having reduced the play actor in him to a minimum'" (p. 40). On the other hand, he declares later that his father's forthrightness and disregard for prudence in talking with his superiors in the diplomatic corps was the reverse of the medal which bore shamanism on its face. This second comment is somewhat less than helpful, since he seems to accept the imputation of cynicism which the other comment rejects—and still without our knowing precisely what the imputation means. We are thus left facing the fact that shamanism is mentioned as though it offered a key to understanding Vincent Berger and then is precipitately dropped from the discussion.

But is it? True, there are no further overtly specific references, but, on the other hand, there is the pattern of Berger's experience of life, which corresponds to that of the shaman's initiation at least in that it is the pattern of Withdrawal, Enlightenment, and Return. After this initiation into one of the archetypal forms of human experience, Berger is especially qualified to reply to the central question of Malraux's meditation on the idea of Man. He is one of the three whose testimony on the question will be treated as having special relevance. *And the other two will be men whose experience has also followed the pattern of the shaman's initiation.*

One of these does not testify in person: Dietrich Berger has committed suicide before the opening of the conference. Some years before, however, the old man had made a pilgrimage to Rome, intent on presenting to the

Pope himself certain differences which he had had with the local priest over regulations in the village church. The audience, following the long journey afoot, had been a complete failure. Overawed by the Pontiff's presence, Dietrich had not managed to say a single word! In a rage he had returned home to Reichbach by express, and from that day on the whole town could observe the marked change in his conduct. Thenceforward he had never entered the church again. Rain or shine, summer or winter, he had heard mass standing outside the building, as if he had renounced the church but not the sacraments. There was also a noticeable connection between the strangeness of his conduct and the respect mixed with awe in which he was held by the townspeople.

His suicide occasions a pivotal conversation between Vincent Berger and Dietrich's brother, Walter. The evening before he killed himself the old man had told his brother that, "whatever might happen," if he had to choose a life for himself he would choose no other than the one he had lived. "Whatever might happen" obviously referred to his self-destruction. After the event, the family had found beside Dietrich's body not only the bottle of veronal from which he had taken a fatal dose, but also a supply of strychnine and a loaded revolver. Such things had spoken eloquently of his constant determination. But at the same time he had left a note testifying to a certain inconstancy: he had originally written that he wanted no religious service at burial—and subsequently crossed out the negative. Walter, as a professional intellectual, is deeply distressed and puzzled by the obscurity of the motive: Why had Dietrich crossed out the words? What was his secret? "Essentially," Walter declares, "a man is what he hides." "A man is what he does," Vincent replies almost brutally (p. 67). And this will be the unspoken testimony of Dietrich Berger, which he is qualified to give (according to the present reading) by virtue of his having undergone the initiation of Withdrawal, Enlightenment, and Return. We do not know the nature of his enlightenment, i.e., what he learned at Rome, but we do know that, like his son's, in Ghazni, *it was precipitated by a failure to communicate.* And we do know the tenor of the testimony. "The truth is in words," will express the attitude of the intellectuals. "For the truth about man, look not to words but to acts," will be old Berger's reply. How important the reply is will become apparent on the Eastern Front of the first great war.

Meanwhile, the other significant witness is the German anthropologist, Möllberg—whom Mme Magny has identified with the late Leo Frobenius.[2] Möllberg is just returned from a trip to Africa, and the intellectuals of the

[2] "Malraux le fascinateur," *Esprit*, 16ᵉ année, No. 10 (October 1948), p. 523.

colloquy are agog because it has been reported that he has now finished his great synthesis on the nature of civilization. He is supposed to be ready to prove that the notion of man's being continuously identical with himself is entirely tenable. But when Vincent Berger meets Möllberg on the eve of the conference, he learns that the great man has changed his mind; Africa has demonstrated to him that civilizations are born, flourish, and die without passing on their triumphs each one to the next. He has scattered his manuscript page by page across the African wilds. "Appropriately," he says, "the victor is wearing the spoils of the vanquished" (p. 79).

Thus for a third time we are in the presence of a man whose experience is like the shaman's, a third instance of Withdrawal, Enlightenment, and Return. The three occurrences would seem ample justification for taking Malraux's seemingly incidental remark about Vincent Berger's shamanism very seriously indeed.

Since the characters of *Les Noyers* are so evidently reincarnations of characters in Malraux's other novels, *Les Noyers* constitutes a pressing invitation to turn back to see how often the same pattern of experience occurs in them also.

With the exception of *Man's Hope*, every one of Malraux's stories recapitulates two-thirds, at least, of the experience pattern of the shaman. The little men in *Lunes en papier* journey to Death's dark kingdom through terrible surrealist vicissitudes, and discover that Death herself is not immortal. The narrator of *Royaume farfelu* marches to the siege of the undefended city, and learns that human effort, even when unopposed, is doomed to frustration. In *La Tentation de l'occident*, "A.D." goes all the way to China to learn that Man (or Western Man at least) is condemned to be balked by the Absurd. Both *The Conquerors* and *The Royal Way* begin on shipboard, with a central character on his way to the Orient; he arrives, and undergoes an experience that gives him a new and grim perception of life. In *Man's Fate*, when Kyo, Katow, and Tchen realize that something has gone very wrong with the Shanghai insurrection, the action stops so that Kyo and Tchen may go off to Hankow to learn the real nature of the cause they fight for; they come back to Shanghai knowing the hopelessness of their plight. In *Days of Wrath*, Kassner's withdrawal takes the form not of a voyage but of a reclusion: the revelation that one is never completely alone comes while he is shut up in prison. Thus in each novel there is a Withdrawal and an Enlightenment. There is also a Return, but it is not always easily discernible. To see it well, we have to study the much-abused abstraction, "Malraux's Hero." The point is that, despite much current opinion, there is not just one "Hero" type in his work; there are at least two, and only one of these two enjoys the privilege of Return. No small part of his success comes from his having contrived to build his fictions around the destiny of significant human figures. In our time the novel has tended to concede the point that the human being has no particular, individual significance. The hero is often supplanted by a collective (see Dos Passos and Jules Romains) or by an unheroic nonentity (Kafka, Camus). But Malraux has attempted the opposite. This attempt has enthralled his critics from Emmanuel Berl to Roger Stéphane and brought down on us much irresponsible chatter.

Small doubt that the heroes of all of Malraux's books have much in common. They have their great intelligence and lucidity—for people who are alleged to have so much trouble communicating with each other, they communicate uncommonly well with the reader. They have their eternal grimness and their lack of humor. They are all eaten by obsessions. They are largely above physical appetite, to an extent almost Racinian: sex is not an appetite to them but an idea; the soldiers in *Man's Hope* are probably the only military men in recent history not to worry constantly about rations. They are usually lonely, in the cosmic sense of alienation—and if, in the ordinary sense, they are not alone, and have wives, children, or parents, they suffer for having them. With one exception, Kassner, they are all refugees from the bourgeoisie who have rejected their class, renounced its values, and set out to destroy it. They have moved out of the world familiar to the reader into the China of Revolution, the Germany of the Nazi terror, the Spain of the Civil War, the Near East of the Turkish Renaissance. Their world is one, that is, where the recourse of a man in a dispute is never to due process of law. So far so good.

But the zeal with which the critics have gone at them has made distortion inevitable. The heroes of the two earliest novels stand out with great relief because there is little else in the stories to obstruct the view. Perken and Garine are always on the stage, always in sharp focus—inveterate scene stealers. Consequently the composite Hero (the hero with the capital letter) looks much more like them than he does like Kyo, Kassner, Manuel, or Vincent Berger, not to say Claude Vannec or young Berger. We get a picture of men unhampered by scruple, thirsty for power, irrevocably committed to the Nietzschean idea of living dangerously—cosmic adventurers entirely guided by the search for their own intimate satisfaction. But the characters in *Man's Fate* and the novels that follow it hardly belong in the same category. Kyo Gisors is not engaged in a quest for personal power, and his conviction that what he is doing is for the good of his fellows involves him in a moral system. In *Days of Wrath* and *Man's Hope*, Fascism appears as a great evil, so that Kassner in the one and the Republicans in the other book are righting a wrong and their acts have a moral status. Kyo, Kassner, and Manuel are far from living as they do for the mere hell of it. If there is an adventurer in the later books it is Vincent Berger, and while at the start Berger reminds us greatly of Garine and Perken, he emerges later as a sadly distressed individual who has entirely shed the adventurer's role. In short, the concept of the single "Hero" type has been overdone.

But the disadvantage of so much insistence on the hero is not merely that a number of very diverse individuals have been forced into one cramped category. In the process, the importance of a number of other important characters has been obscured. It is not the hero of *The Conquerors* or of *The Royal Way* who makes the journey or receives the revelation. The voyager and the recipient is the companion of the hero. The anonymous narrator of *The Conquerors* and Claude Vannec in *The Royal Way* are relatively inexperienced men who have joined fortunes with men older in precisely the experience the younger ones are seeking. They stand in the relation of neophyte to initiate. In the course of the story the Initiate meets his final destiny before the eyes of the Neophyte and the latter thus comes into possession of the particular bit of knowledge which seems to be the subject of the novel—or better, to borrow Jean Hytier's term and twist it a little—its pretext.[3]

This peculiar variety of personal relationship persists throughout Malraux's novels. In *Man's Fate* there seem to be two Neophytes, Kyo and Tchen, and two Initiates, old Gisors and Katow. (Katow has been through this whole experience of revolution before, even to the point of being shot at by a firing squad.) But here we come upon an essential difference. It is now the neophytes who, instead of watching their elders live through an ultimate ordeal which they merely share, will live out the ordeal themselves.

In *Days of Wrath* Kassner is the Neophyte. The Initiate is the unknown in the adjoining cell who taps out the message of hope. Here the pattern rejoins that of the early novels. The Initiate dies once the revelation is accomplished—or at least so we assume, since Kassner hears the guard interrupt the tapping, hears the cry and the beating, and then hears nothing more.

Even in *Man's Hope*, although there is no pattern of Withdrawal, Enlightenment, and Return, the relationship of Neophyte and Initiate turns

[3] *Les Arts de littérature*, p. 31.

up. Manuel learns the trade of war from the old soldier Jimenez; Luigi Scali learns from old Alvear that revolution is not enough; Hernandez learns from Garcia what his own fate must be.

And Vincent Berger is both Neophyte and Initiate. He is the Neophyte as we read his story. But in the eyes of the younger man who tells the story the father is the Initiate. During that wild night in the tank, it is the son who is the Neophyte, verifying the truth previously revealed to the father.

As early as *The Conquerors* there is a hint of Malraux's persuasion that to these characters who go through special experiences the world is not what it seems to the rest of us. Garine and the anonymous narrator are in Marseille on the eve of the former's departure for the Orient to "attach himself to a great action." They stop before the window of a bookshop piled full of Russian novels. Garine speaks: "These writers all have the defect of never having killed anyone. If their characters suffer because they have killed men, it is because the world has not changed—almost—for them. I say *almost*. In reality, I think they would see their world completely transformed, the perspectives changed. It would become the world not of a man who has 'committed a crime,' but of a man who has killed. This world that is not transformed—not enough anyhow—I just can't believe in" (p. 82). One wonders why the remark is made at all. It has nothing visible to do with the development of the story, and reveals almost nothing about Garine. But for us, knowing the later novels, its gratuity adds to its significance; the observation may be unimportant to the story, but it is not unimportant to Malraux.

The very first episode of *Man's Fate* involves a man who is in the act of changing his world by the means specified in Garine's remark above. When Tchen murders the man in the hotel room he discovers that there are two worlds—the world of ordinary men and the world of the murderer—that they are very different from each other, and that he has condemned himself to live in the second. All the events of the remainder of his brief life stem from this discovery. And Tchen's story constitutes, in a way, a prolonged development of the implications of the remark passed by Garine at Marseille.

Up to this point, of course, what we have seen appears to be highly private and not particularly loaded with general significance. But two years after *Man's Fate*, Malraux brings Kassner out of the Nazi prison and through the storm over the mountains back to Prague. Kassner has lived through a moment when there seemed no hope of seeing Prague, and his wife Anna, again. But he is seeing Prague and he will see Anna, a familiar city and a beloved face. What he finds as he leaves the airfield is something completely unreal:

He could not recover either himself or the world. Behind a curtain, a woman was ironing quietly, with great attention. There were shirts and laundry, then, and hot irons in this strange place called the earth . . . And also hands (he was in front of a glove shop now), hands that did everything. There was nothing around him that hands had not touched or created. The earth was peopled by hands . . . He went . . . into a tobacco shop, bought cigarettes, lighted one at once, and found his unreal world again in the smoke: a milliner's window, a clockmaker's (hours for sale, for those not imprisoned), a café. People. (P. 78.)

Obviously the experience of returning to a once familiar, now unfamiliar place is not the same as committing murder. But the *feeling* a man has after he has murdered may, in Malraux's view, be extremely similar to the feeling which accompanies the return after some other ordeal. The proof of this is in *Les Noyers de l'Altenburg*. After his defeat in the Orient, Vincent Berger has taken ship, eventually disembarked at Marseille, and, for want of better to do, has gone out to stroll in the street. After six years of absence from Europe he is overwhelmed by the number of women, and by the elegance and "immodesty" of their clinging costumes, as well as by the sounds of tango music, the smells and sights and sounds of the Canebière, and even the contents of the shop windows. He feels at once detached from all this life and yet liberated by it, just as he had felt liberated by his first confession years before. It is as if he had been tossed up "into the streets of Babylon." He feels, as we learn when the mood recurs later in the story, a "stranger on the earth."

This mood is identical with Kassner's mood as he walks the streets of Prague. *Les Noyers* also identifies it as the mood of the man who has committed murder. For Berger has just read the medical testimony in the trial of some murderers, in which the criminals themselves have been quoted on the psychology of murder: "The dead individual has no importance. But afterward something you don't expect happens, the simplest things, the streets for instance, the dogs . . ." Without finishing the sentence, Vincent Berger recognizes the murderer's state of heightened consciousness as his own. "Spilled blood had the power to break through the omnipotent unawareness that permits us to live; my father had experienced the same burst of recognition, welling up from the extreme depths of his being" (p. 58).

The effect of certain experiences, then, is to endow the individual with clear, fresh, undulled vision. The experience need not necessarily be a killing. Vincent Berger and Kassner may possibly have killed men, but that is not what has brought on the state of exalted awareness. These two have in common the experience of an ordeal. Murder is one kind of ordeal for the murderer, as Tchen found out; but there are others. The specific character-istic trait of the Malraux hero, whether his name is Garine or Perken, Kyo or Katow, Kassner, Manuel, or Vincent Berger, is no more that he lives according to the precepts of Nietzsche or Dostoevski or both, or that he has been a professional adventurer or led an insurrection, than that he has submitted to the ordeal and thereby gained the vision. From the ordeal comes the special significance of what he has done, the special authority with which he speaks.

And we note that among the characters who have this authority there are certain ones who are even more privileged than the others. They re-main, after the ordeal is over, to tell the story. For them the pattern of the shaman's experience is complete in its three parts of Withdrawal, Enlighten-ment, and Return. They are the narrator of *The Conquerors*, Claude Vannec, and the younger Berger.

Malraux's interpreters, who have been extremely voluble on the subject of the resemblance between Malraux and his heroes, have said considerably less about the similarity between these fictional neophyte figures and the Malraux who studies archaeology and writes books. Yet Claude Vannec is an archaeologist who has trouble with the colonial authorities when he goes out on an expedition to Indochina, and although no emphasis is placed on the fact, a passing remark in the conversation with Rensky makes it clear that the Narrator is also an archaeologist who, like Vannec, has come out East to repair his feeble financial condition. Young Berger, though not a professional archaeologist, has an inordinately complete comprehension of the subject for an amateur. Meanwhile Vannec finds some Khmer statues, the Narrator mixes in Communist insurrection, and young Berger fights the first part of World War II in the tank corps—all of which details have a place in Malraux's own biography. Vannec and Berger even have grandfathers, unmistakably shaped on the same model, whom each feels to have possessed a secret, special knowledge of the meaning of life, and the model is old Alphonse Malraux who died in Dunkerque in 1909. Van-nec and the Narrator go through what is more or less the shaman's experi-ence: each separates himself from his kind, undertakes a protracted voyage, shares an ordeal, and emerges, so far as one can judge, an enlightened man; young Berger does not go on a trip, but he does undergo a reclusion (in the P.W. camp) and during it perceives the meaning of something which has already happened to him (the ordeal in the trapped tank). Earlier he has had one of those moments of great clarity of vision (in the farmyard on the

morning after the ordeal). There is about each of these characters, consequently, not only something that suggests the characteristic pattern of the
shaman's experience, but also something that suggests what we have heard,
to date, about Malraux's own.

The first chapter of this book ends with a promise to return, eventually,
to the subject of Malraux's legend. That "Legend of a Life of Action,"
which we said would have to be interpreted in the light of Malraux's other
creations, reveals the contours of the now familiar pattern. Its central figure,
from one angle at least, looks remarkably like many of the characters in the
novels. Vincent Berger's strength, and also his weakness, lay (we learned
early in *Les Noyers*) in his being something of a shaman. Malraux's lie
nowhere else.

Strip the legend of its gossipy details and what is left?

Essentially the story of a special personality. In its wildest flights, of
course, the legend does not quite make Malraux an epileptic, and thus it
deprives him of part of the standard equipment of the authentic primitive
shaman, but it leaves no doubt as to the intensity of his personality. The
rapidity of his intelligence and the almost compulsive flow of his conversation are constantly cited. Exterior symptoms of interior tension—his
chain smoking, his nervous mannerisms, his special tricks of speech—never
go unmentioned. His political opponents habitually characterize him as
"feverish." He qualifies completely as an individual out of the ordinary
run. The possessor of the personality undertakes a long journey, and is
absent from his haunts for a long period. During the absence he undergoes
great hardship and danger. The details are vague. One is never quite sure
just what the dangers were or how great was the hardship, but all versions
of the legend insist that dangers and hardship there were. Some sort of
ordeal waited for him in Asia, possibly the ordeal by anguish through humiliation, but in any case an ordeal. Then he returns, speaking as if he
possessed special enlightenment. He writes about man's fate in parables,
somewhat oracularly, rising above the logic of the unenlightened, express-
ing a vision. Almost immediately he acquires prestige within his group.
After a few years he is referred to as the "Witness." And he not only becomes a leader but, as time passes, becomes progressively more willing to
tell his fellows what direction to take, and what to do. In brief, the legend
that has grown up about Malraux is one more version of the shaman's experience, in general line more complete than the experience appears to be
in any of the novels.

This is not to say that Malraux is subject to hallucinations. He does
not confuse himself with the figure of the primitive miracle man, or any-

thing of the sort. We are talking only of a type of personality and a form of the imagination, a configuration which, judging from the evidence of *Les Noyers*, Malraux recognizes. He is amply qualified to recognize it, by a familiarity with anthropological literature which dates, almost certainly, from his years at the School for Oriental Languages, and by his own studies of art, which have always borne a marked anthropological cast. He has read Frobenius, whose *History of African Civilization* caught the imagination of so many European intellectuals, and whom some critics believe to be the model for Möllberg in *Les Noyers*. And it is precisely this same Frobenius, one of the boldest (his enemies add "and least responsible") generalizers among recognized anthropologists, who proposes the notion that shamanism is one of the two fundamental dispositions which the human mind can assume toward what is outside the mind; he calls shamanism the disposition of the individual temperamentally unable to accept the natural order of reality. If Malraux takes such ideas at all seriously, how could he have failed to recognize himself? And what is the habit which I have called the fundamental characteristic of his writing, the habit of juxtaposing with an account of one man's defeat an image somehow suggestive of man's victory, but the refusal to "accept the natural order of reality"? The studies of the anthropologists offer him an explanation of his personality, and of the shape of his own career, in terms of the eternally human.

Hence the powerful element of unity which, for all the evidence of Malraux's evolution, pervades everything he has written. Like the shaman, he is the possessor of a special knowledge. Thanks to a peculiarly decisive experience, he has seen what the world is, and what man's particular place is in it. Each of his writings is an effort to communicate this vision of man's world.

The vision is an exceedingly grim one. Our world is one of violence. We are here as on a darkling plain, certainly. But there is no good in appealing to love. (Note that there is not one important woman character in Malraux's novels; May, Kyo's wife, comes the nearest to being one, and even she remains decidedly secondary.) Not love but suffering is the rule. And the suffering is irremediable. Cruelty is everywhere: all men experience it, and all men are capable of inflicting it. Each is tortured by his private anxieties and obsessions. And at the end there is death and nothing more. This is man's destiny.

Yet man does not have to accept the destiny that is forced upon him. He can repudiate it. He can behave, if the strength is in him, as if he were not its victim. He can attain human dignity, and a feeling of brotherhood with other men. He can, in other words, refuse to bow. And this refusal to incline to destiny has marked the human race.

This is the vision that all of Malraux's novels report—and of which *Les Noyers de l'Altenburg*, through Vincent Berger's experience, and the explicit identification of Malraux with the same human type, forces us to be particularly aware. Because of its revealing the presence and the nature of the vision, *Les Noyers* is a necessary key to the full meaning of the novels that precede it.

For the same reason, it is the necessary preface to Malraux's writings about the psychology of art.

CHAPTER SEVEN

Art and Destiny

> *"Our time realizes that art is one of the fundamental defenses against our fate."*
>
> —MALRAUX TO AN INTERVIEWER, *Arts,*
> November 30, 1951

EVERYONE has suspected for years that the vision of man counted as heavily for Malraux in his essays on art as in his novels, but only recently have critics begun to say so forthrightly. The subject was perilous. *The Psychology of Art* was a finished job in no sense of the word. It had been written in fragments, and these had been assembled in the volumes in a way that suggested haste to get to press. As studies they were blighted by the difficulty in ordering materials that is characteristic of Malraux's work in general. Critics were long obliged to work with what amounted to a preliminary draft in which the expression of the vision, if not the vision itself, was incoherent. The essay on modern methods of reproduction and their effect on our knowledge of art, like the essay on the development of modern art, seemed only thinly connected with his discourses on the meaning of style, the relation of style to culture, and the process by which artists achieve originality. Attempts to paraphrase and summarize only emphasized the incoherence, to the point where one critic complained that Malraux had made clear only that French was no longer the language of clear expression.[1] The shrewdest hedged their comments with reservations: no judgment formed without Volume III could be anything but tentative. And when at length they got Volume III, they learned from it that the work of revision was already in progress. It was still necessary to postpone judgment.

Malraux's message remained breathless, oracular, and elliptical. His style was still the style of the novels. Transitions were frequently omitted. Paragraphs often ended in suspension points which invited the reader to complete the author's thought. The basic technique, which consisted of placing side by side pieces of art, possibly originating thousands of years apart in time and thousands of miles apart in space, so that they might offer their own testimony, was recognizably similar to the elliptical juxtapositions of the novels. Only when the reader was already convinced that, given the shamanistic shape of Malraux's imagination, the work must contain a view of man, did he begin to see the vision take form. Even for

---

[1] Henri Peyre, "La Saison littéraire," *French Review*, XXII (December 1948), 101.

those who were looking for it, the vision remained incoherent; this is clear from the number of sympathetic and intelligent French critics who took *The Psychology of Art* to be a "Spenglerian" book.

Actually, Malraux's thesis—whatever else it may have been—was the exact opposite of Spengler's. The critics had been led astray, most probably, by an almost universal misreading not of the *Psychology* but of *Les Noyers*. For the winner of the argument at the Priory is not Vincent Berger but the anthropologist Möllberg, the man who left the pages of his "Civilization as Conquest and Destiny" scattered page by page across the African plain. Berger quits the colloquy at intermission precisely because Möllberg's arguments have stopped him, as well as the other participants, dead in their tracks. They have not been able to invoke one single binding argument for the continuity of cultures and the continuous identity of man. The knowledge vouchsafed Vincent Berger by the symbolic walnut trees is nothing that he can present in refutation of Möllberg's position, because it belongs to another order of knowledge. Möllberg's view, if not entirely Spengler's, at least corroborates the main thesis of *The Decline of the West*: civilizations do not develop one out of another; they merely germinate, flourish, and decay without significant transmissions. This is what Vincent Berger knows, but knows *irrationally*, not to be true.

The *rational* refutation of Möllberg and Spengler is *The Psychology of Art*. Actually the intention of refuting Spengler antedates *Les Noyers* by many years. Malraux urged the necessity of such a refutation upon his friend Berl as early as 1928.[2] His recourse to the study of art as a means of refuting a philosophy of history constitutes the great originality of the *Psychology*.

Synthetic treatments of art, organized to substantiate a philosophical thesis, are at least as old as Taine and familiar through the more recent works of Elie Faure. Malraux's innovation lies in the discovery that through the study of art the argument against Spengler can be recast outside the confines of political history. If, for example, the decline of the Roman world is an argument in favor of Spengler, there is an argument against him in showing that the so-called regression of Romanesque art was not a regression but the development, out of the old one, of the characteristic expression of a new culture.

Hence the importance of the three ideas that recur regularly throughout

[2] See Emmanuel Berl, *La Culture en péril*. The dedicatory letter to Malraux recalls conversations on the subject going back to 1928, and adds that since 1942 Malraux had been saying that the most pressing of intellectual tasks was the refutation of Spengler.

the three volumes: a style is an inseparable badge of a culture; no culture develops its style *ex nihilo* but "conquers" it, "wresting" it from a culture that has preceded; an artist begins to be an artist not by imitating nature but by imitating artists who have gone before him. Obviously the third proposition not only gives the three volumes their common title but also stands as the universal principle of the psychology of art which legitimizes the second—one style develops out of another because artists begin by imitation—and the first is significant only as an axiom which confers upon the second its special importance. These are the central themes, and however far in given instances Malraux may wander from the main argument, what he is saying is generally intelligible with reference to one or another of them.

Beneath all three ideas lies Malraux's intention to work through to his conclusion about man, his long-standing concern about man's fate. His first novel, so he wrote in reply to Trotsky, had been written to "denounce man's fate"; the same phrase appears early in *The Psychology of Art*: ". . . that [the denunciation] of the human predicament, in art, [leads] to the destruction of the forms which accept it" (I, 127). In both cases, the French words are *accuser la condition humaine*. In the second case, he is stating the principal theme of the work which is, in a sense, his *Faust*.

From an opening statement on the significance of the museum as we have known it since the nineteenth century he moves to the composition of an imaginary, and ideal, one—the one "without walls." Museums, he alleges, have imposed a new relationship between the viewer and the work of art by taking away the original function of the work and by separating the individual work from everything but other works of art. Models fade in importance and the portrait becomes a picture; more generally, the subject becomes a matter of indifference. The relationship between viewer and thing viewed automatically becomes more intellectualized. New methods of reproduction extend the original possibilities of the museum. The masterpiece is no longer judged against an ideal, but against the other works of its particular style, and, in the same way, what is the best work of an artist is determined by comparison with the rest of his work. Then, when one sees enough examples of a given style together—as is now easily possible—one is able to see what are the great masterpieces *of the style* and to prefer them to the alleged masterpieces which owe their reputations to their similarity with masterpieces of *other* styles. According to Malraux, this changes the orientation of our ideas about art: Gothic statues, for example, are inferior to Greek only if we think of them as imitations of the Greek. And we are at last able to base our judgments on the knowledge of the world's entire fund of art. By being transportable, photographs bring the complete treasure to hand, and by magnifying or reducing the originals to a common scale, they emphasize the common qualities of style. Color photography further reveals the use of color for stylistic expression in such things as Byzantine painting, Gothic glass, and Persian rugs. These qualities make the ideal museum not only possible but also vastly significant.

In it will go all the art—that is, all the styles—in which our time finds special meaning. This includes all of modern art, which Malraux defines as the art that does not try to be fiction or anything else except itself; and with it he puts the arts of Egypt, of the Euphrates, of Byzantium, the art of the savage, the pre-Phidian, Cretan, Assyrian, Babylonian, pre-Columbian and prehistoric, as well as the drawings on the old Greek vases, the art of the steppes, Roman frescoes, and Chinese, Japanese, and Indian sculpture. With these he would put the *Pietàs* of Villeneuve and of Nouhans, and the work of El Greco, Georges de Latour, Uccello, Le Nain, Vermeer, Chardin, Masaccio, Piero della Francesca, and Daumier, the painters in whom Malraux sees the forerunners of the moderns. He would exclude Hellenistic and Roman art, Italian eclecticism, the Bolognese school, the English followers of Van Dyke, and the nineteenth-century Academics. These, he says, have "lost their virtue." He might "perhaps" exclude Raphael, for the same reason. He would also exclude the great Greeks because they were so fully in accord with the world they knew, and the painters of "a world reconciled with God" precisely because they were reconciled. The arts and artists he retains as especially "ours" are those who were "in disaccord," who were "not reconciled," or who "put the world in question."

In other words, Malraux is interrogating, in an extremely roundabout way, the tastes and preferences of our time, asking of course what these tastes reveal about art, but more urgently still what they reveal about us. In his inquest, style becomes paramount, for, he says, "style no longer appears to us as merely the common character of a school or an epoch—the consequence or the ornament of a vision—but as the fundamental thing that the school or the epoch was searching for . . ." He adds that he is ready to define art as "that by virtue of which form becomes style."

Much that Malraux says in the first volume presupposes in the reader an acceptance of the psychological relationship between a time and its art, and between the artist and his matter, which he treats at length only in the second—just as many of his remarks on the tragic significance of our preferences are fully intelligible only when he returns to them in the third. His exposition is anything but rectilinear. *The Psychology of Art* appears to have grown by a process of retouching and enlargement, as if, on rereading his first volume, Malraux had decided both that given details needed development and that, instead of inserting the development where the logic of his discourse required it, he might better defer it to a later volume. Half of the third volume consists of supplementary studies, which the reader is invited to insert at appropriate points in his reading of earlier passages. The second volume leads back from modern art, where the first ended, to the arts of Byzantium and Macedonian India, the Romanesque and the Gothic and the Chinese, in a long demonstration of how styles correspond to the attitudes of nations or times toward the Eternal, how so many are dominated by an impulse to "escape from the human," and how one style "wrested" from another what it needed for its own characteristic expression. The third volume in turn swings back to modern art by way of the European painters who were its forerunners—but with a lengthy side-excursion into primitive art—and thence to Malraux's conclusion regarding the nature of modern art. Repetitions are necessarily numerous.

Whether Malraux is right in the instances he chooses as illustration is a matter for professionals of the subject. Many of his technical affirmations have been contested. What is incontestable is that he sees the establishment of a style as a conquest. (He uses the verb *arracher*, to wrest or tear, constantly.) And given his view that a style expresses the most intimate aspirations of its civilization, civilization must be conquest also, the victory of values over rival values. Similarly, the development of the artist himself also involves a conquest. Artists, Malraux maintains, begin by learning, not from observation of the world around them but from other artists. Each one achieves his originality, "begins to speak with his own voice," when he "tears" away from the art he has known. Creation is a struggle between an imitated form and the form that is potential in the artist. Modes of vision are a delusion, according to Malraux; the exterior world does not look different to one artist from what it looks to another; the artist sees what he wants to see, and as his style makes him want to see it. The mark of the true artist is his obscure but fanatical desire to break, at all costs, with the style in which he has been formed. This is the essential psychological factor in the creative personality, and comes very close to constituting the psychology of art.

Except for a few moments in which men came to accept their human destiny, Malraux feels, the process of creation has also reflected the determination of "the only animal who knows he is going to die" to recreate the world in a form acceptable to the human; it imposes a human order. Art is, in such cases, a refusal to accept the world as the artist finds it.

Such a refusal, to Malraux, is a refusal to accept the human condition. We have returned to the subject of human destiny.

Now, with the beginning of the third volume, Malraux returns to modern art through the sources from which it takes its special character. The power that the art of a given civilization has to "wrest" from the earlier arts what is significant to it, Malraux calls "annexation," and his intention is now to explain, in terms already broadly hinted at, the "annexations" performed by Occidental artists since the middle of the nineteenth century, not only upon historically earlier styles but upon the arts of the primitive cultures which, Malraux believes, can be said to have existed "outside history." Added to his doctrine regarding style, and the transmission which takes place from culture to culture through the annexation of elements of style, this concept of the man who, far from being left behind by history, has never been part of history at all, completes his response to Spengler. The fact that our art reaches back in the past to take what it needs joins the fact that it reaches across simultaneously existing cultures to refute the argument for "closed" cultures. And at long last, when the refutation is completed, Malraux mentions Spengler's name (III, 146).

But art is not merely an "anti-history." It is also an "anti-destiny." And its character as a defiance of man's destiny is the principal distingushing characteristic of our modern art. Since the middle of the nineteenth century, art has been, he says, an "Absolute," i.e., its own end. It has enjoyed the possibility, unique in history, of choosing what it will "annex" from a heritage now world wide and as ancient as the centuries. The mood of annexation has been followed by one of questioning (Cézanne has been followed by Picasso), but the interrogation focuses upon what we have annexed. And the choice of what we would annex, and subsequently interrogate, has invariably fallen upon those arts which have *refused to accept man's fate*. Our art is a refusal to accept chaos and thus expresses a will to impose an order, man's order, upon the chaos he is condemned to live in. Modern art, Malraux says, is agnostic: it sees nothing behind or beyond the chaos, no pre-established order to be sought out, and in this sense admits nothing eternal . . . except the eternal refusal to accept the ultimate disorder. The mark of the human, he believes, is not in Saint-Exupéry's affirmative "I have done what no animal could have done," but rather in the ability to refuse.

At this point, Malraux's prose comes close to being poetry, and he falls into the slow, compulsive rhythms which recall those of the most intense passages in his novels:

Nous savons bien que ce mot tire son accent de ce qu'il exprime notre dé-

pendance, et la part mortelle de tout ce qui doit mourir. Il y a dans notre conscience une faille tantôt éclatante et tantôt secrète, qu'aucun dieu ne protège
toujours: les saints appellent aridité leur désespoir, et «Pourquoi m'as-tu aban-
donné?» est, pour le christianisme, le cri de l'homme même. Le temps coule peut-
être vers l'éternité, et sûrement vers la mort. Mais le destin n'est pas la mort, il est
fait de tout ce qui impose à l'homme la conscience de son néant, et d'abord sa solitude; c'est pourquoi, contre lui, l'homme s'est si souvent réfugié dans l'amour; c'est
pourquoi les religions défendent l'homme contre lui—même lorsqu'elles ne le défendent pas contre la mort—en le reliant à Dieu ou à l'univers. Nous connaissons
la part de l'homme qui se veut toute-puissance et immortalité. Nous savons que
l'homme ne prend pas conscience de lui-même par les mêmes voies que du monde;
et que chacun est pour soi-même un monstre de rêves. (III, 146.)

Well we know that this word gets its tone from the fact that it expresses our
dependence and expresses the mortality of everything that must die. We know that
in ourselves there is a weak point that no god can watch over constantly: the saints
call their despair aridness, and "Why hast thou forsaken me?" is, for the Christian,
the cry of man himself. Time sweeps on, perhaps toward eternity, and certainly
toward death. But destiny is not death—it is made up of everything that makes
man aware of his nothingness, and, first of all, of his solitude; that is why man has
so often taken refuge in love, and why religions protect man against his destiny—
even when they do not defend him against death—by making him a bond with
God and the universe. We know the side of man that wants to be omnipotent
and immortal. We know that man's awareness of himself is not formed in the same
way as his awareness of the world; and we know that for himself each one is a
monster of dreams.

As the style recalls the earlier works with such force, so the sense of
Malraux's statements picks up the old motifs and even echoes the old
phrases. Solitude and love, death and destiny, and man's old desire to
enjoy the exemptions of a god are present in the passage just above. Immediately following the quoted lines Malraux recalls Kyo's story in *Man's
Fate*. Four pages later he is saying that the *quality* of man is the ultimate
object of culture, and we are thrown back into the scene between Scali and
old Alvear in *Man's Hope* where the two students of art discuss the ultimate
objects of Revolution during the burning of Madrid. Earlier he has picked
up a whole phrase from *Man's Fate*: "We know that the Tahitians were
much less cruel than the Confucian sages who promulgated so many frightful laws . . ." (III, 91), and on the same page occur two sentences which
have the tone, though not the sense, of Möllberg's speech about the Gothic
wood-sculptures in *Les Noyers*: "Such and such a wooden Breton crucifix
(not the Crucifixion groups), or the Christ of Nowy Targ, are Christian

only in appearance. They are less a part of degenerative Christian art than the expression of a multimillennial feeling about life."

These recalls and echoes are so many that they must be in the text by design. They suggest that *The Psychology of Art* must have represented to him, at the time of writing, something like a testament—not by any means that he intended to write nothing more, but that, if anything prevented further writing, these pages could stand as his final utterance upon the themes that have always been his special concern.

If this is so, then the word *destin*, upon which everything hinges at the end of *The Psychology of Art*, should undergo further scrutiny. This destiny which he sees the modern artist confront as representative of Western man, he defines as "everything which imposes on man the awareness of his own insignificance (*néant*)." Elsewhere in the last volume he makes destiny the equivalent of *chaos*. These words should be kept in mind as we turn back to a passage in the second volume where Malraux speaks of the early Christians and their willingness to accept martyrdom in the name of a belief which permitted them to deny that man's suffering is meaningless. ". . . Pour le mendiant, pour l'humilié, pour l'infirme [he writes] quelque chose a [it] été plus nécessaire même que l'autre monde: *échapper à l'absurdité et à la solitude* de la douleur sans espoir" (II, 118). The italics are mine. Modern art's refusal comes extremely close, here, to being a refusal of the Absurd, written with a capital.

The note at the end of *The Twilight of the Absolute* had made it clear that Malraux was not completely satisfied with his work. There would be a new version, he promised, and the changes made would ensure a better ordering of the materials. The note sounded as if the work of revision would be mainly a paste-and-shears job, and quite possibly such a job was all that Malraux originally intended. He had realized that, as a discourse on the nature of art, *Psychology of Art* suffered from the lack of continuity and flow that had characterized this work as it had the novels.

But while *The Twilight of the Absolute* was in the printer's hands Malraux fell ill. The months of convalescence were long. As late as June 1951, he could take only a limited part in the first electoral campaign in which the Gaullists participated as a full-fledged political party. Thus he had time on his hands, and the work of revision went far beyond what he seems at first to have intended. *Les Voix du Silence* is not only a reordered *Psychology of Art*; it is a third longer than the *Psychology*, and—between the effect of the reordering and the effect of the additions—is really a very different book. The reader is much less frequently confronted by ellipses which place the burden of responsibility for the meaning squarely upon him; in general, Malraux's prose is now much less sibylline. Explanation frequently removes the oracular nature of the original utterance or, at least, chastens it.

There are now four parts instead of three. Part One is still *The Museum Without Walls*, but with more exclusive attention to the idea of the "museum" itself and much less digression into subjects properly the matter of later divisions. Part Two, originally *The Creative Act*, has now become two parts, "Les Métamorphoses d'Apollon" and "La Création artistique." The French title of the last is the one translated in the *Psychology* as *The Creative Act*, but the matter is vastly different—Malraux has now separated the subject of the evolution of styles from the problem of the artist's originality. "Les Métamorphoses d'Apollon" is entirely devoted to the relation of one style to another and "La Création artistique" to how the artist comes "to speak with his own voice"; the essential theses are not changed but a certain confusion is eliminated. Finally, "The Twilight of the Absolute" remains devoted to the subject treated under the same title, but is strengthened by the presence of material rescued from the previous parts, where it appears now to have been completely out of place.

In other words, *Les Voix du silence* is no longer a collection of essays on more or less related subjects, written at various times and places; it is much more a book. The logic of its development is clearly evident. Part One establishes the condition which makes the subsequent parts possible; Part Two examines the development of art as the expression of cultures; Part Three explains, in terms of what the artist, as artist, must do, how the process in Part Two operates; and Part Four draws the conclusions about the meaning of art and the fundamental nature of man.

In a way, *Les Voix du silence* is less exciting reading than its predecessor. It gains in clarity over the earlier version, but it is heavier because of the added detail, slower because of the accumulated explanations. No doubt many of the latter are designed to meet objections raised in criticisms of the *Psychology*. No doubt also that, as a discussion of art, *Les Voix* is a "sounder," less vulnerable book than the earlier version. One cannot avoid the feeling that it was written for a slightly different audience—the professionals of the subject.

In so far as it is written for the professionals, they must be the ones to judge it, just as they alone could judge some aspects of *The Psychology of Art*. Relatively few of those readers who were originally attracted to Malraux by the power of his novels will possess the detailed familiarity with the fine arts which alone can qualify one to pass judgment. And yet

Les Voix du silence, like the *Psychology,* is at once prose discourse and poem—and of the poem it is our business to take account.

Actually, the poetic nature of the later version is more hidden. In increasing the amount of detail, Malraux has had to subdue his language. The verb *arracher,* which recurs so frequently in the *Psychology* that it can almost be said to constitute a leitmotiv, now appears much less frequently, as does another of Malraux's favorite words, *obsédant.* And in general, the tone of explanation in the first three parts rather crowds out the ejaculatory tone (the tone in which one affirms that a thing is because it is. One is aware that the tension has, in general, been relaxed.

But in the rearrangement of the fourth part, the process is reversed. The tension increases again, and actually gains in effect through the contrast with the earlier parts of the book. This is not a quality that can be demonstrated by the juxtaposition of sample passages taken from the contrasting parts, because the effect of the final pages is cumulative and fully available only if the conclusion is read at length. But there is no question: the whole of *Les Voix du silence* is meant to lead up to the full, somber poetry of the last part, and to the final sentence of the book. At the end of the second volume of *The Psychology of Art,* with a whole volume yet to come, Malraux had written: "Et cette main, dont les millénaires suivent le tremblement dans le crépuscule, tremble d'une des formes secrètes, et les plus hautes, de la force et de l'honneur d'être homme."

"And that hand, trembling in the twilight as the accumulated centuries stand by, trembles with one of the secret forms, and with one of the finest, of the power and the glory of being a man." This sentence now appears (with one word changed: *suivent* has been replaced by *accompagnent,* without changing the essential meaning) as the last sentence, the very last, of *Les Voix du silence.* A part of this sentence has already appeared in this book, as epigraph to the chapter on *Man's Fate.* It could doubtless have been used, with equal appropriateness, as epigraph to any of the other chapters. For *Les Voix du silence* turns out to be, as one comes to the last page, another treatment of Malraux's eternal subject, the subject of all his tragic poetry.

For art, as Malraux summed up his view for a newspaper interviewer[3] when *Les Voix du silence* was published, is one of the most potent weapons at man's disposal for resisting, and refusing, his destiny. Destiny takes many forms: history (Spengler's history) is one; the Absurd is another.

We are not far here from hearing the words of Garine: "One can live in the Absurd, but not in an acceptance of the Absurd." And the modern

[3] *Arts,* No. 335 (November 30, 1951), p. 1.

artist, as Malraux pictures him, becomes a kindred figure to "A.D.," the character in *La Tentation de l'occident* who at the end of that book is left sitting in "the Chinese night," promising himself never to quail before the absurdity he has discovered to be man's lot. The picture of the artist standing upon his refusal reminds us of Kassner and his violent struggle against insanity; the prison in which the hero of *Days of Wrath* is confined seems to stand as a symbol for the destiny within which all men are confined. One even sees an added relevance now in Katow's demonstration, at the end of *Man's Fate*, that a man can literally transcend the circumstances of his ignominy.

Thus Malraux's "message," as we get it from the art books, reflects the view of man which he has constantly proposed in his novels ever since his return from the crucial sojourn in the Orient, back in 1927. His books are all expressions of the same enlightenment, the fruits of the same ordeal, the aftermath of the same withdrawal. This is the sense in which they can be said to be unified, in spite of the obvious evolution that has gone on over the years. And this unity, doubtless, explains his great prestige among his kind, and the impressive number of his readers. We read him for the pleasure of seeing the peculiar problems and predicaments of our time ordered, under the form of art, so as to reveal the truth that they have been man's problems from all eternity. Better, it seems, than anyone else writing today, Malraux has told us that eternity includes the twentieth century.

Appendix, Bibliography
and Index

Appendix: Malraux's Politics

M OST recent discussions of Malraux's politics have assumed that his
appearance in the entourage of General de Gaulle constituted an
abrupt and violent about-face. Critics could not forget that he had put
in the mouth of Manuel, in *Man's Hope*, ominous words to the effect that a
determined pessimist, unless he has "a fidelity back of him," is or will be a
Fascist. They felt that in abandoning Communism he had also abandoned
his "fidelities." In consequence they feared the worst.

Now that the political furor has subsided a bit, the evidence that
Malraux abandoned everything he had been faithful to is rather less impressive. The party he broke with between 1939 and 1945 was hardly
the party that had had his sympathy—small difference whether or not he
ever held a party card—back in 1924–25. In 1924 the arteries of the party
of Stalin *and* Trotsky had not yet hardened, and the questions who was
orthodox and who heretic were still open. Over the intervening years they
were to be closed, bloodily, and Malraux's novels themselves might be read,
by those so disposed, as a history of the process. Malraux has argued,
eloquently, that it is Communism that has changed more than he.[1]

Meanwhile, is it so entirely clear that he has abandoned the extreme
Left for the extreme Right? The disposition of De Gaulle's Rassemblement
Populaire Français has not been tested at this writing. Its constituents
come both from the Right and from the Left. We know perfectly well
what they are against: they are anti-Communist. But what are they for?
And is there cohesion enough in their body to stand the strain of assuming governmental power, or would the weight of a positive program put
into action bring about a split? And if we cannot answer these questions,
just how certain is it that Malraux and his party should be placed so far
to the Right?

What Malraux has written since 1945 surely does not have a Rightist
resonance. The books on art refute the views of Spengler. Of the two,
which more clearly reflects the Fascist *Weltanschauung*, *The Decline of
the West* or the belief in the continuity of man and his culture? These
ideas on art, it should be noted, are ideas which Malraux began to express
long before his break with the Communists. They may well survive the
termination of Malraux's association with De Gaulle.

[1] See the "Address to Intellectuals" delivered at the Salle Pleyel, March 5, 1948, and reprinted in the Grasset (1949) edition of *The Conquerors*.

What we know about Malraux's politics at this moment is what we know about those of his party: he is belligerently opposed to Stalinist Communism. But have we ever known more about his politics, actually, than what they were opposed to? I doubt it.

Before his departure for Indochina he seems to have been politically unformed, vague. The fact that he wrote a preface to a politically oriented book by Maurras indicates little, especially since we lack any sort of supporting evidence. And the reflection of his politics in his first novel is also vague; his revolutionaries are Communists, to be sure, but it is as revolutionaries rather than as Communists that they interest him. One could sum up his first attachment to Communism as a revolt against European values, the rupture discussed at length in this book.

And to the extent that the politics of *Man's Fate* can be summed up at all, they also are best expressed negatively: Stalin's Communist International is responsible for the deaths of Kyo, Katow, and Tchen. *Man's Fate* can hardly be said to recommend Stalin.

But *Man's Hope*? Certainly the book, in its propaganda aspect at least, pleads the necessity of following the Communists. But is it pro-Stalinist? Or is it rather anti-Fascist? The more we contemplate Malraux's attitudes of the 'thirties, the more we are tempted to define them negatively: he was for Stalin *because* he was against Fascism. Fascism was the greater danger. When graver danger threatened more immediately from another quarter, Malraux changed his political orientation.

One way to put it would be to say that Malraux's politics seems always to have been a politics of refusal. He has chosen his shifting political colors with reference to what, at any particular time, he could *not* accept. The focus of his "fidelities" has not lain in the parties themselves, but in a set of values which—according to the moment—one party or another has appeared best able to protect. What those values are is implicit in all of his work, explicit in his writings upon art. The essential question which bothered so many Frenchmen between 1945 and 1950, when *le cas Malraux* was so violently actual, was poorly put: instead of asking what to fear of a man who had no loyalties, it should have asked what Malraux's loyalties really were.

Bibliography

By Malraux:

This listing is not complete; I have not seen some of the small magazines in which certain early writings are supposed to have appeared. It enlarges and corrects, however, the bibliography in *Biblio*, 16e année, No. 10 (December 1948), pp. 8–9. Purely journalistic writings and articles later reprinted in books are not listed.

"La Genèse des chants de Maldoror," *Action*, No. 3 (April 1920), pp. 13–14.

"Mobilités," *Action*, No. 4 (July 1920), pp. 13–14.

"Prologue," *Action*, No. 5 (October 1920), pp. 18–20. (A first version of the opening pages of *Lunes en papier*.)

Lunes en papier. Simon, 1921.

"Journal d'un pompier du jeu de massacre," *Action*, No. 8 (August 1921), pp. 16–18. (A fragment apparently intended for a book to be called *Écrits pour une idole à trompe*. This title is listed in several bibliographies but I have never seen it and the alleged author informs me that it was never published.)

"Aspects d'André Gide," *Action*, 3e année [not numbered] (March-April 1922), pp. 17–21.

"Introduction," *Mademoiselle Monk*, by Charles Maurras. Stock, 1923.

La Tentation de l'occident. Grasset, 1926.

"D'une jeunesse européenne," in *Écrits*, with other essays by André Chamson, Jean Grenier, and Henri Petit, and three poems by P.-J. Jouve; seventieth and last volume of *Les Cahiers verts*. Grasset, 1927.

"Ecrit pour un ours en peluche," *900*, No. 4 (Summer 1927). (I have not seen the periodical but have used a typescript furnished by Malraux.)

"Le Voyage aux iles fortunées," *Commerce*, cahier 12 (Summer 1927), pp. 95–131. (Varies only slightly from first part of *Royaume farfelu*.)

✻*Les Conquérants*. Grasset, 1928.

Royaume farfelu. Gallimard, 1928.

"Où le cœur se partage, par Marcel Arland," *Nouvelle Revue Française*, 15e année, No. 173 (February 1, 1928), pp. 250–52.

"L'Imposture, par Georges Bernanos," *Nouvelle Revue Française*, 15e année, No. 174 (March 1, 1928), pp. 406–8.

"Contes, historiettes et fabliaux," "Dialogue d'un prêtre et d'un moribond, par le Marquis de Sade," *Nouvelle Revue Française*, 15e année, No. 177 (June 1, 1928), pp. 853–55.

"L'Enfant et l'écuyère, par Franz Hellens," *Nouvelle Revue Française*, 15ᵉ année, No. 179 (August 1, 1928), pp. 291–92.

"Battling le ténébreux, par Alexandre Vialatte," *Nouvelle Revue Française*, 16ᵉ année, No. 183 (December 1, 1928), pp. 869–70.

"Journal de voyage d'un philosophe, par Hermann Keyserling," *Nouvelle Revue Française*, 16ᵉ année, No. 189 (June 1, 1929), pp. 884–86.

"Les Conquérants, fragment inédit," *Bifur*, No. 4 (December 31, 1929), pp. 5–15.

✳*La Voie royale*. Grasset, 1930.

"Réponse à Léon Trotsky," *Nouvelle Revue Française*, 19ᵉ année, No. 211 (April 1, 1931), pp. 501–7.

"Préface," *L'Amant de Lady Chatterley*, by D. H. Lawrence. Gallimard, 1932.

"Jeune Chine," *Nouvelle Revue Française*, 20ᵉ année, No. 220 (January 1, 1932), pp. 5–7.

"Documents secrets, par Franz Hellens," *Nouvelle Revue Française*, 20ᵉ année, No. 224 (April 1, 1932), pp. 915–16.

✳*La Condition humaine*. Gallimard, 1933.

"Exposition Fautrier," *Nouvelle Revue Française*, 21ᵉ année, No. 233 (February 1, 1933), pp. 345–46.

"A l'hôtel des sensations inédites," *Marianne*, December 13, 1933.

"Préface," *Sanctuaire*, by William Faulkner. Gallimard, 1933.

"Les Traqués, par M. Matveev," *Nouvelle Revue Française*, 22ᵉ année, No. 249 (June 1, 1934), pp. 1014–16.

"L'Art est une conquête," *Commune*, Nos. 13–14 (September-October 1934), pp. 68–71.

"L'Attitude de l'artiste," *Commune*, No. 15 (November 1934), pp. 166–75.

Le Temps du mépris. Gallimard, 1935.

"L'Œuvre d'art," *Commune*, No. 23 (July 1935), pp. 264–66.

"Réponse aux 64," *Commune*, No. 27 (December 1935), pp. 410–16.

    See: "L'Intelligence française devant le Guerre d'Ethiopie,—pour la défense de l'Occident," *Le Temps*, October 4, 1935. A manifesto in favor of Mussolini signed by Henri Massis, Charles Maurras, André Rousseaux, Thierry Meaulnier, Gabriel Marcel, and others.

"Préface," *Indochine S.O.S.*, by Andrée Viollis. Gallimard, 1935.

De Dimitrov à Thälmann: Echec au Fascisme. Bureau d'éditions, 4 rue Saint-Germain-l'Auxerreois. Undated pamphlet.

Boukharine. Les problèmes fondamentaux de la culture contemporaine. Association pour l'étude de la culture soviétique, 6 Place du Panthéon. Undated. (I have not seen this pamphlet.)

✳*L'Espoir*. Gallimard, 1937.

Tableau de la littérature française. Gallimard, 1939. (Contains Malraux's chapter on Choderlos de Laclos. Gide, who wrote the Preface for the volume, refers to the book as Malraux's enterprise. See *Journal*, September 1, 1928.)

✳ *La Lutte avec l'Ange*, J. Lausanne-Yverdon, Editions du haut pays, 1943. (First publication of *Les Noyers de l'Altenburg*.)

Œuvres complètes. Geneva: Skira, 1945. (Contains only the fiction.)

"Préface," *Messages personnels*, by Bergeret and Grégoire. Bordeaux: Bière, 1945.

"L'Homme et la culture artistique," *Les Conférences de l'Unesco*. Fontaine, 1947. Pp. 75–89. (Address delivered at the Sorbonne, November 4, 1946. The same volume contains a reply to Malraux by Louis Aragon, "Les Elites contre la culture," pp. 91–106.)

"L'Espoir, Film d'André Malraux," *Ecrits de France*, No. 2 (1946), pp. 138–42. (Fragments of the film from the scenario made at Barcelona in 1938.)

Scènes choisies. Gallimard, 1946.

Esquisse d'une psychologie du cinema. Gallimard, 1946.

Goya. Desseins du musée du Prado. Geneva: Skira, 1947.

Le Musée imaginaire, Volume I of *La Psychologie de l'art*. Geneva: Skira, 1947.

Romans. Pléiade edition, 1947.

La Création artistique. Volume II of *La Psychologie de l'art*. Geneva: Skira, 1949.

Les Conquérants. Grasset, 1949. "Version definitive." (With "Postface," which consists largely of his speech of March 5, 1948, in defense of Gaullism.)

"Culture," *Liberté de l'esprit*, No. 1 (February 1949), pp. 1–2.

"N'était-ce donc que ça," *Liberté de l'esprit*, Nos. 3, 4, and 5 (April, May, and June, 1949), pp. 49–51, 86–87, 117–18. (On T. E. Lawrence. In part a reprint from *Saisons*, 1946.)

The Case for De Gaulle. Random House, 1949, with James Burnham. A "dialogue."

La Monnaie de l'absolu, Volume III of *La Psychologie de l'art*. Skira, 1950.

Saturne. Gallimard, 1950. (His essay on Goya.)

"Dix ans après," *Liberté de l'esprit*, Nos. 11–12 (June-July 1950), p. 103. (Reprinted from *Rassemblement*, June 18, 1948.)

Les Voix du silence. Gallimard, 1951.

About Malraux:

Listed here are only items mentioned in the course of this study, plus a few titles which the reader will find particularly helpful. For a very complete listing of writings about Malraux, see the successive annual volumes of *Bibliography of Critical and Biographical References for the Study of Contemporary French Literature* (Stechert-Hafner, 1949——).

ABEND, HALLETT. *My Life in China, 1926–1941*. Harcourt-Brace, 1943.

ALBÉRÈS, R.-M. *Portrait de notre héros*. Le Portulan, 1945.

ARLAND, MARCEL. "Sur un nouveau mal du siècle," *Nouvelle Revue Française*, 11e année, No. 125 (February 1, 1924), pp. 149–58.

BARRÈS, MAURICE. *Un homme libre*. Emile-Paul, 1889.

BERL, EMMANUEL. *La Culture en péril*. La Table Ronde, 1948.

——. *La Mort de la pensée bourgeoise*. Grasset, 1929.

BRIEUX, J.-J. "La Chine de Mao Tse-tung," *Esprit*, 17e année, No. 11 (November 1949), pp. 766–86.

BURGUM, EDWIN BERRY. *The Novel and the World's Dilemma*. Oxford University Press, 1947.

CHASE, RICHARD V. *The Quest for Myth*. Louisiana State University Press, 1949.

CHIAROMONTE, NICOLA. "Malraux and the Demons of Action," *Partisan Review*, XV (July 1948), 776–89; and XV (August 1948), 912–23.

EHRENBURG, ILYA. *Duhamel, Gide, etc. vus par un écrivain de l'U.R.S.S.* Gallimard, 1934.

FERGUSSON, FRANCIS, *The Idea of a Theater*. Princeton University Press, 1949.

FROHOCK, W. M. "Notes on Malraux's Symbols," *Romanic Review*, XLII (December 1951), 274–81.

——. "Note for a Malraux Bibliography," *Modern Language Notes*, LXV (June 1950), 392–95.

GIDE, ANDRÉ. *Journal*. In the absence of a definitive French edition the annotated American edition (Alfred A. Knopf, translated by Justin O'Brien) is likely to be most useful.

GILBERT, OSCAR-PAUL. *Mortelle Asie*. Flammarion, 1951.

GRENIER, JEAN. *Essai sur l'esprit d'orthodoxie*. Gallimard, 1938.

GROETHUYSEN, BERNARD. "Les Conquérants; Royaume farfelu," *Nouvelle Revue Française*, 16e année, No. 187 (April 1, 1929), pp. 558–63.

HYTIER, JEAN. *Les Arts de littérature*. Charlot, 1941.

ISAACS, HAROLD R., *The Tragedy of the Chinese Revolution*. Revised edition, Stanford University Press, 1951.

LEVIN, HARRY. *James Joyce*. New Directions, 1941.

——. "From Priam to Birotteau," *Yale French Studies*, VI (December 1950), 75–82.

MAGNY, CLAUDE-EDMONDE. *Histoire du roman français depuis 1918*. Editions du Seuil, 1950.

——. "Malraux le fascinateur," *Esprit*, 16e année, No. 10 (October 1948), pp. 513–34.

MALRAUX, CLARA. *Portrait de Grisélidis*. Colbert, 1945.

MAURIAC, CLAUDE. *Malraux ou le mal du héros*. Grasset, 1946.

PEYRE, HENRI. "La Saison littéraire," *French Review*, XXII (December 1948), 97–102.

PICON, GAËTAN. *André Malraux*. Gallimard, 1945.

RAHV, PHILIP. *Image and Idea*. New Directions, 1949.

SACHS, MAURICE. *Au temps du bœuf sur le toit*. Nouvelle Revue Critique, 1937.

SACHS, MAURICE. *Le Sabbat*. Corréa, 1946.

SAINT-CLAIR, M. (MME THÉO VAN RYSSELBERGHE). *Galerie Privée*. Gallimard, 1947.

SAVANE, MARCEL. *André Malraux*. Richard-Masse, 1946.

SIMON, JEAN-PIERRE. *L'Homme en procès*. Editions du Seuil, 1950.

SIMON, PAUL. *Le Mouvement communiste en Chine*. Recueil Sirey, 1939.

STÉPHANE, ROGER. *Portrait de l'aventurier*. Sagittaire, 1950.

————. "Malraux et la Révolution," *Esprit*, 16ᵉ année, No. 10 (October 1948), pp. 461–68.

TROTSKY, LEON. "La Révolution étranglée," *Nouvelle Revue Française*, 19ᵉ année, No. 211 (April 1, 1931), pp. 488–501.

Index